WOODROW WILSON CENTER SERIES

Northern Ireland and the politics of reconciliation

Other books in the series

Northern Ireland
and the politics
of reconciliation

Edited by
DERMOT KEOGH and MICHAEL H. HALTZEL

 WOODROW WILSON CENTER PRESS

AND

 CAMBRIDGE
UNIVERSITY PRESS

Published by the Press Syndicate of the University of Cambridge
The Pitt Building, Trumpington Street, Cambridge CB2 1 RP
40 West 20th Street, New York, NY 10011–4211, USA
10 Stamford Road, Oakleigh, Melbourne 3166, Australia

Woodrow Wilson Center Press
Editorial Offices
370 L'Enfant Promenade,SW
Washington, DC 20024–2518 USA

First published 1993

Reprinted 1994

Printed in the United States of America

Library of Congress Cataloging-in-Publication Data is available

A catalog record for this book is available from the British Library.

ISBN 0-521-44430-6 hardback
ISBN 0-521-45933-8 paperback

This book is dedicated to the memory of John Whyte.

Contents

Acknowledgments

The idea for the publication of this volume came from the participants at a conference, "Anglo-Irish Relations and Northern Ireland," held in May 1990 in Washington, D.C., and Airlie, Virginia, and organized by the West European Studies program of the Woodrow Wilson International Center for Scholars. Throughout the planning and organization of the conference and preparation of this book, the editors were helped greatly by many members of the diplomatic corps of Ireland, the United Kingdom, and the United States.

A special vote of thanks is due to the Irish ambassador to the United States at that time, Padraic MacKernan, who was a strong supporter of the conference idea from the very beginning. He took a personal interest in developing the program and was an active participant in the proceedings. He later encouraged the publication of the volume.

The press officer at the Irish Embassy in the late 1980s, Declan Kelleher, worked to bring the idea of a major conference on Ireland and Northern Ireland to a successful conclusion. His professionalism was much appreciated by the organizers, as was the work of his immediate predecessor, Kevin Dowling, who first suggested the idea of a conference in 1986. At Iveagh House, Dublin, Richard O'Brien—now Irish ambassador to Poland—helped the organizers carry the conference plans forward to a successful conclusion. Thanks are also owed to Noel Dorr, Ted Barrington, and Ann Anderson, and other members of the Irish diplomatic service too numerous to mention for their support and assistance.

Sherard Cowper-Coles, British Embassy, Washington, was a strong supporter of the idea of a conference and greatly assisted the organizers' efforts to provide official British representation at the proceedings. We also wish to record our thanks to the Northern Ireland Office and the Foreign Office for participating in the proceedings.

Thanks are also due to Kenneth Longmyer, desk officer for Ireland at the U.S. Department of State in 1990, for his valuable help.

In Dublin, Professor Brian Farrell, Politics Department, University College, Dublin, helped shape the final program and put the organizers in contact with a number of important sources. His hospitality is much appreciated. Dr. Miriam Hederman O'Brien also gave her support to the organization of the conference. Her advice was invaluable. In London, Marigold Johnson, executive secretary of the British-Irish Association, was most helpful in identifying policy-makers who contributed to the success of the conference.

The organizers would also like to thank former Irish prime minister Dr. Garret FitzGerald, leader of the Irish Labour Party Dick Spring, Ken Maginnis of the Official Unionist Party, and the many others who participated in the Airlie House conference.

The conference was funded by grants from the Bank of Ireland and the United States Congress Special Wilson Center Conference Fund. Our thanks go to Professor Louden Ryan, former governor of the Bank of Ireland, who supported the conference idea and participated in the proceedings. The organizers are also grateful to John Bastable, head of the New York office of Aer Lingus, for providing major support in the form of transatlantic airline tickets. All such support was greatly appreciated by the participants.

The editors would like to thank Samuel F. Wells, Jr., and Mike Lacey of the Woodrow Wilson Center for their help in the production of this volume.

A great debt is owed to Charlotte Thompson and Susan Nugent of the West European Studies program of the Woodrow Wilson Center, who prepared and executed the arrangements for the conference. The participants were very appreciative and asked to have their gratitude publicly recorded.

The editors wish to thank two former postgraduates of the Department of Modern History, University College, Cork, Dr. David Ryan and Finbarr O'Shea, and Charlotte Holland of the Department of Irish History, who helped in the preparation of the manuscript. We acknowledge with thanks the assistance of Dick Rowson of the Woodrow Wilson Center Press in the publication of this volume.

Finally, we thank the contributors who prepared the specially commissioned chapters for this volume.

Northern Ireland and the politics of reconciliation

Introduction

DERMOT KEOGH and MICHAEL H. HALTZEL

The violence in Northern Ireland since the late 1960s has provided academics with a new term, *Ulsterization*. Although this word defies rigorous definition, it is meant to convey the idea of an intractable intercommunity conflict. The apparently unsolvable nature of the "problem"—another much used term—has been an unspoken assumption underlying much of the media coverage of Northern Ireland since 1969, the year the civil rights movement brought the inequalities and injustices of that state to international attention. This volume challenges the notion that the situation in Northern Ireland has deteriorated irrevocably since the late 1960s. The diplomats, academics, civil servants, and politicians who contributed chapters differ sometimes in their historical perceptions and political starting points, but all share the view that it is possible to develop and strengthen the framework in which peaceful coexistence, if not reconciliation, can be achieved.

The origins of the conflict in Northern Ireland are explored by Roy Foster in this volume's opening chapter, "Anglo-Irish Relations and Northern Ireland: Historical Perspectives." Foster argues that the figurative kaleidoscope should be shaken so that the shapes and colors might reveal "new patterns" of meaning. Histories written from behind the barricades of the conflicting traditions will not provide the ideas from which new understandings can develop; such writing will only deepen divisions. Foster pro-

DERMOT KEOGH is Jean Monnet Professor of European Integration Studies, Department of Modern History, University College, Cork. He has written many books, including *The Rise of the Irish Working Class: The Dublin Trade Union Movement and Labour Leadership 1890–1914; The Vatican, the Bishops, and Irish Politics 1919–39; Church and Politics in Latin America; Ireland and Europe 1919–1989;* and *Twentieth Century Ireland.* He is a former Fellow of the Woodrow Wilson Center.

MICHAEL H. HALTZEL is Chief of the European Division of the Library of Congress, Washington, D.C., and former Director of West European Studies at the Woodrow Wilson International Center for Scholars. He is the author of *Der Abbau der deutschen ständischen Selbstverwaltung in den Ostseeprovinzen Russlands 1855–1905.*

1

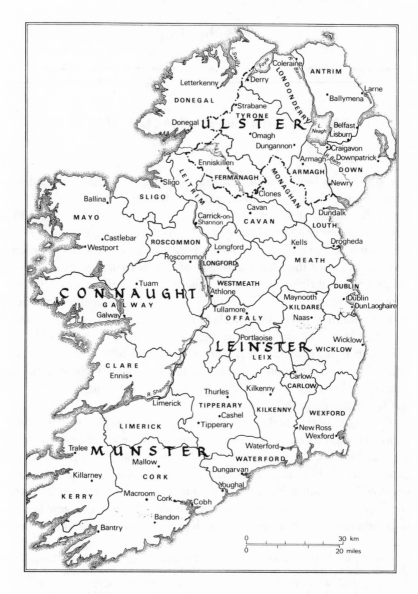

Ireland (from *Ireland 1912–1985: Politics and Society,* by J. J. Lee. Cambridge:
Cambridge University Press, 1989)

vides the reader with a review of perspectives and a challenge to interrogate traditional attitudes on both sides of the Irish Sea.

Academic reflection and historical investigations into the cause of the conflict are not arbitrary and peripheral activities remote from the search for a peaceful solution. By 1992 the death toll in Northern Ireland since the outbreak of "the troubles" in 1969 had exceeded three thousand. Scholars and artists have an obligation to use their powers of analysis to contribute to a fuller understanding of the past, the better to slow the spread of prejudice. The Derry-born poet Seamus Heaney has discharged that responsibility consistently in his work. His poem, "Orange Drums, Tyrone, 1966," captures better than any statistic the bitterness and hatred that fuel the violence on one side of the conflict in Northern Ireland:

> The lambeg balloons at his belly, weighs
> Him back on his haunches, lodging thunder
> Grossly there between his chin and his knees.
> He is raised up by what he buckles under.
>
> Each arm extended by a seasoned rod,
> He parades behind it. And though the
> drummers
> Are granted passage through the nodding
> crowd
> It is the drums preside, like giant tumours.
>
> To every cocked ear, expert in its greed,
> His battered signature subscribes "No Pope."
> The pigskin's scourged until his knuckles bleed.
> The air is pounding like a stethoscope.[1]

The air certainly pounded like a stethoscope in the latter part of the 1960s, when the Northern Ireland Civil Rights Association (NICRA) was founded to highlight sectarianism and discrimination against members of the nationalist community. Martin Luther King, Jr., was a model for the marchers. Sit-ins were staged to highlight discrimination in favor of the majority Protestant community in the allocation of public housing. In January 1969, a Selma-to-Montgomery–style march was made from Belfast to Derry. Marchers were attacked at Burntollet near Derry by a mob which included in its ranks off-duty police auxiliaries known as the

---

[1]"Orange Drums, Tyrone, 1966," from *Poems 1965–1975* by Seamus Heaney. Copyright © 1975, 1980 by Seamus Heaney. Reprinted by permission of Farrar, Straus & Giroux, Inc., and Faber & Faber, Ltd.

B-Specials. This force was loathed by the minority Catholic community. The marchers, among other things, sought "one man, one vote." This was a demand to end the property franchise in local elections which discriminated heavily against the poorer minority community.[2] The attack on the marchers provoked riots in Derry. The violence continued until law and order broke down in Belfast in August 1969 and the British Army had to be called in to halt sectarian attacks on the minority community.

Why did the civil rights movement disintegrate in the early 1970s? Why did constitutionalists fail to force through change with sufficient speed to preempt the rise of physical-force nationalism? Why did the Irish Republican Army (IRA), represented by rival wings after 1970— the Provisionals and the Officials—gain so much strength in those early years? These questions require careful analysis. Their answers may be found in part by examining the ambivalence in Ireland toward the use of the gun in politics. Another part of the answer may be located in an analysis of the mystique surrounding violence in a nation that won its independence by the gun and the bomb, a mystique that lasted into the early 1970s. Another point of departure for the analysis of the period would be to situate the IRA in its wider European context, where that organization can be seen as supportive of nazism and fascism during World War II. The phobias of the modern IRA are reminiscent of fascist doctrine from the 1920s and 1930s. To the 1970s Sinn Féin leader, Daithí Ó Conaill, members of the majority Protestant community were simply part of a colonial class that gave its allegiance to Britain:

The reality is that they are a colon class. They are the settler class that arose out of the plantation. Republicans accept that fact, and the fact that they are of colonial breed. But they've been here for so long that they're part and parcel of the Irish nation, and we feel their place is in the body politic as such, in the nation as a whole.[3]

But Ó Conaill considered that the "colons" had to be brought into line in the way that pro-French Algerians were dealt with when they attempted to thwart the granting of independence to their country.[4] The simplistic

[2]See Michael Farrell, *Northern Ireland: The Orange State*, 2nd ed. (London, 1980), pp. 277ff.; John Whyte, *Interpreting Northern Ireland* (Oxford, England, 1990); and Padraig O'Malley, *The Uncivil Wars: Ireland Today* (Belfast, 1983).
[3]Quoted in O'Malley, *Uncivil Wars*, p. 298.
[4]Ibid., pp. 298–9.

answer provided by the IRA is that only unification can end the conflict between communities in Northern Ireland.

It suits "republicans"—whose respectable enlightenment tradition the Provisional IRA has attempted to hijack—to perpetuate the perception that Irish history is cyclical and that the pattern of events in Northern Ireland over the past three decades is a vicious circle in which violence is endemic. The "armed struggle" is presented, therefore, as the inevitable consequence of an "unjust" political situation. This mistaken analysis is reinforced by certain aspects of media coverage, whose unspoken assumption concerning events in the North is, "The more things change, the more they remain the same." When the international media gather to report particularly gruesome events—protracted hunger strikes, no-warning bombings of civilians, serial sectarian killings, etc.—the temptation is to report such events as if social and political relations in Northern Ireland were stagnant and entrenched. But that only reinforces a view of Northern Ireland which asserts dogmatically that sectarianism is as prevalent today as it was in the early 1920s or mid-1960s. That is not a view accepted by contributors to this volume.

In the first three years of "the troubles," 1969 to 1972, significant changes took place in Northern Ireland. Anthony Kenny has outlined these developments in his book, *The Road to Hillsborough:*

The Electoral Law Act of 1969 provided for adult suffrage in local elections; the ratepayer's franchise was abolished. All local government boundaries and wards were redrawn. A Parliamentary Ombudsman and a Commissioner for Complaints were appointed. Following a report by the explorer Lord Hunt, the Royal Ulster Constabulary was thoroughly overhauled. The force was disarmed, and a new representative police authority set up; the Ulster Special Constabulary was abolished, and a new part-time security force, the Ulster Defence Regiment, was set up within the British Army; the police role in prosecutions was modified and later replaced by an independent Director of Public Prosecutions for Northern Ireland. A Ministry of Community Relations was set up, and also an independent Community Relations Commission. The 1970 Prevention of Incitement to Hatred Act contained the equivalent of the criminal provisions of the English Race Relations Act of 1965. In 1971 a Housing Executive was set up to deal with public authority housebuilding and to allocate houses on an objective points system.[5]

The subsequent introduction of direct rule from Westminster expedited a program of limited reform. But that expedient has been turned into a

[5]Anthony Kenny, *The Road to Hillsborough: The Shaping of the Anglo-Irish Agreement* (Oxford, England, 1986), pp. 26–7.

semipermanent system of government over the past two decades. In "A Constitutional Background to the Northern Ireland Crisis," Alan J. Ward argues that time may be running out for those in Northern Ireland who wish to establish for the state a new constitution capable of winning the consent of both communities. Full integration is the alternative. But such stark alternatives have not altered the fact that Northern Ireland was permitted to muddle through the late 1970s and 1980s with an excessive reliance on force and counterinsurgency tactics. The latter aspect is investigated in Charles Townshend's contribution to this volume, "The Supreme Law: Public Safety and State Security in Northern Ireland."

John Whyte, who died in New York on his way to the conference that generated the contributions to this book, wrote of the complexities and the intractability of the Northern problem in his chapter, "Dynamics of Social and Political Change in Northern Ireland." Whyte was ideally placed to address this topic, having spent many years as professor of political science at Queen's University, Belfast. Although Whyte was pessimistic about the short term, he retained a constructive and hopeful attitude, claiming that it was reasonable to speak of society in Northern Ireland as "dynamic" rather than "static." All sorts of changes were going on—political, demographic, and economic—but they usually worked at cross-purposes and largely canceled each other out. "This conclusion is pessimistic," he acknowledged, "but it is not unrealistic." However unsatisfactory the current situation in Northern Ireland, he concluded that it was not the worst conceivable. John Whyte's death cast a deep sadness over the proceedings of the Airlie House conference. His contribution to the volume provides distinguished testimony to the lifelong humanitarian and scholarly work of one of Ireland's pioneers in political science. In his last book, published posthumously, he had written that perhaps the time had come when we should start looking for a new paradigm.[6] Perhaps his final volume, along with his contribution to this work, will stimulate a new generation of academics to achieve that objective.

Joseph Lee, in his contribution to this volume, "Dynamics of Social and Political Change in the Irish Republic," takes up John Whyte's challenge to seek a new paradigm on which to base an analysis of the Republic of Ireland. Lee's chapter builds upon the research he did for his book,

[6]Whyte, *Interpreting Northern Ireland*. This extensive and wide-ranging work, in press at the time of Professor Whyte's death, is a masterly synthesis and critique of the large corpus of work on Northern Ireland.

Ireland 1912–1985: Politics and Society.[7] In his chapter, he turns his attention to the rapid and complex changes occurring in Irish society, economy, and politics since the mid-1980s. His chapter also helpfully refers to the complicated series of events in the country in the 1980s in the area of church-state relations which received international publicity. Church-state relations is also the theme of Mary Harris's detailed chapter, "The Catholic Church, Minority Rights, and the Founding of the Northern Irish State."

Because of the centrality of religion in the development of the two Irish states, Ireland's leading moral theologian, Enda McDonagh, was invited to reflect on "New Forces for Positive Change in Ireland." McDonagh's analysis draws him to the conclusion that there is a lot that the churches in both states could and should do to realize their essential commitment to the cause of peace and justice. The more obvious areas for concentration, in his view, are education and mixed marriages. A clear commitment to the joint education of adults and children, and of laity and clergy, from the different traditions is necessary, he writes. McDonagh also argues that mixed marriages should be seen as a Christian opportunity rather than as a threat. Writing on the development of the ecumenical movement in Northern Ireland, Josiah Horton Beeman and Robert Mahony expand upon McDonagh's themes in their chapter, "The Institutional Churches and the Process of Reconciliation in Northern Ireland." Their chapter is followed by Terence Brown's analysis of the development of literature and culture in Northern Ireland since 1965: "The Cultural Issue in Northern Ireland, 1965–1991."

The final chapters of this volume focus on the practical side of the politics of reconciliation. Former Irish prime minister (Taoiseach) Garret FitzGerald writes on "The Origins and Rationale of the Anglo-Irish Agreement of 1985." Together with John Hume, the leader of the Social Democratic and Labour Party, FitzGerald had sought throughout the 1970s and into the early 1980s to establish a political framework in which progress could be made toward establishing representative structures in Northern Ireland acceptable to all traditions. The incentive to do so was great indeed. It was estimated in 1983 that more than 2,300 people had been killed in the violence since 1969. Those deaths, in an area with a population of about 1.5 million, were equivalent proportionately to the killing of about 84,000 in Britain, 83,000 in France, or

[7] J. J. Lee, *Ireland, 1912–1985: Politics and Society* (Cambridge, England, 1989).

350,000 in the United States. More than 24,000 had been injured or maimed. From 1969 to 1983 there had been more than 43,000 recorded incidents of shootings, bombings, and arson. The prison population in the North rose from 686 in 1967 to about 2,500 in 1983, proportionately the highest number of prisoners in Western Europe. These figures were provided in the New Ireland Forum report of May 1984.[8] The forum, which involved all of the major constitutional nationalist parties on the island, was the combined initiative of FitzGerald and Hume. It met first in Dublin Castle on 30 May 1983, and it reported a year later after a total of thirteen public and twenty-eight private sessions. One of its more important recommendations was:

> It is clear that a new Ireland will require a new constitution which will ensure that the needs of all traditions are fully met. Society in Ireland as a whole comprises a wider diversity of cultural and political traditions than exists in the South, and the constitution and laws of a new Ireland must accommodate these social and political realities.[9]

FitzGerald and the prime minister of the United Kingdom, Margaret Thatcher, signed the Anglo-Irish Agreement on 15 November 1985 at Hillsborough Castle. FitzGerald's chapter provides a personal insight into the process leading to the agreement. Lord Armstrong, a leading figure on the British side of the negotiations, also makes a short contribution, "Ethnicity, the English, and Northern Ireland: Comments and Reflections." Legal scholar Donald L. Horowitz provides a comparative context in which to examine policy in the face of community conflict ("Conflict and the Incentives to Political Accommodation"), and Paul Arthur discusses the issue, "The Anglo-Irish Agreement: A Device for Territorial Management?"

Aware of the difficulties inherent in the process of reconciliation, the authors of these latter chapters are much exercised by John Whyte's argument that the situation in Northern Ireland—no matter how grim it might seem at times—is not a worst-case scenario. The objective is to avoid at worst the development of another Bosnia or Lebanon in Northern Ireland.

The rapid progress of European integration provides a new speculative context for several contributors to this volume. Lord Armstrong sees the European context as having a greater impact over the longer

[8] New Ireland Forum, *Report* (Dublin, 1984), p. 15.
[9] Ibid., p. 23.

rather than the shorter term. He believes that there is an "opportunity that beckons. It is an opportunity which we have never had before; and that is one of the reasons why we must not be trammeled by history." John Whyte argues that change undoubtedly is being brought about by the greater unity within the European Community: "In a few years' time, one can expect the border between the North and South in Ireland to mean less in practical terms than it does now." Unionists, he states, may be less hostile to joining a united Ireland, or nationalists to remaining in the United Kingdom. He is also quick to recognize that trends toward greater unity at the European level may have only limited impact. National loyalties may not be simply the product of economic issues. Intense emotions may still be a prevalent force, Whyte concludes. And here history may be the dragnet that is trammeling the potential new opportunities that the European Community could provide to the search for a solution.

In contrast, Kerby Miller argues in "Revising Revisionism: Comments and Reflections" that the euphoria over European integration and the triumph of the free market is a fatal delusion. Implicit in this euphoric view, Miller says, is the idea that European integration and its new political structures, coupled with some military repression, may cause the terrorists to be suppressed and the communities to be reconciled. Facilitating this process would be the toleration generated by exposure to other cultures. In most such analyses, Miller warns, the social and economic aspects of marginalization have been ignored—aspects that often generate a tendency toward violence or violent solutions. The process of convergence, Miller argues, be it economic, political, or cultural, goes forward primarily among the island's two elites. There are "certain classes in certain areas" that

have not benefited—indeed, they have been deeply disadvantaged in a variety of real and perceived ways—by the very economic, social, and cultural changes that have persuaded their social superiors to become more ecumenical, integrationist, or inclusive in their conceptions of the meaning of community.

John Hume, a member of both the Westminster and European parliaments, has titled his contribution "A New Ireland in a New Europe." He is unapologetic about his hope for the future of the whole of Ireland within a more closely united Europe. In finding its place in that process of political integration, he argues, Ireland would not be at a point of arrival but rather at a point of departure "on a challenging journey on which it can maturely discharge a responsibility to, and with, the peoples with whom it shares the European continent and the larger world." He does not see Ireland joining the North Atlantic Treaty Organization (NATO). Hume suggests instead that Ireland could play a particular role in promoting and enhancing the possibilities offered by the Conference on Security and Cooperation in Europe (CSCE) process, making common cause not just with other neutral Western states but also with countries of Central and Eastern Europe that wish to escape from the notion of two military conglomerates. In that way, he says, Ireland could complement the efforts of those in NATO member states who wish to work to achieve a real and complete pan-European security offering true peace.

These chapters provide a basis for a debate likely to grow more intense as the dynamics of European integration are played out. Though academics are not noted for an ability to prescribe a path for the future, the intellectual discourse in this volume may help highlight the futility of the various communities on the island of Ireland continuing to live under the tyranny of what Roy Foster has called "imprisoning historical perspectives."

Part I

The "Irish Question": historical perspectives

1

Anglo-Irish relations and Northern Ireland: historical perspectives

ROY FOSTER

Perspectives involve looking at things; and it is a cliché, but nonetheless a true one, that you have to look at Irish history in order to understand the pass to which we have come. But perspective also involves a point of view; and views of history can be obscurantist as well as enlightening. To a historian, looking at Anglo-Irish relations over the last hundred years, it is striking how consistently "history" is produced as an argument, or a witness, at junctures when the discourse should—one might think—be concentrating upon affairs more immediately at hand. Daniel O'Connell, introducing his motion for repeal of the Union in the House of Commons on 22 April 1834, remarked bitterly: "I shall be as brief as I can upon this subject, for it is quite clear, that no man ever yet rose to address a more unwilling audience."[1] But he implacably entered upon a disquisition about Irish history from the year 1172, which takes forty-six columns of *Hansard* before coming anywhere near the present. In the same way, forty years later, Isaac Butt, introducing a motion for home rule, paid comparatively little attention to contemporary arguments for the measure but devoted most of his speech to a learned expatiation on the late-eighteenth-century Irish economy.[2]

The tradition continued; David Lloyd George, opening negotiations with Eamon de Valera, was told that the problem lay rooted in the recent great dispossessions of land perpetrated in Ireland, which turned out to

Roy Foster is Carroll Professor of Irish History at Oxford University. Among his publications are *Modern Ireland 1600–1972* and *The Oxford Illustrated History of Ireland*.

[1]Great Britain, *Hansard Parliamentary Debates*, 3rd ser., 22 (1834):1092ff.
[2]Ibid., 220 (1874):700ff.

have been "in the time of Cromwell." In the treaty debates of December 1921, the same syndrome recurs, as speeches by Mary MacSwiney, Austin Stack, Seán MacEntee, and others demonstrate.[3] And the proceedings of the debates in the House of Commons on the Anglo-Irish Agreement of 1985 carried it on; the strongest speeches, that of John Hume supporting the agreement and that of the late Harold McCusker attacking it, were equally devoted to the argument from history.[4] It is striking, though, that in the debate of 1921 practically all who relied heavily on historical exposition were arguing against the treaty. Those arguing for it, notably Desmond Fitzgerald in a powerful speech,[5] tended to stick to the question at hand. And in the preceding era, the politician who perhaps came nearest to bringing about a modus vivendi between Britain and Ireland, Charles Stewart Parnell, was the one who knew least about Irish history.[6]

Of course, those who quote history do so because they believe history—or their version of it—is on their side. A great deal of ink has been spilt on the question of the uses of Irish history, and the angle of perspective employed. The term *revisionist* has been adopted by the orthodox for those who see certain aspects of Irish history in a manner different from theirs, or who have reinterpreted certain key junctures. It is an irrelevant tag in its way, because there are no professional historians who are not revisionists; and I have consistently argued for the intellectual meaninglessness of the notion.[7] In the very nature of the business, the latest publications of research are now querying the findings of those judged to have been "revisionist" twenty years ago, when they "revised" received versions of the Famine of 1845–50 or the Land War of the

---

[3]See Dáil Éireann Official Report, *Debate on the Treaty Between Great Britain and Ireland* (Dublin, 1922), especially pp. 27, 152.
[4]Great Britain, *Parliamentary Debates* (Commons), 76 (1985–86):785, 910.
[5]*Debate on the Treaty,* pp. 234ff.
[6]See Thomas O'Connor Power, *The Anglo-Irish Quarrel: A Plea for Peace* (London, 1880), for a strong argument that "there is no subject about which Mr. Parnell is so ignorant as that of Irish history." The topic is further debated in F. S. L. Lyons, *Charles Stewart Parnell* (London, 1977), pp. 37–8, and "The Political Ideas of Parnell," *Hist. Jn.* 16, 4 (1973):749–75; see also R. F. Foster, "History and the Irish Question," *Transactions of the Royal Historical Society,* 5th series, 33 (1983):182.
[7]See "We Are All Revisionists Now," *The Irish Review* 1, 1 (1986):1–5. A rather involved attempt to pin down "revisionism" has been made by Brendan Bradshaw in "Nationalism and Historical Scholarship," *Irish Historical Studies* 26 (1989):329–51, but much of this is based on the idea that so-called revisionists believe themselves—inaccurately—to be impartial and value-free, which is a red herring, easily disproved. More germane are the comments of L. M. Cullen in the *Newsletter* of the Economic and Social History Society of Ireland, no. 2, Spring 1990.

1880s.[8] But this does not make their new-wave critics antirevisionist. They may be reasserting some of the judgments held by an earlier generation. But they are not reasserting the imposed political view which Irish history necessarily represented in the irredentist period, when an official national identity had to be constructed from the 1920s. For a historian, the politics do not automatically follow the historical critique.

This is not to say that politics are not inextricably involved with the assessment of historical evidence, because they are; and a political "sense" is an essential ingredient in interpreting it.[9] But the politicizing of history in, for instance, commentaries on Ireland put together for the consumption of some audiences in Britain is a different matter. What we know about the history of Anglo-Irish relations tends to be ignored; deliberate decisions are sometimes taken to exclude *soi-disant* revisionist conclusions, because they are deemed politically unsound.[10] It may sound chauvinist to say so, but such crude maneuvers would not, nowadays, be found in Ireland—North or South. And "revisionist" historians are listened to far more dispassionately by the Irish in Ireland than by their sundered brethren in Britain or America—for psychological and social reasons that are probably obvious.

What I want to outline here is not a "revisionist" agenda, nor a chronological reinterpretation; more, a discussion of historical perspectives on certain recurrent themes. The topic of Anglo-Irish relations is subject to certain specific preoccupations that come up again and again.

---

[8]Thus Joel Mokyr, *Why Ireland Starved: A Quantitative and Analytical History of the Irish Economy 1800–1850* (London, 1983), and Cormac O Gráda, *Ireland Before and After the Famine: Explorations in Economic History 1800–1925* (Manchester, 1988), are challenging recent views of the Famine, and to a certain extent reestablishing the old orthodoxies on firmer quantitative foundations, while K. T. Hoppen, *Ireland since 1800: Conflict and Conformity* (London, 1989), and others are questioning the view of the Land War established in the early 1970s by scholars such as Barbara Solow, *The Land Question and the Irish Economy, 1870–1903* (Cambridge, Mass., 1971).

[9]For instance the Victorian historian Robert Dunlop, when reading the depositions taken at the time of the 1641 insurrection, found his view of them inescapably colored by the politics of 1882. "I began to experience an uncomfortable feeling that my evidence was not so strong as I would have liked it to be. True, the depositions were very explicit and apparently incontrovertible; but I was living in Dublin at a time when the power of the Land League was at its height, and I could not help asking what value depositions taken by a body of Orange magistrates as to nationalist outrages were likely to possess for an impartial estimate of the state of Ireland during the government of Earl Spencer. Was the state of affairs in 1642 more favourable for an impartial enquiry than it was in 1882?" R. Dunlop, *Ireland Under the Commonwealth* (Manchester, 1913), pp. i, vii.

[10]It should be said that the inclusion of Irish history in the new National Curriculum, and the efforts of organizations such as the British Association of Irish Studies, are bringing the debate in Britain more closely up to date with developments in Ireland.

One, for instance, is the idea of a turning point, after which nothing would be quite the same again. The year 1885 was one, when Gladstone took up home rule and made it respectable. Another was 1914, when it became clear that the Liberal government was not going to impose home rule on Ulster by force. Another was 1920–21, when the state of Northern Ireland was set up and subsequently the Anglo-Irish Treaty was signed, which established the twenty-six–county Irish Free State with the powers of an implicitly autonomous dominion. Another was 1972, when the Heath government suspended Stormont and Northern Ireland returned to direct rule from London. But the nearer one approaches the present, the more risky such assertions become. The Maze hunger strikes of 1981 seemed a turning point, at least as regards support for the IRA on the island at large. But so was the European Parliament election of June 1984, when Social Democratic and Labour Party (SDLP) leader John Hume decisively beat Danny Morrison, the Sinn Féin candidate, and called Sinn Féin's bluff that the time had come when its popular support would supplant that of the SDLP. The year 1985, and the Anglo-Irish Agreement signed at Hillsborough, may seem an indisputable turning point. But we cannot yet tell if it will be like that of 1920–21—a fundamental reordering of the relationship between the two countries—or like the Irish Convention of 1917, which clarified only that goodwill, desperate urgency, and constitutional imagination were not enough, faced with the implacable opposition of extremists on both sides.

Other recurrent themes involve the preoccupation with forms of words, and the discovery of a winning constitutional formula that will somehow reconcile the opposites. Here, as always, British self-deception and wishful thinking are every bit as marked as the Irish variety, and with less historical excuse. Thus much of the negotiation around the treaty of 1921 concerned the form of the oath of allegiance to be taken, and ignored the meaning and implications of the Boundary Commission on Northern Ireland. Similar ingenuities preoccupied those who drew up the 1985 Hillsborough agreement, notably regarding any implication that the Irish government accepted the constitutional basis of Northern Ireland.[11] And from the 1880s much effort was spent on discovering variants of the "home rule" formula—"national boards," "home rule all round," and so on—that would enable constitutional virtue to be

[11]See Padraig O'Malley, *Northern Ireland: Questions of Nuance* (Boston, 1990), pp. 4–5, and Anthony Kenny, *The Road to Hillsborough: The Shaping of the Anglo-Irish Agreement* (Oxford, 1986), pp. 96–7.

preserved. Nor is this preoccupation with forms of words the sole preserve of the constitutionalists. The new words used to deal with Irish antipathies and oppositions now tend to be "traditions," "communities," "identities," "exclusions," and (cautiously) "inclusions." There is a danger of euphemism here; some phrases, such as "community worker," have achieved very distinct and special meanings in certain Ulster contexts. And when the ostensibly innocent word "tradition" is adopted it might be worth remembering that historians are increasingly preoccupied with the idea of "the invention of tradition"—the artificiality and recentness of many worldviews and identifications which are assumed to be venerable and therefore unchangeable.[12] In this context, the capacity of the British for reassuring themselves about their own providentialist history is, once more, every bit as striking as the Irish variety; the academic analysis of British nationalism is only just beginning, and none too early. But at the same time, the search for new words as tools with which to approach the Irish past must be encouraging, if it enables the kaleidoscope to be shaken around a little, and the shapes and colors to be disposed in potentially new patterns.

There is room, to begin with, for some new thinking on the idea of the Union—the concept so central to the history of Ireland's relations with Britain over the last two hundred years. At the moment, unions are much in the mind; one enormous experiment in the union of states is proceeding in Western Europe, while in the East, another has crumbled. Looking at Scandinavia, the Netherlands, Finland, and other examples, one is struck by the disparateness of the conditions and factors that create a union—and dissolve it. In the case of Ireland and Britain, several sensitive elements were there from the beginning, and helped jeopardize it at the end. Economic and political exploitation formed the basis of its operation, whether that had been the original intention or not. This was clearly demonstrated by the Famine, when Ireland was treated as an integral part of the Union only insofar as it suited the priorities of British political economy. But there was always the question of contested legitimacy: an argument stated at the outset by the opposition in the old Irish Parliament, later adapted by O'Connell, and finally accepted by Gladstone. There was the argument that the mechanics of the Union held the ring against warring local factions; though this assertion could be

[12]See E. J. Hobsbawm and T. O. Ranger (eds.), *The Invention of Tradition* (Cambridge, England, 1983).

turned on its head by the nationalist opposition, which claimed that the Union actually fomented rather than prevented those warring factions. And there was the fact that throughout its 120-year history, the Union, so constitutionally rigid, in fact changed its nature all the time. One facilitating mechanism for this was the peculiar nature of Irish government—organized in a unique and often experimental (or ad hoc) way, bearing little relation to the government of other areas of the empire, and making nonsense of the often-repeated claim that Ireland was a part of the British state in the same way as, for instance, Yorkshire. Another way in which the terms of the Union changed on the ground, so to speak, was the simple fact that so many Irish people came to live in Britain, or lived between the two islands. Both of these factors remain, complicating Irish-British relations and affecting the situation of that part of the island of Ireland that still adheres to the Union of Great Britain.

Partly because of the way the situation kept changing, adapting the Union was always a tortuous process. Home rule itself was, in a sense, a developing aspiration rather than a set and unshakeable blueprint. By the time of its passing, in 1914, home rule was a refined and complex version of the "simple demand" of Isaac Butt's, and even Parnell's, day— probably because it was now in the real world at last. The freedoms conferred by the treaty of 1921 were wider than those envisaged by home rule, but the opposition took care to claim that it embodied nothing different. Cathal Brugha, for instance, made the point that the "freedom to achieve freedom" argument had been pressed by John Redmond; and this, to Brugha, was an immoral compromise.[13] It also indicated a belief in Britain's fundamental untrustworthiness, which was quite rational in 1921, given the events of the previous decade, but which the subsequent period did not in fact vindicate. For their part, the proponents of the treaty had to claim that they had extracted something qualitatively different from, and better than, the home rule that had been on the table in 1914. If they had not, the implications were too devastating to contemplate, making nonsense of the heroics of the War of Independence. Behind all these arguments lay the question of how long, through oaths of fidelity and commitments to the Commonwealth, the Union could be allowed a sort of prolonged, if progressively enfeebled, life.

There is a left-wing or vulgar-Marxist approach to Ireland that still sees the problem as "the Irish Question" *tout court:* tacitly assuming the

---

[13]*Debate on the Treaty,* p. 66.

Republic to be under effective British rule, a colony continued by other means, principally the means of finance capitalism. Why this shadowy structure should be so closely connected with Britain, rather than be part of the European or international scene usually adverted to in this context, is never clarified; perhaps a clue comes in the way that such rhetoric quickly shifts to the old-fashioned personifications of "England" and "Ireland." As with the repudiation by many Irish emigrants of revisionist views of Irish history, the psychological reasons for this determined evasion are easy to find. It is difficult, if not morally impossible, for the left to admit that an independent Irish state should be so decisively different from the left's vision of what it should be. As part of this process of compensation, such advocates argue that James Connolly—the single Marxist ideologue among the revolutionary leaders of 1916—has somehow been betrayed. They might rather investigate ways he himself may have adapted the socialist analysis of Irish history to the point of abandoning it.

This kind of Green-Marxist view of the Union shades easily into the old republican view of Ireland's unfinished revolution, which puts any shortcomings in independent Ireland down to the fact that it is not really independent at all. From the 1960s, particularly with the Anglo-Irish Free Trade Agreement of 1965, the republican argument has stressed that the Act of Union has been, in a sense, brought in again by the back door; this argument was adverted to even more strongly in the aftermath of the events of 1969.[14] The failure of the Northern Ireland state threw into sharp relief the disasters and negligence apparently inseparable from British conduct of Irish affairs. It was probably inevitable that the development that has really altered the parameters of Irish sovereignty—involvement in the European Community—is more or less ignored, in favor of the ancient historical enemy. The idea of a British master plan to regain Ireland for the Union was subscribed to by both wings of the Irish Republican Army (IRA) in the early 1970s, although they never quite explained why this should be so earnestly desired. The notion of Stormont as a puppet regime, manipulated by the British, was also adhered to against all the evidence; if anything, the opposite was the case. The only way the British government could manipulate Stormont was to abolish it.

[14]See the *United Irishman* for the early months of 1970, as quoted in Henry Patterson, *The Politics of Illusion: Republicanism and Socialism in Modern Ireland* (London, 1989), p. 129.

This was not incompatible with the maintenance of unruffled complacency and deliberate ignorance on the part of British politicians where Northern Ireland was concerned—vividly demonstrated in diaries such as Richard Crossman's, as well as apologias such as James Callaghan's. The unionist approach to the Union is equally unrealistic, to the point of evasion. As in the nineteenth century, it is for unionists a psychological necessity rather than a constitutional arrangement. And here the historian has a role, in trying to uncover the instincts and expectations that have led to this attitude—and possibly in analyzing the profound trauma that lies behind (though this makes the profession sound rather like Hollywood's idea of psychiatrists, operating as detectives in the underworld of the subconscious). Certainly one historical perspective that helps explain this psychological need is the study of religion; and significantly, much interesting work is beginning to appear on religion and society in nineteenth-century Ireland, abandoning the superior attitude of the old positivist approach, and analyzing the mechanisms that reinforce communal identifications and group solidarities.[15]

This makes it all the more important to examine why Orange and Green occasionally united against the British state in the years of the Union. Money was important; campaigns against overtaxation create unlikely allies. So was the demand for local government reform. The ideologues on both the Protestant and Catholic sides also united in opposition to any idea of nonsectarian education, from Edward Stanley's scheme of 1831 right up to the present, when one of the most depressing recent developments has been the anathema delivered by both churches against the initiatives toward integrated education in Northern Ireland. In general, however, what kept the Orange and Green, or unionist and nationalist, sides apart was far more potent than what united them, politically speaking. Politics are not the sum of humanity's social experience; there are cultural levels at which the two traditions were less divided, and more intuitively aware of a common Irishness, than is often allowed.[16] But the question of the Union was political and focused pow-

---

[15]Richard Crossman, *The Crossman Diaries: Selections from the Diaries of a Cabinet Minister, 1964–1970* (London, 1979); James Callaghan, *Time and Chance* (London, 1987). On the study of religion, see, for instance, S. J. Connolly, *Priests and People in Pre-Famine Ireland 1780–1845* (Dublin, 1982), and Peter Brooke, *Ulster Presbyterianism* (Dublin, 1988).

[16]I have explored this idea in a lecture, "Varieties of Irishness," published in Maurna Crozier (ed.), *Cultural Traditions in Northern Ireland* (Belfast, 1989), pp. 5–29.

erful feelings. Even if there were some administrative and even economic arguments to be made for it, these stood for nothing against the often irrational potency of the separatist ideal.

The continuity of this ideal is one of the most thoroughly kicked footballs in historical debates. Most historians would now accept that, while there were recurrent calls for total separation from Britain, usually on the part of an elite minority, the idea of a continuous and represent-ative nationalist wish for independence on the part of "the Irish people" is an anachronism before the early nineteenth century (at the earliest). At the same time, the separatist rhetoric imposes its own reality. Patrick Pearse, in his propagandist essays "Ghosts" and "The Separatist Idea," invented a coherent political tradition of separatism, brilliantly weaving disparate strands in Irish history into a common fabric of Anglophobia; most conspicuously, he reinvented the eighteenth-century radical Theo-bald Wolfe Tone.[17] Pearse was not the only one to take him out of context; Tone made several memorable statements that lent themselves to adoption. For example: "Our freedom must be held at all hazards; if the men of property will not help us they must fall; we will free ourselves by the aid of that large and respectable class of the community—the men of no property."[18] This statement has been taken by twentieth-century radicals as a call to the working class; at least one such has proudly claimed a phrase from it as the title of his autobiography.[19] What Tone in fact meant by "men of no property" was the nonparliamentary classes, who were in the 1790s literally a "respectable class of the community." He was, as so often, throwing a line to the radical middle classes, es-pecially the Belfast merchants and journalists, who shared his political faith. His attitudes toward the proletariat and the Catholic peasantry were a great deal more fearful, and his idealistic crusade came to grief on the rocks of sectarianism. The other great Tone phrase, enshrined by Pearse, recorded his admirable and inspiring wish "to unite the whole people of Ireland, to abolish the memory of all past dissensions and to

[17]This process is discussed in "The Cult of Tone," the conclusion to Marianne Elliott's definitive *Wolfe Tone: Prophet of Irish Independence* (London, 1989), pp. 411–19.
[18]W. T. W. Tone, *The Life of Theobald Wolfe Tone*, 2 vols. (Washington, D. C., 1926), 2:46. See Elliott, *Wolfe Tone*, p. 418, for a discussion of this statement.
[19]C. S. Andrews, *Man of No Property* (Cork, 1982). And Peadar O'Donnell, speaking at Bodenstown in June 1931, took the "men of no property" formulation as the manifesto of the breakaway socialist republican movement, Saor Éire; see *An Phoblacht*, 27 June 1931.

substitute the common name of Irishman in place of the denominations of Protestant, Catholic and Dissenter."[20] What mattered here is not that he was morally right, but that he was politically obtuse.

Yet Tone reemerged, a hundred years after his death, as the inspirational icon of the 1798 centenary celebrations arranged by James Connolly, Maud Gonne, and others, while Pearse apostrophized him as the holiest of the apostles who preached the gospel of Irish separatism. (This is Pearse's imagery, not mine.) What is interesting for our purposes is that the idea of dissolution of the Union was related closely to the idea of purity, and of a regained soul. Oddly enough, James Connolly, Pearse's contemporary and eventual unlikely companion in arms, used the same implicit imagery in his idea of the "Reconquest" of Ireland.[21] Economically and politically, the British connection had polluted Ireland. Connolly was a Marxist, but rather than complete capitalism's contradictions, he wanted Ireland to revert to the purity of a precapitalist order and to rediscover the potential of communal organization which was, in his opinion, part of the Irish national psyche. A rupture with Britain would entail the rediscovery of social and economic innocence. Thus Connolly's socialism is very closely linked to Gaelic revivalism, enabling him to see the peasants of the West as future soldiers in an economic class war—an unlikely prospect, looked at from any other angle.

It is worth instancing these two examples of separatist ideology because they indicate the power of the images and motivations built into the wish to dissolve the Union. Of course, the desire to reclaim a golden past, fantasized through "history," is not at all a distinctively Irish quirk, especially in the late nineteenth century; it is, in many countries and cultures, a classic response to dislocation and modernization.[22] But ironically, the dissolution of the Union was enabled and in a sense precipitated by nineteenth-century processes that had been introduced and facilitated by the Union itself, and that transcended the simple fact of Britain's apparent inability to govern Ireland with sensitivity or even good sense. For instance, the loss of the Irish language through commercialization and modernization was seen by Irish ideologues as a trauma that must be reversed; the language had to be revived if independence were to be gained. But in fact the much decried process of "anglicization," in the

---

[20]Written in Paris in August 1796; see Elliott, *Wolfe Tone*, pp. 309–12, 411.
[21]See James Connolly, *The Reconquest of Ireland* (Dublin, 1915).
[22]See E. J. Hobsbawm's Wiles lectures on nationalism, published as *Nations and Nationalism since 1780* (Cambridge, England, 1990).

loosest sense, itself had helped create nationalism, by bringing about increased literacy, revolutionized communications, a spreading culture of highly politicized provincial newspapers, and a revolutionary though peaceful distribution of land through the land acts from the 1880s on. The creation of what Joseph Lee called a "possessor class"[23] made for an implacably conservative and petty-bourgeois base to Irish society.

The process was aided by emigration, the great social fact of the modern Irish experience, upon which Kerby Miller has written so eloquently. What would have happened if the most energetic and alienated elements of society, those with the least to lose, had stayed at home instead of leaving? (It could be said that we have seen what would have happened—since they stayed home during World War I, helping to bring about a period of sustained revolution in Ireland.) Emigration fostered that search for a golden past which I have mentioned: a nation on the move has to affirm a spiritual home. And emigration also underpinned the embourgeoisement of Irish rural society. The possession of land, achieved by successive land acts up to 1909, had a political implication too, well put by Henry Patterson: "It was precisely because the Irish programme on the land question had been largely met by the British parliament that an Irish constitutional party at Westminster became irrelevant."[24] It was pointed out at the time that "until land purchase was peacefully completed the man who would suggest the withdrawal of the Irish Party from London would make himself the laughing stock of Irish politics."[25] In a sense, where the Union actually worked, it also helped prepare the way for its dissolution.

Moreover, the form which dissolution of the Union took was characteristically idiosyncratic. After 1921, an implicit acceptance of special links and peculiar conditions remained. Special commercial relationships were sustained; Britain's defense and strategic interests in the area were tacitly allowed. Irish residents in Britain had a special constitutional status (an arrangement only recently reciprocated in the Republic). But for good historical reasons, the Irish line on constitutional abstractions continued tough, and often determinedly idealist. Uncomfortable facts—the majority vote for the treaty, the actuality of Partition—were not admitted. When de Valera brought the process of dissolving the Union a few stages

[23]See J. J. Lee, *Ireland 1912–1985* (Cambridge, England, 1989), passim.
[24]Patterson, *The Politics of Illusion*, p. 12.
[25]Paul Bew, *Conflict and Conciliation in Ireland 1890–1910: Parnellites and Radical Agrarians* (Oxford, 1987), p. 239.

further in the 1930s, he was thus enabled to legislate platonically for the six northeastern counties, "pending the re-integration of the national territory." Yet in practical matters the process of dissolution was gentle and rather ambiguous. Reformist and mildly autarkic economic policies gave way to a series of important commercial agreements in the late 1930s. The gradualist constitutional evolution of the Anglo-Irish relationship into the new-look Commonwealth seemed a viable and not unpopular option. The Irish approach to phased disengagement was, in retrospect, both sophisticated and effective. Certainly de Valera's combination of rhetorical separatism and practical caution was extremely popular—far more so than the perfectionist exhortations of the republican left, such as Saor Éire, still trying to "achieve the Reconquest."[26]

It should be remembered, though, that the gradualist policies that led eventually to an Irish republic externally associated with Britain for certain purposes would not have been possible had not Partition preceded the creation of the twenty-six–county state. This removed the huge stumbling block of the Protestant presence, leaving an extraordinarily homogeneous Catholic and rural state where social and cultural differences from the perceived English norm could be, in a sense, reinforced. There was also the fact that English perceptions reliably failed to register the fact that the world actually contained and accommodated other norms. John Stuart Mill's remark that Ireland was in the mainstream of general European developments, and England in an eccentric tributary, has never been registered by his countrymen. The essential cultural difference bedeviled, and continues to bedevil, Anglo-Irish relationships. George Bernard Shaw's play *John Bull's Other Island* is still one of the best commentaries on it; the most recent reactions to, for instance, certain Irish legal decisions offer a continuing illustration. One of the most irreducible differences, and something which English opinion continues to find incomprehensible, is the close relationship of religion to politics. Even the socialist republican Saor Éire, after all, began its 1931 congress with a religious invocation; and the close involvement of priests with extremist nationalism runs from the Fenian period right through to arms-buying activities in 1969,[27] and the 1981 hunger strikes.[28] It is not just an eccentric historic hangover or, as some British opinion has it, an

---

[26]See Patterson, *The Politics of Illusion*, pp. 50–1.
[27]Ibid., p. 122.
[28]See Padraig O'Malley, *Biting at the Grave: The Irish Hunger Strikes and the Politics of Despair* (Boston, 1990).

obscure Irish delusion. It should not be forgotten that the unrest of 1969 and the slow collapse of the Northern Ireland state began not with a campaign for nationalist liberation but rather with a movement for civil rights for Catholics.

There were also continuing differences of social structure and practice that made Ireland deeply foreign to the British mind. (If the judge and jury who sentenced the Birmingham Six had read, for instance, Conrad Arensberg's anthropological work on rural Irish society, they might have taken a different view of the defendants' fatal insistence on returning to Belfast for a funeral: in their culture, it was a simple social obligation.) Statements about Irish social ideals in the twentieth century continued to be ostentatiously bizarre to the English mind; the *Manchester Guardian* was told by de Valera in 1928 that he hoped "to free Ireland from the domination of the grosser appetites and induce a mood of spiritual exaltation for a return to Spartan standards."[29] The point here is not if this was feasible or even, really, representative; Joseph Lee has remarked that if Irish values were to be deemed spiritual, then spirituality must be redefined as covetousness tempered only by sloth.[30] But the point is that it was considered an appropriate way to frame a political agenda; and that such statements helped reinforce the British view of the Irish as a race apart. The fact that the British were perceived by most of Europe as a race apart rarely entered the question.

For the purposes of this argument, this also reminds us of Connolly's preoccupation with differentiating Ireland socially and economically from Britain, as well as politically. If you were a Marxist or a Gaelic revivalist, some sort of blueprint for this was at hand. If you were neither, however, you silently assented to some kind of continuing relationship with Britain; accepted that the Irish agricultural economy would be conditioned by the proximity of British markets; and saw many of your family established in London and Manchester, even if they always came—as they put it— "home" for Christmas. The firm imposition of a distinctively Irish cultural ethos in education and religion met the psychological and political needs of nationhood; the social and religious coherence of the country made for an enviable stability, reinforced, as before independence, by emigration. Neutrality during World War II affirmed the reality of Irish autonomy. Yet economic links remained extremely close; the 1965 legislation

[29]Reported in the *Round Table* 18 (May 1928).
[30]Lee, *Ireland*, p. 522.

establishing a free trade area just slipped through, although some far-left republican prophets fulminated against it. The special Anglo-Irish relationship, as subtle and persistent in its way as the impulse to national independence, somehow sustained itself. It was inevitable that this should be so; but it also meant that traditional British attitudes to Ireland, usually obtuse as well as condescending, were sustained as well.

And from the Irish side, some doublethink was strategically necessary. Reality would never live up to the nationalist ideal, as some old republicans admitted: "We lived in dreams always; we never enjoyed them. I dreamed of an Ireland that never existed and never would exist."[31] From the days of the Irish Free State on, the need to compensate for inevitable anglicization was demonstrated by the official effort to emphasize Irishness. (The official guide to the Irish Free State, edited by Bulmer Hobson, is a particularly vivid example.)[32] Again, this is by no means an exclusively Irish phenomenon; all states that achieve independence disappoint their nationalists. The efforts of, for instance, the Finnish government in national image-building during the 1930s strike a very familiar note for an Irish reader.[33] But this is where Northern Ireland played a vital part in the difficult tissue of Anglo-Irish misunderstandings; its very existence could provide a convenient reason why utopia had not been attained. "Pending the re-integration of the national territory," life must necessarily be imperfect. The aspiration of unity provided a reason for present failings, as well as an idealist policy for the future. But in the face of the rank impossibility of a political "solution," the purist republican ethos essentially had to rely on violence.

Violence, the strategy for cutting the Gordian knot, is a response to conditions of psychological rather than actual desperation, and once more it raises the vexed question of the argument from history. Nor should the legitimization of violence be seen as the sole responsibility of the Irish. British policy often implicitly endorsed it, officially as well as unofficially. And it could be articulated in ways other than the manipulation of "law and order." Gladstone characteristically outraged many contemporaries when he stated that it was the Fenian outrages such as the bomb

---

[31]Denis McCullough quoted in Tom Garvin, *Nationalist Revolutionaries in Ireland* (Oxford, 1988), p. xi.
[32]*Saorstát Éireann Irish Free State Official Handbook* (Dublin, 1932), a beautiful and richly illustrated volume ironically celebrating a "state" whose days were already numbered.
[33]See David Kirby, "Nationalism and National Identity in the New States of Europe: The Examples of Austria, Finland and Ireland," in P. M. R. Stirk (ed.), *European Unity in Context* (New York, 1989), p. 120.

attack on Clerkenwell jail that made him turn his mind to seeking remedies for Ireland. This did not, in fact, accurately reflect the chronology of his interest in Ireland.[34] But the admission was rapidly seized upon as the necessary justification for the use of violence, and not only by Irish nationalists. The woman suffragists in 1912 used the parallel, and quoted Gladstone approvingly: "Sir, is it not the case that in all great movements in human affairs even the just cause is marked and spotted with much that is to be regretted?" Elsewhere he had remarked that without violence, "the liberties of this country would never have been attained." This was much more to the suffragists' taste than being told sharply by Lloyd George that "the Irish never had a chance of succeeding until Mr. Parnell engaged in constitutional agitation."[35] And in fact Parnell himself was a frequent if careful user of the argument that the British would listen only to violence, or the threat of it. Less expectedly, so was Redmond.[36] And so have been the apologists for colonial resistance movements all over the world, notably Kenya.[37]

The case for proving that violence is counterproductive is difficult to make, largely because it relies on counterfactual speculation. Without 1916, and with the Irish Party involved in drafting the home rule legislation of 1920, how far would its terms have approximated to the 1921 treaty achieved by violence? And how far would Labour governments in the 1920s, and Neville Chamberlain's in the 1930s, have accepted the evolution of Ireland's relationship to Britain in any case? And was Partition reinforced by the events of 1916–21, whereas it might have been muted by a federal-home-rule-within-the-empire arrangement such as that drafted in 1920? No one can answer these questions; violence in this period changed the terms and created the structure for political action. In fact, the way it came about was partly a deliberate short-

[34]See J. R. Vincent, "Gladstone and Ireland," *Proceedings of the British Academy* 63 (1977):193–238.
[35]Brian Harrison, "Violence and the Suffragettes," in his *Peaceable Kingdom: Stability and Change in Modern Britain* (Oxford, 1982), p. 37.
[36]See a speech at Maryborough, October 1901: "My guiding principle in public life is perfectly simple. I have no faith, and never had, in any English political party. I have no faith, and never had, in English benevolence towards Ireland. I have no faith, and never had, in the possibility of any class of our population getting justice in the smallest particular for mere reason or argument or persuasion. No! We have never got anything, from the days of O'Connell down to today, without labour or suffering or sacrifice on our part, or without making a movement dangerous and menacing towards England." Quoted in Liam de Paor, *Unfinished Business: Ireland Today and Tomorrow* (London, 1990), p. 21.
[37]See John Lonsdale, "Mau Maus of the Mind: Making Mau Mau and Remaking Kenya," *Journal of African History* 31, 3 (November 1990):393–421.

circuiting of the drift toward nonviolent action. Dan Breen, who led the attack on the Royal Irish Constabulary at Soloheadbeg that traditionally "began" the War of Independence, recounted frankly in the first edition of his autobiography why he took this action. It was, he said, because his companions were taking to politics—a term he employs with some contempt. This telling observation was missing in later editions of his book, but it remains enlightening.[38]

As Breen realized, the state would have to meet violence with violence. By some reckonings, the government had already shown in its reaction to Carson's rebellion that it would listen to force, and indeed would back down in front of it. The ineptness with which it retreated before violent threats, on the one hand, and responded to them by employing its own underhand violence, on the other, characterized British policy until the withdrawal of the army garrison in 1922. Both elements have been equally and lamentably noticeable in policy in Northern Ireland since 1969.

This is one of the factors which conditions the republican mind against political negotiation or compromise: "The Republic" stands, in a sense, for the negation of politics. It is striking how clearly this is affirmed by the guardians of the pure republican flame in the treaty debates.[39] Similarly, the debate of the General Army Convention of the IRA in November 1925 provided many tirades against "mere politics." The vote against the abstention policy at another IRA convention in December 1969 aroused a similar reaction. The theological adherence to the Second Dáil, refusing to admit the legitimacy of anything that had happened since, enforced a repudiation of all politics as corrupt and corrupting. The corollary of this was a commitment to violent tactics until they magically stopped being necessary with the "re-integration of the national territory."

It should be noted, once again, that the record of British government policy in 1916–21, and its covert approach to Northern Ireland in the ensuing period, adds some historical weight to the argument. But the idea that violence is the realistic response to the situation is, I think, fundamentally unhistorical, and indeed unrealistic. The easy solutions that are posited, by their very nature, deny the real conflicts and ignore the basic conundrum. As in the nineteenth century, those who embrace

---

[38]Dan Breen, *My Fight for Irish Freedom* (Dublin, 1924), pp. 32–3.
[39]See *Debate on the Treaty*, p. 128 (Mary MacSwiney) and pp. 228–9 (Liam Mellowes).

solutions which rely on violence, whether the slogan is "Clear out the trouble-makers" or "Drive the oppressor into the sea," are inevitably shifting the ground and identifying an easier enemy than the one who really constitutes the problem. This applies just as much to draconian British governments as to visionary republican nationalists. It is equally true of Gladstone invoking martial law against the supposed "village ruffians" who provoked land agitation in the 1880s, and of the 1916 rebels preferring to attack a British government that had put home rule on the statute book, rather than take on the Ulster Volunteer Force that was actually blocking its way. As the sterility of the extremist option becomes clearer, and intellectual opinion in the Republic and the North is more and more prepared to see the ambiguities, difficulties, and obstacles that bedevil the traditional versions of our histories, it is interesting to notice unfashionable subjects coming back into the historical spotlight—among them John Redmond, and the political era between the fall of Parnell in 1891 and the Easter Rising in 1916. This is beginning to be seen, not necessarily as a demoralized and sterile landscape, redeemed by the Easter sacrifice, but as a period when new options were tried, new alliances cautiously tested out, and traditional identities debated and examined.[40]

This brings us back to historical perspectives on Anglo-Irish relations, and indeed to the questions of historical revision with which I began this chapter. In some ways, historical reinterpretations in Ireland over the last generation gave a number of hostages to fortune. Perhaps too much faith was put in the brave-new-world expectations of the 1960s, and later in the *bien-pensant* liberal-Protestant bias of many of the practitioners of the art, who tended to elide some of the more awkward confrontations of Irish history. It is interesting that the most rebarbative questioning of historical pieties tends to come from the traditionally Catholic and nationalist ethos of University College, Dublin, and University College, Cork, and even from St. Patrick's College, Maynooth, whereas the most graceful smoothing over of jagged outlines originally came from tradi-

---

[40]Bew, *Conflict and Conciliation;* also R. F. Foster, "Anglo-Irish Literature, Gaelic Nationalism and Irish Politics in the 1890s," in *Ireland under the Union: Proceedings of the Second Joint Meeting of the Royal Irish Academy and the British Academy, London, 1986* (Oxford, 1989), pp. 61–82; *Modern Ireland 1600–1972* (London, 1988), chapter 18; and "Varieties of Irishness," cited in footnote 16. The current debate on the abandonment of Articles 2 and 3 from the Irish constitution (claiming the territory of Northern Ireland) has produced some memorable "impossibilist" rhetoric—see for instance, a letter from Captain Gibbons to *The Irish Times,* 11 May 1990.

tionally Protestant and unionist Trinity College, Dublin, and Queen's University, Belfast: perhaps another sign that old identities have been interrogated. It should also be pointed out that initial examination of the basis of Irish nationalism, geographic, social and religious, tended to come at first from scholars working outside Ireland altogether.[41]

We have arrived, however, at a point where historical perspectives on Anglo-Irish relations, and on Irish history in general, have thrown some interesting light from new angles, and asserted some provocative parallels. Oliver MacDonagh has written a brilliant book on England and Ireland in which he compares the 1970s to the 1790s—that era of recurrent crises, missed chances, and reactionary obtuseness on both sides.[42] Liam de Paor has noted parallels between the politics of Ireland during the 1980s and the Redmond era, and has compared the current condition of Irish constitutional relations to Britain with the situation of flux following 1916.[43] Elsewhere I have likened the atmosphere of cultural activity and the potential for a cross-cultural debate currently opening up in Ireland to the ferments of early twentieth-century Ireland, when much of the most interesting developments were taking place outside the formal arena of politics, as was acutely noted by one of the principal brokers in the cultural debate. "I understand and sympathise with the fixed passion of the politician for his theory of an Irish State," wrote AE in 1912,

but I do not believe he will gain the results he hopes for unless his state is composed of people who may truly be called citizens; and citizenship in the true sense is created much more by the non-political movements than by the political movements in our time. The highest developments of humanity, of civic and patriotic life the world has known, have been in the small states, in communities no larger than Sligo.[44]

In Ireland, the study of history might ideally be used for such "non-political" explorations; but it remains resolutely a political issue. I was struck recently by reading a reflection on national history:

[41]Notably Erhard Rumpf, *Nationalism and Socialism in Twentieth-Century Ireland* (English translation, edited by A. C. Hepburn, Liverpool, 1977); M. W. Heslinga, *The Irish Border as a Cultural Divide* (Assen, Netherlands, 1962); Charles Townshend, *Political Violence in Ireland: Government and Resistance since 1848* (Oxford, 1983); David Fitzpatrick, *Politics and Irish Life: Provincial Experience of War and Revolution, 1913–1921* (Dublin, 1977).

[42]Oliver MacDonagh, *States of Mind: A Study of Anglo-Irish Conflict 1780–1980* (London, 1983).

[43]De Paor, *Unfinished Business*, pp. 16, 137.

[44]AE [George Russell], *Co-operation and Nationality* (Dublin, 1912), pp. 59–60.

We need history that promises signposts to identity, moorings in the rapids of progress.... History holds for [us] the chance to find ourselves again.... Today the issue is the salvation of our intellectual personality ... the calculability of our policy, the inner good sense of our political culture, and last of all the continuity of our fatally threatened constitution of freedom.... The cultural politics of the sixties sowed the storm, and today we are reaping the whirlwind. If we fail to agree on an elemental cultural curriculum, which can prepare the way for continuity and consensus in our country, and which can prepare once again the measure and mode of patriotism, then [this country] may well find that the best part of its history is behind it.[45]

This plea for a politically acceptable history, nurtured for state-building purposes, might be the manifesto of an Irish antirevisionist, or possibly a conservative critique of the new National Curriculum in English schools. As it happens, it is neither: it is a plea by a prominent German historian, Michael Stürmer, who believes that too much examination of the German past is leading to national demoralization, and who reacts against those German revisionists who have brought the forbidden subject of nazism into the foreground of general treatments of German history in the nineteenth and twentieth centuries. The question of historical interpretation in Germany is so highly politicized as to have affected federal elections since the early 1980s. It is worth remembering that controversy over the legitimate use of the national past, and who has the right to reinterpret it, is not a peculiarly Irish phenomenon. To fully possess your history, you may have to give some of it up.

It is also worth noting that, despite fashionable nostrums to the contrary, there is no such thing as an "end" to history; even if one form of struggle ends, or changes its mode, a static millennium does not automatically arrive. This is as unrealistic as the idea of a past golden age, which I have mentioned earlier as characterizing received notions of Irish and Anglo-Irish history: the theory that social, political, and economic relationships were rightly and happily ordered before someone came along from outside and spoiled everything. I have mentioned how this lies behind the apparently socialist analysis by James Connolly (who was much influenced by Alice Stopford Green's resolutely unhistorical tract, *The Making of Ireland and Its Undoing*);[46] but it is a fantasy indulged

[45]Michael Stürmer, *Dissonanzen des Fortschritts: Essays über Geschichte und Politik in Deutschland* (Munich, 1986), p. 276, quoted in Geoff Eley, "Nazism, Politics and Public Memory: Thoughts on the West German *Historikerstreit*, 1986–1987," *Past and Present* 129 (November 1988): 181.

[46]Alice Stopford Green, *The Making of Ireland and Its Undoing 1200–1600* (1908; reprint, Salem, N.H., 1977).

in by both sides. The golden age has been variously perceived as before the Normans, before the Plantations, before O'Connell, before the Land War, before 1916, before the civil rights marches of 1968, or before the British troops arrived in 1969. And it is interesting that those who try to recapture the supposed golden-age spirit are condemned to re-create an artificially exclusive environment: whether it is the Victorian landlord's idea of a model estate without any "land agitators" living on it; the Gaelic revivalists' fantasy of life in the West of Ireland; the idealized version sometimes presented of social relations in Northern Ireland under the old Stormont regime; or the romantic accounts already appearing of the 1989 West Belfast Festival. Again, the judgment holds good against British and Irish, unionist and nationalist, alike. And it is the denial of plurality, variousness, and ambiguity that seems unrealistic. By contrast, acceptance of the complex strata of identities laid down by the irreversible accumulations of history seems a pragmatic response, not just a well-meaning liberal cliché.

It is at least mildly encouraging that in 1989, 12 August and the traditionally Protestant celebration of the Apprentice Boys anniversary in Derry were presented as a shared event in the history of the city, with the support of the nationalist-controlled city council;[47] and that in 1990 celebration of the tricentenary of the Battle of the Boyne was organized at Drogheda with the local Fianna Fáil councillors taking a leading part. But the worry is that the popular view of the history of Anglo-Irish relations, Northern Ireland, and much else will not accommodate the ambiguities and uncertainties, and that professional history-writing will remain too tentative and too specialized to please those who demand history as a tonic for the national soul, like the German professor quoted above. As I noted at the beginning, historical perspectives can obscure as well as illuminate. To escape imprisoning historical perspectives requires deliberate refocusing. If the history of recent Anglo-Irish relations demonstrates anything, it is, first, the necessity for interrogation of traditional attitudes on both sides of the Irish Sea as well as on both sides of the border, and second, the fact that there are at last some small signs that this is beginning to happen.

[47]In 1990, however, the commemoration of the Siege of Derry, organized by the Social Democratic and Labour Party, was boycotted by unionist councillors.

2

A constitutional background
to the Northern Ireland crisis

ALAN J. WARD

Scholars are inclined to discuss the roots of the present problem in Northern Ireland in terms of Irish nationalism and Irish identity. This chapter, however, concentrates on the more mundane subject of constitutional relations. It reviews attempts since the late eighteenth century to create an Anglo-Irish relationship that would satisfy Irish demands for self-government while protecting important British interests in Ireland, including the Protestant minority. It is an elementary if often ignored fact that, when viewed from the perspective of a settlement that has to satisfy more than one party, the intractability of the Irish problem becomes particularly evident.

One can date the belief that Ireland should be subordinated to English, or British, interests to the twelfth century, but the conquest of the country was not completed until the early seventeenth century, by which time it had developed its own political institutions. The two countries existed under one crown as separate kingdoms with separate parliaments, but Britain could never accept the principle of Ireland's constitutional co-equality and used three forms of control to manage Ireland as a de facto colony prior to 1782. The first was the royal prerogative, exercised by the lord lieutenant acting as the agent of the British executive in Ireland. The second was manipulation of the Irish political class, using the influence and patronage of the crown to provide honors, offices, and pensions

ALAN J. WARD is Professor of Government at The College of William and Mary, Williamsburg, Virginia. He is the author of *Ireland and Anglo-American Relations, 1899–1921; The Easter Rising, 1916: Revolution and Irish Nationalism;* and *Northern Ireland: Living with the Crisis.*

to Irish politicians in return for their political support. The third was control of Irish legislation. Poynings' Law of 1494, an act of the Irish Parliament, required all Irish acts to be approved by the king in council in London before their passage in Ireland, and the Declaratory Act of 1720, an act of the British Parliament, asserted Britain's right to legislate for Ireland.

THE "CONSTITUTION OF 1782"

For a moment it appeared that Ireland's subordination would end when Britain, faced with the intimidating pressure of the 40,000-member militia known as the Volunteers, agreed in 1782 to the amendment of Poynings' Law in the Irish Parliament and the repeal of the Declaratory Act in London. These two changes, often known as the "Constitution of 1782," gave Ireland virtual legislative independence, but Britain was now faced in Ireland with a constitutional problem much like the one it had recently failed to solve in its American colonies. How could self-government for an important part of the British Empire be reconciled with the protection of vital British interests? Ireland was an important element in Britain's imperial economic design, and its control was considered essential to British security: security for the empire against piecemeal disintegration, for Britain's trade routes in the Atlantic, and for the British Isles themselves, threatened by hostile powers in continental Europe.

The plan offered to Ireland was essentially the one that had been offered, too late, to the American colonies a few years earlier. Ireland could have full domestic legislative autonomy in return for formal agreements concerning trade, a contribution to imperial defense, and a reserve power for the British Parliament that would be used to defend the integrity of the crown and the empire. In Vincent Harlow's words, the British government had already "probed their way step by step towards the idea of Britain as the superintendent of a group of subordinate commonwealths."[1]

The Americans had rejected the British formula, and so did the Irish patriot leaders when it was offered to them in 1783. Henry Grattan, for example, insisted that a shared crown would provide all the assurance of security Britain could reasonably require. The British government did not share his confidence and quickly reverted to two of the forms of

[1]Vincent T. Harlow, *The Founding of the Second British Empire, 1763–1793* (London, 1952), 1:493.

control it had previously used to manage Irish politics in the British interest: the royal prerogative and patronage. Irish foreign relations and defense were still matters for the prerogative, and Britain, through the lord lieutenant, continued to manipulate the Irish political class with patronage.

There were already some in the 1790s who argued against British manipulation by suggesting that Ireland should be governed "responsibly," as was Britain to a degree, by a ministry having the support of its own legislature rather than by Englishmen appointed by and responsible to the government in London. Prime Minister William Pitt disagreed, fearing that a responsible Irish executive might disagree with Britain on important policy issues. But he also feared the existing situation because the Irish Parliament was only tenuously subject to British manipulation. Pitt knew, to quote Harlow again, that "whenever public opinion became inflamed, the [Irish] oligarchy took fright, and the laboriously constructed majority of the Viceroy . . . disintegrated."[2]

By the late 1790s, neither British control of the royal prerogative nor its manipulation of the Irish political class could secure the country as the United Irishmen turned to revolution and the French landed in Ireland. To guarantee British security, therefore, Pitt made the ultimate use of patronage to purchase a majority for union in the Irish Parliament in 1800.

Hindsight suggests that an important opportunity was lost between 1782 and 1800. Had Ireland's political leaders accepted formally what they were prepared to accept in practice, which is to say, membership in the British imperial system, the country probably would have entered the nineteenth century as a subordinate but self-governing entity, much like a self-governing colony. It was from essentially this constitutional status that Australia, Canada, and New Zealand gradually worked their way to full independence in the nineteenth century. Ireland's leaders chose not to associate with Britain on these terms in the 1780s, and a venal political class allowed itself to be bribed into abandoning the ancient Irish Parliament in 1800.

THE UNION AND IRISH EXCEPTIONALISM

Union in 1801 ought to have simplified the Anglo-Irish constitutional relationship but it failed dismally because it was approached in a truly

[2]Ibid., p. 55.

bizarre way. The Union did nothing to eradicate the sense that Ireland was a discrete political community. The country was governed in many respects as a crown colony because it was still seen as a security problem. Irish representatives sat in the United Kingdom Parliament but the lord lieutenant continued to preside over a vice-regal court and an Irish administration in Dublin. There continued to be, for a while, an Irish treasury, an Irish currency, and an Irish chancellor of the exchequer. At first the home secretary assumed he would have responsibility for law and order in Ireland, as in Britain, but this authority was actually entrusted to the lord lieutenant, who still had prerogative powers. During the entire period of the Union, therefore, Irish administration was an extreme example of "Irish exceptionalism": the treatment of Ireland as an exceptional case in forms of government, in the continuous application of special laws to police popular disturbances, and in a host of remedial measures to address its social and economic problems.

Irish exceptionalism created an enormous amount of extra work for the United Kingdom Parliament. For example, from 1800 to 1830 more than one hundred commissions and sixty-one parliamentary committees investigated Irish problems, and in the parliamentary session of 1823 alone forty-nine of eighty-four business days were devoted to Irish subjects.[3] All this effort failed to produce any solutions because there was no consensus on the causes of Ireland's problems and their cure. Jenkins notes, for example, that British governments from 1812 to 1830 could only be formed by agreeing to take no collective positions on Ireland, and even those most responsible for administering the country, the chief secretary, under secretary, and lord lieutenant, were to be found in opposite camps.[4] The result was piecemeal relief and piecemeal repression, neither of which amounted to anything resembling an Irish policy. This absence of consensus delayed Catholic emancipation until it was forced on the government by popular pressure in 1829, and by then a powerful Catholic nationalist movement had been created.

THE REPEAL MOVEMENT AND HOME RULE

The first manifestation of Catholic nationalism after emancipation was the repeal agitation led by Daniel O'Connell in the 1830s and 1840s.

[3]Brian Jenkins, *Era of Emancipation: British Government of Ireland, 1812–1830* (Kingston, Ont., and Montreal, P.Q., 1988), p. 177.
[4]Ibid., p. 303.

This was imaginatively organized, but there was always confusion over the precise constitutional relationship with Britain that the repeal movement was seeking. It is clear that O'Connell himself was not an Irish separatist and he spoke most often of his desire for a local Irish legislature to attend to purely Irish interests. In 1844 he framed this in federal terms, seeing the repeal of the Union as a technical first step toward establishment of a new federation which would provide, he wrote, "for questions of Imperial, colonial, military, naval, and of foreign alliance and policy, a congressional or federative parliament, in which Ireland should have her fair share and proportion of representation and power."[5] Others in the repeal movement favored a simple return to the so-called Constitution of 1782.

O'Connell failed to secure constitutional reform because he had very few supporters, Irish or British, in Parliament, but reform acts in 1867 and 1884 enlarged the Catholic electorate, and by the mid-1880s there were more than eighty Irish nationalist members of Parliament, led by Charles Stewart Parnell and committed to home rule, which is to say, to the creation of a subordinate parliament in Ireland. By 1886 this group held the balance of power in the House of Commons and the Liberal prime minister, William Gladstone, responded by introducing a comprehensive proposal for the devolution of legislative powers to Ireland.

Gladstone's 1886 home rule bill was largely his own work and formed the nucleus of each of the subsequent home rule bills. The 1886 bill was defeated by Liberal unionist defections in the House of Commons. The 1893 bill passed the House of Commons only to be soundly defeated in the House of Lords. The 1912 bill became law in 1914, over the Lords' veto, but met with the threat of armed resistance from Ulster Protestants and was suspended for the duration of World War I. It was subsequently abandoned, but formed the basis for the Government of Ireland Act of 1920, which created two Irish parliaments, one in Dublin and one in Belfast. This act was brought into operation in Northern Ireland in 1921 but was rejected by Sinn Féin in the South.

All the home rule bills provided that the United Kingdom would legislate for imperial and British affairs while an Irish parliament would "make laws for the peace, order and good government of Ireland" subject to the recognized supremacy of the United Kingdom Parliament and to certain exclusions. The Irish would not be allowed to legislate concerning

[5]W. J. Fitzpatrick (ed.), *Correspondence of Daniel O'Connell* (London, 1888), 2:446.

the crown, honors and titles, foreign and colonial relations, defense, trade and navigation, customs and excise, or the terms of the home rule act itself. Ireland, whether immediately or shortly, would control the post office, the police, and the judiciary, but the Judicial Committee of the United Kingdom Privy Council would be the final court of appeal and would determine which parliament would have jurisdiction in any matter. Finally, and to protect Irish Protestants, the bills provided that no Irish parliament might make laws to establish, endow, or restrict religion, set religious tests for office, require children to receive religious instruction in public schools, or restrict the equal protection and due process of law.

The debates in Parliament on the home rule bills were largely about two related questions. First, would the Irish accept the subordinate status accorded to their parliament and the restrictions on its powers? Second, would it be possible, in practice, to prevent the Irish from expanding the powers of an Irish parliament in violation of the terms of the act, or even from using it as a launch pad for secession? The majority of Irish histories take a rather uncritical view of home rule but at the time unionists answered no, decisively, to both questions, and their position was defensible. Indeed, seen from the perspective of a stable Anglo-Irish relationship, all the home rule bills had three flaws likely to cause friction between Britain and Ireland and encourage Irish separatism: the representation formula for the United Kingdom Parliament, the financial formula, and the formal constitutional relationship between the United Kingdom and Ireland.

The first flaw, the representation formula, is simply described. If the Irish were to be represented in the United Kingdom Parliament at Westminster with full powers, they would participate not only in the governance of the United Kingdom as a whole but also in the domestic governance of Great Britain. Their votes would help determine legislation for Britain, and their members might, as in 1886 and 1910, decide which party would form its government. But if Ireland were denied seats in the United Kingdom Parliament on these grounds, it would be reduced to the status of a self-governing colony, which would strengthen its case for independence.

Various formulae were offered to overcome the representation dilemma. They ranged from no Irish representation at Westminster, except for debates on home rule itself, to full Irish representation with very limited voting rights, to full representation and full voting rights, to the formula actually enacted in the 1914 and 1920 acts, partial representation with full voting rights. But any formula was going to be unsatisfactory, either because it would give Ireland too much power in British affairs or too little power in United Kingdom affairs. There was no satisfactory solution to this problem short of a comprehensive plan of devolution to Scotland, Wales, England, and Ireland, "home rule all round." This would leave the United Kingdom Parliament with no regional responsibilities. Such a plan was acceptable in principle to Gladstone and Asquith, and to the House of Commons itself in 1919, but the fundamental reconstruction of the constitution that it required was never introduced.

The second flaw in home rule was the proposed financial relationship between the United Kingdom and Ireland. Home rule bills always denied Ireland any major taxing powers, including customs and excise, and this meant that there were likely to be conflicts between the United Kingdom and Ireland over the supply and use of money. No nationalist leader accepted the financial terms as final, and in 1912 John Redmond said, "[Home rule] is a provisional settlement.... When the time for revision does come ... we will be entitled to complete power for Ireland over the whole of our financial system."[6]

The third flaw in home rule was the ambiguity of the proposed constitutional relationship between Britain and Ireland. When might the United Kingdom assert the parliamentary supremacy recognized in the bills? Liberal governments insisted that intervention would be used only in the most extreme case, a contingency that would never arise because, by satisfying Irish nationalism, home rule would bind Ireland closer to the Union than before. The unionists countered that Irish nationalists could not be trusted to respect home rule and that no Liberal government, certainly no Liberal government dependent itself on Irish support for its majority at Westminster, would ever intervene in Ireland to protect the Protestant minority. Liberals also insisted that the provisions for religious freedom and due process built into home rule would be sufficient to protect Irish Protestants, but this took a very narrow view of the Protestants' fears of a Catholic-dominated parliament in Dublin. They believed that a Dublin parliament would jeopardize all that the Union protected: their religion, certainly, but also their property, their status, and their identity. There was no way to accommodate all these concerns in a piece of legislation, and the Liberals could only counter by accusing

[6]R. J. Lawrence, *The Government of Northern Ireland: Public Finance and Public Services, 1921–1964* (Oxford, England, 1965), p. 181.

unionists of exaggeration. "Given perversity on the one hand and pedantry on the other," said Prime Minister Herbert Henry Asquith in 1913, "there is not a Constitution in the world which could not be wrecked in a week."[7]

Had home rule been imposed in 1886, 1893, or 1914, would it have finally resolved the problem of the Anglo-Irish relationship? Probably not. In another work I conclude:

Rather than settling the problem of the British-Irish relationship...home rule might have been the focus of powerful centrifugal forces as Parnell and his successors demanded greater autonomy for Ireland. Talented Irish politicians would have looked for their political fortunes to Dublin, not to Westminster, because no Irishman would have been allowed to govern Britain. In Dublin they would have operated within the flexible framework of colonial home rule and responsible government which had already brought the self-governing colonies to the brink of independence by 1886. And had Parnell become Prime Minister of Ireland, with the backing of three quarters of the Irish parliament and the support of what was, organizationally, probably the most advanced political party in the world, it is difficult to imagine a list of reserved matters in a British statute restraining him for very long.[8]

Colonial experience also confirms the view that home rule probably would have been, as the unionists argued, a step toward Irish independence. Home rule proposed a constitution for what would have been, in many respects, a self-governing Irish colony. For example, the lord lieutenant would have had essentially the powers of a colonial governor: to appoint ministers, summon and dissolve parliament, propose money bills, and give the royal assent. But the constitutional subordination of the colonies did not guarantee the integrity of the British Empire because the key to independence was the introduction of responsible government by specific instructions to the colonial governor from the crown, not by a change in colonial constitutional law. That is to say, the British conceded that the colonies would be governed by responsible executives drawn from their own legislatures, and once that was accomplished executive power moved inexorably to the colonial governments and away from the governor, the agent of the United Kingdom. Unionists such as A. V. Dicey understood this process perfectly well because although the independence of the colonies was not formalized until the Statute of Westminster in 1931, it had been set in motion in Canada in 1848.[9] In this

[7]*The Times* (London), 16 January 1913.
[8]Alan J. Ward, "Models of Government and Anglo-Irish Relations," *Albion* 20 (1988): 34.
[9]See, for example, A. V. Dicey, *A Leap in the Dark* (London, 1911).

context it is significant that the Irish home rule bill of 1893 came very close to defining responsible government in constitutional law for the first time in the British Empire by requiring the lord lieutenant to assent to legislation on the advice of the Executive Council of the Privy Council, essentially a responsible cabinet.

During the home rule debates it was argued that Ireland was too close to Britain, too important militarily, economically, and politically, to follow or be allowed to follow the colonies' course to dominion status and independence. But given the intensity of Ireland's nationalism, the sentiment of an oppressed people unmatched in the colonies, Nicholas Mansergh was right to conclude: "While the Irish enjoyed less freedom [than the self-governing colonies], they were likely, despite the modesty of their immediate claims, in the long run to demand more than their colonial counterparts."[10] It was exactly this interpretation of Irish nationalism that caused unionists to shudder when Parnell declared, in January 1885, "No man has the right to fix the boundary to the march of a nation."[11] As home rule approached, unionists began to prepare for civil war.

THE PARTITION DEBATE IN 1914

Was there any way to accommodate the unionists' fears without denying Irish nationalism? There was a way, partition, although it is unlikely that it would have inhibited nationalist Ireland's evolution to independence. But it was natural that unionists would eventually embrace partition to escape a Catholic-dominated Irish parliament, even if this required the sacrifice of the Protestant minority outside Ulster. At the Buckingham Palace Conference of July 1914, called in a last attempt to find a solution by agreement, the home rule debate was reduced to two formulas for partition, which contained the seeds of a settlement. For the government and the Irish Parliamentary Party, respectively, Prime Minister Asquith and John Redmond were ready to consider temporary exclusion for six counties for a period of six years. This implied an important concession because, in normal circumstances, the six years would have included a general election, and had the Conservatives won they would have amended home rule to exclude at least some northern counties permanently.

For the Conservatives and unionists, respectively, Andrew Bonar Law

[10]Nicholas Mansergh, *The Commonwealth Experience,* 2nd. ed. (London, 1982), 1:225.
[11]Paul Bew, *C. S. Parnell* (Dublin, 1980), p. 70.

and Sir Edward Carson countered with a proposal containing an equally important concession, that six of Ulster's nine counties should be permanently excluded from home rule unless they were to choose, on a county-by-county basis, to accept home rule. Because two of the six contained Catholic majorities, this proposal would probably have led to the permanent exclusion of only four counties, not the six ultimately included in Northern Ireland.

The subject of partition had been broached, therefore, and a resolute government might have driven a limited, four-county partition plan through the gap at this point, with the partitioned portion of the North continuing as a fully integrated part of the United Kingdom. But the outbreak of war in Europe in 1914 gave Asquith an opportunity to defer action. Home rule for a united Ireland was enacted into law but suspended pending the end of the war, and by then, of course, everything had changed. Irish nationalism had moved beyond home rule to demand outright independence in the aftermath of the 1916 Easter Rising, and the Liberals had begun their descent into the political wilderness. They were replaced in government by a Lloyd George-led coalition dependent on Conservative and unionist support in Parliament.

DEVOLUTION TO NORTHERN IRELAND

The partition proposals in 1914 and wartime discussions of federalism opened the way for the Government of Ireland Act of 1920, which created two home rule parliaments in 1921, one in Belfast and one in Dublin. The unionists had not asked for a Northern Ireland parliament in 1914, but one was created in 1921 to assure foreign, primarily American, opinion that self-determination was being recognized for the whole of Ireland, albeit in two parts. Had Northern Ireland remained wholly integrated into the broad political system of the United Kingdom, as was envisaged in the partition proposals of 1914, it might have been spared the sectarian politics of a self-governing region.

Once the principle of partition was accepted, the unionists who dominated the Lloyd George cabinet were able to insist on a Northern Ireland of six counties. Although only four contained unionist majorities, in the six counties as a whole there was a comfortable unionist majority. A council of Ireland, with representatives from both parliaments, was proposed to coordinate all-Ireland affairs, and Lloyd George hoped that it would lead the way to a united Ireland under home rule.

The Northern Ireland Parliament convened on 22 June 1921, but the convening of its counterpart in Dublin six days later was boycotted by Sinn Féin, which had won all but 4 of the 128 seats. Devolution was out of the question in the South, therefore, and the United Kingdom government resumed control of the twenty-six counties until the Anglo-Irish Treaty of December 1921 opened the way for the Irish Free State and Irish independence in 1922. The story of how the United Kingdom and the Free State struggled to define a new constitutional relationship after 1921 is fascinating, but must be set aside in favor of the issue of the constitutional relationship between the United Kingdom and Northern Ireland.

Ironically, Northern Ireland provides the only example of home rule in practice. The Government of Ireland Act created a bicameral legislature and a responsible executive in Northern Ireland. The governor exercised the royal prerogative on the advice of a cabinet drawn from the legislature. The Northern Ireland Parliament had power to legislate for "the peace, order and good government of Northern Ireland," subject to essentially the same exceptions contained in all the previous home rule bills concerning the crown, freedom of religion, trade, foreign relations, and defense. As in the 1893 bill and the suspended 1914 act, the supremacy of the United Kingdom Parliament was recognized explicitly.

Unionists had always argued that the future of the Union would turn not on formal constitutional arrangements but on the probability that the nationalist majority would use home rule as a vehicle for independence. This, at least, was not a problem in Northern Ireland because the province, as it came to be known by unionists, was created to permit the Protestant majority to remain in the Union. Nonetheless, the history of Northern Ireland as a self-governing entity demonstrates that the three flaws in Irish home rule identified earlier persisted, albeit in muted form.

The representation problem existed but was negligible because of the small numbers involved. Northern Ireland was assigned only twelve members in the United Kingdom House of Commons, plus one university member for a time, rather than the seventeen or eighteen its numbers would have justified. The government argued in 1920, as it had in 1914, that Ireland did not need full representation at Westminster because it would have a parliament of its own, but in principle this reasoning left Northern Ireland underrepresented in United Kingdom affairs and overrepresented in British affairs. It was not until 1979, after the abolition of its own parliament, that Northern Ireland was assigned an appropriate seventeen seats. Ironically, by then, Northern Irish representatives were free to participate in the government of Britain but not, under the terms of direct rule, in the government of Northern Ireland.

The issue of financial relations also produced no crippling conflict with the United Kingdom because Northern Ireland was in an extremely weak bargaining position. The Government of Ireland Act reserved all important taxes to the United Kingdom Parliament, amounting to 90 percent of the six counties' revenues. Northern Ireland services, all of which fell within the legislative purview of the Northern Ireland Parliament, therefore had to be supported by grants from the United Kingdom Treasury. However, the depressed state of Northern Ireland's economy required a net annual subsidy to Northern Ireland, which reached £72 million in 1968–69; this meant that it had no choice but to accept grants on terms set in London. As R. J. Lawrence concluded: "Northern Ireland... evaded rather than refuted the Unionist thesis that Home Rule is impractical. That thesis rested on the natural assumption that a regional legislature would insist on making full use of its powers. Ulster preferred close cooperation."[12]

It is when the third of the flaws in home rule is considered—the ambiguous constitutional relationship between the United Kingdom and Ireland—that the inherent weakness of home rule becomes dramatically apparent in Northern Ireland. During the home rule debates, unionists had consistently argued that the supremacy of the United Kingdom Parliament and the protections for the minority, religious freedom, and due process of law built into the bills would not adequately protect the complex interests of the Protestant minority. Unionists did not trust the United Kingdom government to intervene to protect them from the anticipated excesses of a Dublin parliament, and their suspicions were fueled by Liberal governments much more anxious to assure nationalists that there would be no intervention than to assure unionists that they would be protected.

When might the United Kingdom intervene? When would a royal veto or the supreme power of Parliament be invoked against a home rule government or parliament? Neither routinely nor to block legislation the United Kingdom did not like, said James Bryce, the chief secretary, in 1893. The supremacy of Parliament would be "a power to be kept in

---

[12]Lawrence, *The Government of Northern Ireland*, p. 181.

reserve, only to be used if the gravest case should arise—and in particular if the restrictive provisions of the Bill should be transgressed." Bryce trusted that a constitutional convention would emerge to guarantee this restrictive interpretation.[13]

The history of Northern Ireland shows that Bryce's interpretation gave little protection to the minority that ultimately emerged under home rule, not the unionists of Ireland as a whole but the nationalists of a partitioned Northern Ireland. All the issues that led to the civil rights movement of the 1960s and the ultimate collapse of the Northern Ireland political system fell within the statutory authority of the Northern Ireland Parliament—housing, job discrimination, local government, and the police. Because Northern Ireland did not trespass upon the restrictive provisions of the Government of Ireland Act, the United Kingdom could only intervene by overriding the legislative authority of the Northern Ireland Parliament, something it would not do. The speaker of the United Kingdom House of Commons, for example, strictly enforced a convention that no parliamentary questions would be allowed on subjects reserved to Northern Ireland. Furthermore, Calvert noted in 1968, United Kingdom governments never legislated for Northern Ireland in subject areas transferred to Northern Ireland in the 1920 act without the consent of the Northern Ireland government. There is evidence that they sometimes used pressure, including threats of financial sanctions, to secure that consent for social and economic legislation, but not to secure lasting relief for the nationalist minority.[14]

It was not until the late 1960s, in response to the civil rights agitation and the violent reaction of unionists, that the United Kingdom seriously addressed itself to the grievances of the minority in Northern Ireland, and that decision exacerbated the crisis. When Terence O'Neill, Northern Ireland's prime minister, dismissed William Craig from his government in 1968 because of Craig's opposition to British prime minister Harold Wilson's demand for reforms in local government, housing, employment practices, and the police, all subjects reserved to Northern Ireland in the 1920 act, Craig insisted: "I would resist any effort by any government in Great Britain, whatever its complexion might be, to exercise power in any way to interfere with the proper jurisdiction of the Government of

[13]*Hansard Parliamentary Debates*, 4th ser., 8 (1893):1427.
[14]Harry G. Calvert, *Constitutional Law in Northern Ireland* (London, 1968), pp. 88–9.

Northern Ireland. It is merely a reserve of power to deal with an emergency situation."[15] To Craig, the events of 1968 did not constitute a crisis. O'Neill won on this occasion, and reforms were begun, but they were soon to cost him his leadership of the Ulster Unionist Party, which deeply resented the intervention from London. O'Neill's successors, James Chichester-Clark and Brian Faulkner, had no more success than he at implementing reform without provoking unionist resistance, and in 1972 the Northern Ireland (Temporary Provisions) Act suspended the Northern Ireland Parliament. The supremacy of the United Kingdom Parliament had finally been asserted, not simply to override the authority of the Northern Ireland Parliament on particular issues but to extinguish it. The 1972 act vested all government powers in the newly created office of secretary of state for Northern Ireland. Lacking a legislature to make laws, Northern Ireland was now to be governed by orders in council having "the same validity and effect."[16] The system quickly came to be known as direct rule, meaning direct rule from Westminster.

CONSTITUTIONAL CONTORTIONS, 1973–1993

In no period of United Kingdom history has there been more constitutional controversy and innovation than in the years since the introduction of direct rule in Northern Ireland. Indeed, one might start in 1969, when the Royal Commission on the Constitution began to sit under the chairmanship of Lord Kilbrandon, who was also to chair an independent inquiry on Northern Ireland, sponsored by the British-Irish Association, which reported in 1984. More than two decades have now passed, with a bewildering number of commissions, reports, white papers, discussion documents, bills, and acts of Parliament, most of them not devoted to Northern Ireland. The Kilbrandon Commission reported in 1973, for example, that there should be devolved assemblies in Scotland and Wales. Three white papers later, devolution was enacted for Scotland and Wales in 1978 only to be rejected by referendum in both countries in March 1979.[17] It is easy to forget that these Scottish and Welsh bills were being

---

[15]Martin Wallace, *Northern Ireland: Fifty Years of Self-Government* (New York, 1971), p. 39.
[16]Brigid Hadfield, *The Constitution of Northern Ireland* (Belfast, 1989), pp. 100–1.
[17]The 52 percent of Scottish voters who approved devolution fell well short of the referendum requirement that 40 percent of the electorate vote yes. In Wales only 20 percent of those who voted supported devolution.

conceived and rejected during the period of intense constitutional controversy in Ireland.

Following suspension of the Northern Ireland Parliament in 1972, the search for a successor began almost immediately because United Kingdom governments have never seriously contemplated the complete integration of Northern Ireland into the British political system. Official policy is to devolve power to Northern Ireland when peace is restored, in part to accommodate the wishes of the people there but also to avoid the burden of legislating for a region that is still seen as an exceptional place requiring exceptional measures. But no matter how much some unionists may argue for a return to devolution with majority rule, the classical home rule model is now recognized to be impossible in a community divided on sectarian lines. In January 1974, therefore, the so-called power-sharing assembly formally came into being. This body collapsed during a unionist-led general strike in May. It could not survive unionist outrage at the Sunningdale Agreement of 9 December 1973, in which representatives of the United Kingdom, the Irish Republic, and the Northern Ireland executive-designate agreed to recognize an all-Ireland dimension in an Irish settlement. Article 7 of the agreement provided that there would be a "Council of Ministers with executive and harmonizing functions and a consultative role, and a Consultative Assembly with advisory and review functions."[18]

Direct rule was reintroduced from 1974 to 1982. In 1975, the Northern Ireland Constitutional Convention was convened to allow the Northern Irish themselves to find a solution to their dilemma, but the United Ulster Unionist Council, a clear majority, and the nationalist Social Democratic and Labour Party (SDLP) supported contradictory positions. Consequently, the majority report was rejected by the government because it did not "command sufficiently widespread acceptance throughout the community to provide stable and effective government."[19]

This period of direct rule was followed by the "rolling devolution" of the Northern Ireland Act of 1982. This act provided for yet another Northern Ireland Assembly with "scrutinising, deliberative and consultative" functions,[20] and provided for partial or substantial devolution of legislative and executive functions to Northern Ireland subject to the development of a degree of cross-community consensus. Such consensus

---

[18]Hadfield, *The Constitution of Northern Ireland*, p. 113.
[19]Ibid., p. 128.
[20]Ibid., p. 152.

never materialized. The Assembly was elaborately organized to permit almost endless scrutiny, deliberation, and consultation, but it had no legislative power and was boycotted throughout by both the SDLP and Sinn Féin. Unionists finally brought it to a halt in 1986, their objection this time being the Anglo-Irish Agreement of 1985, which restated many of the understandings of the Sunningdale Agreement and created an intergovernmental conference through which the government of the Irish Republic is given a formal consultative role in Northern Irish affairs.[21] The Anglo-Irish Agreement also provides, in Article 4(b), "that responsibility in respect of certain matters within the powers of the Secretary of State for Northern Ireland should be devolved within Northern Ireland on a basis which would secure widespread acceptance throughout the community," but as of April 1993 there was no sign of progress on a new constitutional framework. The novel constitutional formulation in the Anglo-Irish Agreement, which recognizes United Kingdom sovereignty in Northern Ireland while providing for a formal consultative role for the Irish Republic in Northern Ireland's affairs, is the major obstacle to unionist cooperation.

This brief recitation gives some sense of the complex issues involved in Scottish, Welsh, and Irish devolution since 1972, but it does not exhaust the list of constitutional problems facing the United Kingdom. From 1970 to 1972 the Conservative government of Edward Heath was also engaged in negotiating entry into the European Community. The United Kingdom entered the EC on 1 January 1973, only to find the issue of membership reopened by Harold Wilson's Labour government in 1974. The terms of entry were renegotiated and were put to a referendum in 1975, which finally confirmed membership.

During these years, therefore, the United Kingdom was faced with two levels of constitutional challenge. At one level it struggled to come to terms with the problems of regional self-government in Northern Ireland, Scotland, and Wales. At another level it was faced with the issue of the European Community. It met neither challenge with particular efficiency, although the entry into the EC, a particularly graceless affair, was finally achieved. The attempts to come to terms with regional nationalism failed entirely, in large part because they were, as every attempt to manage Ireland has been for two hundred years, acts of political expediency under pressure rather than principled attempts at creative

[21]Ibid., pp. 261–8.

constitution-making. All the devolution proposals put forward by United Kingdom governments since 1886 have been responses to political crises involving challenges to the state and, with the exception of the Government of Ireland Act of 1920, to the governing party as well. Arthur Balfour argued in 1914, "Home rule is not a constitutional remedy, it is a parliamentary device";[22] therefore it is no surprise that the flaws associated with Irish home rule were reproduced almost exactly in the Scottish home rule act of 1978.

The result of all this activity in the past twenty years has been constitutional incoherence on a grand scale. Imagine what the constitutional structure of the United Kingdom would now be if the initiatives of the 1970s had all succeeded. Northern Ireland's internal affairs would be the responsibility of a subordinate assembly and a power-sharing executive that could accomplish nothing without the cooperation of sworn enemies and the consent of the minority. Scotland's internal affairs would be the responsibility of a classical home-rule assembly and a responsible executive drawn from that legislature. Wales would be administered by committees drawn from a Welsh assembly with no legislative powers. England would be governed by the United Kingdom Parliament, in which the Scots and Welsh would be substantially overrepresented, and by a government drawn from that Parliament. If Labour, that government would be dependent on Scottish and Welsh members of Parliament for its majority. The affairs of the United Kingdom as a whole would also be the responsibility of the United Kingdom Parliament and government, assuming that they could find time in a schedule already full of English business. Finally, the whole country would be subject to laws and regulations set by the European Community. This complexity would be owed to the alleged genius of a "flexible constitution," and the one certain outcome is that power would have moved to the army of civil servants and lawyers necessary to manage such exotic constitutional arrangements. The United Kingdom is blessed, perhaps, that so little came to pass.

However, the outcome is the absence of a final settlement of the long-standing constitutional problem posed in Northern Ireland. Of the alternatives applied to date, the present one, direct rule by orders in council, is unacceptable in the long run because it deprives the Northern Irish of the right, through their representatives in the United Kingdom Parliament,

[22]Arthur Balfour, *Nationality and Home Rule* (London, 1914), p. 19.

to participate in their provincial government. Traditional home rule with majority rule is unacceptable to the minority in such a scheme, whether nationalist as now or unionist at some point in the next century. Power-sharing can only work in a community divided along sectarian lines if accompanied by the kinds of incentives for the major parties to collaborate, engineered through the electoral system, which Donald L. Horowitz discusses elsewhere in this book. These will be difficult to arrange, and the effort has yet to begin.

The future is unclear, but there is one significant incentive for the constitutionalist parties in Northern Ireland to agree upon some kind of constitutional settlement—the threat that direct rule will surely evolve into Northern Ireland's complete integration into the British political system unless the Northern Irish themselves can agree on an alternative. Integration is not the official policy of the United Kingdom government, and it has been rejected by all major parties in Northern Ireland. The nationalists reject it because it would harm the prospects for a union of the two Irelands, and unionists because they are unwilling to entrust their vital interests to the United Kingdom Parliament so long as there is a possibility of their dominating a Northern Ireland political system themselves. But for anti-integrationists there are some ominous signs at Westminster. Northern Ireland has lost its governor and now has a secretary of state, just like Scotland and Wales. The House of Commons has established a Northern Ireland Committee on the model of the Scottish and Welsh committees to deal with Northern Ireland business. It has also authorized select committees to consider orders in council issued by the secretary of state for Northern Ireland and "to examine the expenditures, administration and policy of the principal government departments ... and associated public bodies, and similar matters within the responsibilities of the Secretary of State for Northern Ireland."[23] In addition, the convention in Parliament that members may not question the government on the internal affairs of Northern Ireland has been abandoned. Parliament is steadily intruding itself into Northern Irish affairs, something it would not do before 1972, and it would now be only a short step in law to legislate that the United Kingdom Parliament should make laws for Northern Ireland concerning matters presently reserved to the secretary of state. As time goes by, the people of Northern Ireland, who have

[23]Hadfield, *The Constitution of Northern Ireland*, pp. 251–8, lists changes in House of Commons rules. At the time Hadfield's book was published, 1989, the Northern Ireland Committee had not sat since 1985.

generally been well served by direct rule, will raise few objections. The politicians of Northern Ireland therefore may already be facing a choice between full integration into the United Kingdom and a new constitution for the province that can win the consent of both communities. Time is running out.

3

Revising revisionism:
comments and reflections

KERBY A. MILLER

Roy Foster has argued that the term *revisionist,* as applied to recent Irish historical scholarship, has become so generic and imprecise as to be almost meaningless. Certainly, his and Alan J. Ward's chapters are "revisionist" in that each rearranges and analyzes events in Irish history in ways alien to traditional nationalist interpretations. The major differences in their approaches, however, suggest that the term *revisionist* should be refined rather than abandoned.

Ward contends that from at least the eighteenth century on, Anglo-Irish constitutional and legal relations were characterized by profound and persistent contradictions, which stemmed in part from British uncertainty over whether Ireland should be treated as an equal, integral part of the United Kingdom or as a subordinate colony to be exploited, chastised, or reformed in accordance with changing British economic, strategic, and political interests. At crucial junctures in Anglo-Irish history, particularly 1783–1829 and 1912–23, unfortunate political and constitutional choices were made. Partly because of Irish inflexibility and partly because Ireland and its problems were perceived as annoying distractions by nearly all British leaders, their ill-fated policies were too often motivated by what Ward describes as "political expediency under pressure." Nevertheless, the tone of Ward's chapter is largely positive, for one implication of his analysis is the potential of constructive statesmanship, even when those engaged represent political cultures and his-

KERBY A. MILLER is Professor of History at the University of Missouri. He has written many articles on Irish and Irish-American social history, and he is the author of *Emigrants and Exiles: Ireland and the Irish Exodus to North America* (1985).

torical traditions as disparate and as antagonistic in many respects as have been those of the British and Irish.

For statesmanship to be constructive, however, the equal validity of the cultures, traditions, and interests of all parties must be acknowledged. In this respect, too often Anglo-Irish or Irish nationalist-unionist dialogues have been deficient. Foster's chapter is a stimulating examination of the political cultures that helped produce the political impasses and constitutional conundrums Ward describes. Although Foster lays bare traditional Irish nationalism's ironic, contradictory, and irrational qualities, he does not submit the political cultures of Ulster unionists or of Britain's governing classes to similar, sustained dissection. As a result, we see the foibles and hypocrisies on only one side of a malign, tripartite dialectic: those aspects that seem, in Foster's words, "characteristically idiosyncratic" and "ostentatiously bizarre to the English mind." By that exacting standard, it might appear that Irish nationalism has been illegitimate, that the Irish should even be ashamed of a nation-state based on such puerile political traditions: on the childishly futile efforts of "Gaelic ideologues" or their "vulgar-Marxist" critics to stem the benign and inevitable processes of economic, political, and cultural "modernization" under English auspices.

Although one must applaud Foster's desire to free us from "imprisoning historical perspectives," if the present task of objective Irish historians is to feed the popular heart on ambiguities and uncertainties instead of hoary fantasies, these historians should take care that that salutary diet—and the consequent heartburn of confusion and guilt—are fairly distributed among all those who share responsibility for the violence and political morass of contemporary Northern Ireland. Otherwise, the consequence may not be healthy compromises among equally self-respecting and self-confident "traditions" or "identities," but rather the triumph of old, self-righteous certainties on one side over new, paralyzing self-doubts on the other. After all, if the Thatcher and Reagan eras have taught anything, it is that policies and rhetoric based on ideological rigidity, even on willful ignorance, bring enormous if perhaps short-term political dividends. In that context, it may not pay the Irish to be quite as enlightened or as apologetic as some critics might wish.

As Foster has said, "Historical perspectives can obscure as well as illuminate," and with all deference to his enormous scholarly achievements, in some respects his perspective is as obscurantist as the old nationalist traditions he decries. For example, his analysis of the irrational features of Irish nationalism is remarkably divorced from the historical circumstances that produced and shaped that political culture.

Indulge a flight of historical fancy, for example, and loosely transpose the history of Ireland after the United Irishmen's rising of 1798 onto the history of the United States after the American Civil War of 1861–65. On both occasions, separatist movements were crushed by central governments, with the acquiescence or assistance of indigenous elements in the rebellious provinces. The casualty lists in the two countries were proportionately similar. Suppose, however, that in America in 1861–65, as in Ireland in 1796–98, the great majority of deaths occurred on the losing side, and not in pitched battles, but as the result of state-sponsored terrorism before, during, and after the rebellion itself. Imagine also that in America the victorious federal government had confiscated 90 percent of the Southern land, transferring ownership of plantations and farms to Northern entrepreneurs and creditors, ex-Union soldiers, and Southern loyalists, thus reducing the great majority of Southern whites to the status of tenants, sharecroppers, and laborers. Suppose in addition that, at least for a time, the victors had imposed various degrees of legal, political, and economic restrictions on the vanquished, while simultaneously developing elaborate cultural and ethnic-based ideological justifications for the latter's "natural" inferiority and for their own ascendancy. Imagine as well that during the next forty years the development of a Northern-dominated capitalism, conditioned by falling cotton prices, produced increasing misery among most of the dispossessed and their descendants, culminating, say, in a corn or grain famine around 1900, during which (proportionate to Irish experience in 1845–55) about two million Southerners would die and another four and one-half million would emigrate by 1910. Assume, too, that during the next sixty years the federal government (despite strong objections by Southern loyalists) gradually and grudgingly dismantled the legal structures of Yankee ascendancy, eventually allowed the remaining Southerners to repurchase the lands their ancestors had lost, and even offered the "natives" a degree of regional autonomy—except, say, in Louisiana, where the "unionists" who dominated the thriving port of New Orleans and its hinterland threatened rebellion unless their area was excluded from the government's "home rule" proposal. Suppose as well, that in the meantime the South had lost another nine or ten million people to emigration, and that the region and its declining population had become so integrated with Northern industrial and finance capitalism, and so pervaded by Northern cultural influences, that "responsible" middle-class Southern leaders (often members of the clergy, because of the legacy of political suppression and social trauma) had little room to maneuver in their region's "special relationship" with the North. As a result, suppose finally that more extreme and often violent separatist movements flourished, both among certain disadvantaged sectors of the Southern population and among its large, self-styled exile or emigrant communities abroad.

This may be historical revisionism with a vengeance, but my point in making this counterfactual comparison is to argue by analogy that in non-Irish contexts, unburdened by the current violence in Ulster, few observers would suggest that varieties of political and cultural nationalism which emerged in such historical circumstances lacked rational bases and moral legitimacy—however distressing their practical and rhetorical excesses might be. Indeed, given Ireland's bitter history, it is remarkable that Irish nationalism, in origin and theory at least, has been so inclusive and relatively free of racial arguments. By contrast, and to return to my analogy, with far less historical justification than had Ireland's Catholics, white Southerners after the American Civil War invented traditions and created myths of the "Old South" and the "Lost Cause" that were more tendentious—and much more systematically brutal in their application to the "minority community" of Southern blacks—than any dark dreams concocted by Patrick Pearse and James Connolly in early-twentieth-century Ireland.

To argue that Irish nationalism—and Ulster unionism or British nationalism—must be understood in their historical contexts is not to deny the importance in their own right of these conflicting cultures or identities. It has been argued that the roots of Northern Ireland's current crisis can be traced to the historical construction of three competing ethnic groups—Irish Catholic, Ulster Protestant, and English (often mistakenly termed British)—each clinging to distinct interpretations of Anglo-Irish history, each with separate institutions and traditions shaped in part by negation of the others. This is a valuable perspective, but it has led some contributors to this volume to insist that solutions to the problems of Anglo-Irish-Ulster relations can only be found by jettisoning history, by obliterating the memories and traditions, "real" or invented, that validate these separate and antagonistic ethnic identities. Some have suggested that this necessary process of cultural deconstruction can be furthered by popular exposure to alternative identities, to a spirit of religious toleration, or, most frequently, to the processes of economic and political

integration that currently pervade Western Europe and that, by implication, are creating a transnational bourgeoisie freed from the parochial
shackles that generate ethnic, religious, and national conflicts.

One possible fallacy of this benign scenario is that most contributors
seem to have assumed that, until deconstructed by the agencies of progress, each ethnic culture has been static and monolithic. However, ethnicity's internal dynamics and the historical, regional, and social-class
variations and possibilities within each ethnic identity have gone unex-
amined. More crucially, we have not recognized that although ethnic
cultures draw on past and purportedly timeless traditions, they are not
merely situational but, most important, they emerge and mutate according to shifts in their groups' external and internal economic and political
relationships. Indeed, it is the economic and social dimensions of the
Anglo-Irish-Ulster crises, past and present, that are most neglected in this
volume.

A perception of Irish nationalist and Ulster unionist cultures as static
and monolithic is understandable, given the long-term trends toward
cultural homogenization, generally, as well as the intense pressures since
1968 for communal solidarity in Northern Ireland. However, the regional
and class differentiations in ethnic identities have been historically important. For example, in the 1790s certain classes of Irish Protestants,
living in certain areas, defined their ethnic identity not only as "Irish"
but as at least theoretically inclusive with respect to the island's Catholics
and as antagonistic to British imperial interests, institutions, and political
culture. Indeed, my reading of several thousand letters written by early-
nineteenth-century Ulster emigrants suggests that the relatively homogeneous Protestant/unionist ethnic identity that later appeared may have
been made possible only by the massive departures of those who forswore
the tribalism that characterized the Orange Order. Also, the history of
Ulster politics in the late nineteenth century demonstrated that internal
differences remained, and even today the Official Unionist and Democratic Unionist parties, with socially and regionally differentiated constituencies, express the ideals and interests of the "Protestant community"
in subtly but significantly distinct ways. Likewise, as Ken Maginnis has
pointed out, the defection of some elite sectors of the Official Unionist
Party to the Conservative Party, now organizing in Northern Ireland,
indicates how differently Ulster Protestants define group identity and
interests. One could make similar analyses on the Catholic, nationalist
side, but the point is that ethnic cultures have always been dynamic,

situational, and internally differentiated along class, regional, and other lines.

But how and why are ethnic identities constructed? Who defines ethnicity and the ethnic group's salient traditions, institutional expressions, and economic and political interests? A fully adequate answer would be prohibitively long and complex for this chapter, but at the risk of gross oversimplification I would argue that those who have the greatest economic and political status in any group will play the leading role in defining the meaning and interests of the community they dominate socially and invent culturally. Albeit in a dialectical relationship with other social classes, it is the socioeconomic elites within each group (whether landlords, merchants, and industrialists in the Ulster unionist case, or strong farmers, shopkeepers, and professionals, including religious, in the Irish Catholic case) who will synthesize inherited traditions and present exigencies into a cultural matrix imposed through education, politics, religion, the organization of work, and the interpretation and manipulation of shared symbols. This process is common to all societies, but in a multiethnic polity such as Ireland or the United Kingdom it may be especially essential for at least two reasons: first, to define and mobilize one culturally organized group in competition with others for economic and political advantages; and, second, within each group to impose the dominant class's definitions of "proper" thought and behavior on its own social inferiors, to ensure their loyalty or at least acquiescence to an unequal, intraethnic distribution of resources.

However, what determines how each society's or subsociety's dominant classes define the terms and boundaries of "community"? As relatively inclusive or exclusive? With group membership determined, as in the American case, by voluntary loyalty to transethnic economic and political norms? Or, as in the Irish case, according to largely immutable religious and cultural characteristics? The answer depends mainly on the economic and political contexts in which different ethnic groups or, more precisely, their dominant classes, operate. Thus again, in the late eighteenth century, East Ulster Presbyterian merchants and manufacturers tried to define their community as inclusively "Irish" and anti-British when they perceived their status and way of life more threatened by imperial policies than by Catholic competition. However, in the localized and relatively "underdeveloped" Ulster society of that era, they were unable to exercise cultural hegemony over most rural Protestants who clung to residual, pro-British identities, based in turn on situations and interests different from those of Belfast's entrepreneurs. Ironically, in the nineteenth century, when urbanization, industrialization, and the spread of literacy markedly increased the influence of East Ulster's socioeconomic elites, they had become so thoroughly and favorably integrated into British capitalism and the political union that protected those economic links that their definition of ethnic identity altered in accordance with their changing interests and hegemonic imperatives: becoming inclusive (unionist) with respect to Great Britain, but exclusive with respect to Ireland's Catholics, whose own middle classes were simultaneously inventing an exclusive Catholic/Gaelic nationalist identity as they realized that the economic disadvantages and political frustrations that they suffered under the Act of Union, as well as their need to suppress agrarian violence among their poorer coreligionists, necessitated communal solidarity and mobilization around symbols and goals defined by the Catholic bourgeoisie.

However, as Foster points out, nationalists' and unionists' rhetoric was usually tempered by their leaders' practical caution, producing contradictions resulting partly from the conflicting socioeconomic interests and outlooks within each group, as well as from the arcadian character of the rhetoric itself. Even more important, by the early twentieth century Ireland had become so enmeshed in a web of "special relationships"— economic, cultural, strategic—with Britain, relationships largely beneficial to the Irish Free State's governing or, in Joseph Lee's phrase, "possessing classes" (the non-possessors having obligingly emigrated), that rigidly nationalist or antipartition policies (as opposed to rhetoric) had become both impractical and undesirable. Of course, Ulster unionists eschewed both the policies and the rhetoric of nationalism, with their ethnic interests and identity safeguarded by their continued links to the crown and, ironically, by a degree of local autonomy that ensured their ascendancy over the Six Counties' nationalist minority. Indeed, in the 1950s and 1960s it appeared that the governing classes on both sides of the border were prepared to modify their ethnic political cultures in mutually inclusive directions, as Northern Ireland's prime minister, Terence O'Neill, and his Southern Irish counterpart, Seán Lemass, both realized that radically changing economic circumstances, both within and outside their island, necessitated the full integration of their economies to an emerging international capitalism, which in turn mandated the erosion of parochial barriers and the exclusivist identities that had justified their creation and maintenance. Thus, as the economic and political imperatives of Ireland's dominant classes, nationalist and unionist, have changed in relation to each other, to the dynamics of their respective communities, and to Britain and the rest of the world, so also has their conceptualization of ethnicity contracted or expanded accordingly.

The process of economic, political, and cultural convergence among the island's two elites has continued, despite or perhaps more urgently because of "the troubles" in Ulster since 1968. Otherwise, Britain's and Ireland's joint commitment to European integration with all its profound implications would be inexplicable.

However, in light of that convergence, how can we explain the outbreak in 1968 and the persistence of violence in Ulster: the conflict between adherents to extreme, exclusive, and seemingly now-atavistic ethnic identities and political cultures? Of course, a host of specific incidents precipitated and perpetuate this crisis. More broadly, one could suggest that symbolic and institutional expressions of exclusive ethnicities have a life and importance of their own, continuing to guide behavior and thought long after what one might regard as their objective reasons for existence have passed. But far more important is that in each ethnic group certain classes in certain areas have not benefited—indeed, they have been deeply disadvantaged in a variety of real and perceived ways— by the very economic, social, and cultural changes that have persuaded their social superiors to become more ecumenical, integrationist, or inclusive in their conceptions of the meaning of community. Generally, these are the people, from the high-unemployment neighborhoods of West and East Belfast, from the poor hill-farms of South Armagh and Fermanagh, who fill the ranks of the paramilitary organizations. Thus, although John Cope speaks of the British and Irish governments' desire to "marginalise the terrorists," I suggest that in most cases they and their families were already marginalized before they became terrorists by impersonal forces far greater and more profound than any which the powers of law and order can now apply. Having for generations been "taught," to put it crudely, that their interests, their identities, their entire way of life—as poor as it was, or as fulfilling as their dreams might imagine it once was or could still be—depended on the maintenance or the pursuit of certain old ethnic and mutually exclusive "truths," it seems entirely predictable that at least some of them would react violently against the traditionally defined targets of their fears and frustrations, instead of against the more pervasive but impersonal processes that were marginalizing them.

The historical development of agrarian, industrial, and now postindustrial capitalism has created similarly marginalized groups in all societies. Usually, the threats they pose to "social stability" (an ironic label for a process that, for the marginalized, is ruthlessly destabilizing) are successfully "managed" in a variety of ways, including, in the Irish case, massive emigration by the disadvantaged and disinherited. Perhaps in a bizarre sense it is to the credit of the Irish, both republicans and loyalists, that at least some of them have refused a quiet consignment to the dustbin of "progress." However brutal or misdirected their efforts, at least they have understood that links exist between economic conditions and political structures—unlike so many of their American or British counterparts, mesmerized by the seemingly intractable and impersonal power of the marketplace, who retreat into hopeless apathy, common criminality, or the dead ends of spuriously traditional "family" or religious politics that reinforce a conservative political order.

In conclusion, my point has been to challenge the prevalent tendency in this volume to analyze the "Irish problem," past and present, with little or no reference to economic and social issues. The implicit assumption that a combination of military repression, new political structures, and, most important, steady "progress," "enlightenment," and "modernization" (i.e., through European economic and political integration) will suppress the terrorists, reconcile the two communities, and attenuate their ethnocultural conflicts, bears challenging. However, the real processes that words such as "progress" represent have different results for different sectors of the Ulster Catholic and Protestant people, according to their ability to derive positive material and psychological advantages from them. Unless they can derive what Paul Arthur has called "equality of esteem," including self- as well as mutual regard, then they will continue to turn to more traditional sources of solace, identity, and violence. Moreover, I suggest that unless we address these fundamental economic and social problems and inequalities inherent in "modernization," we will not only fail to find long-term solutions to the Northern Ireland crisis, but we also may witness similar explosions of nationalist, racist, and fascist ideologies and movements among other frustrated and marginalized groups throughout post–Cold War Europe. If history teaches anything, it is that the current euphoria over impending West European integration and the triumph of the "free market" is a fatal delusion, because it will be—as it always has been—the uneven and unsettling workings of the market itself that are central to the problems discussed in this volume. But perhaps that is one reason—alongside desires to forget events such as the Famine, whose memories feed the fires of Irish republicanism—why other contributors urge us to ignore history and focus instead on what they see as the dawn of a timeless new era of permanently triumphant international capitalism.

4

―――――――――――――――――――――――――――

The Catholic church, minority rights, and the founding of the Northern Irish state

MARY HARRIS

The Catholic church's response to the founding of the Northern Irish state was expressed in terms of the need to defend minority rights. A number of areas caused the church particular concern. The first was education, which it considered a religious right. There were also fears that unionist-controlled local government would discriminate against Catholics. In the years between the 1916 Easter Rising and the Anglo-Irish Treaty of 1921, the Catholic church, like the Catholic laity, moved to an increasingly "advanced" nationalist position and came to regard partition as a violation of Ireland's right to self-government. Furthermore, the periodic outbreaks of intercommunity violence caused the church concern over the prospect of being left to the mercy of a Belfast government.

In the quarter century leading up to the establishment of the Northern Irish state, the Catholic church in the North East, particularly in defense of its control over education, had acted as a defender of Catholic rights. The education system set up in Ireland under Edward Stanley's scheme of 1831 had been nondenominational; nonetheless, by the end of the nineteenth century most schools were in fact run by clerical managers, and the church did not want to lose any of its hard-earned gains. Articles in the press and in such journals as the *Irish Ecclesiastical Record*, the *Catholic Bulletin*, and the weekly *Irish Catholic* frequently recalled previous centuries when much of education was geared to anglicizing the Irish and converting them to Protestantism. The secularizing trends of

MARY HARRIS is Lecturer in Irish Studies at the University of North London. A historian, she specializes in study of the Catholic church in Northern Ireland.

other countries and the struggles of the Catholic church to provide Catholic education throughout the world were also reported, and left the Irish Catholic church wary of the educational implications of any political change.

Developments in 1918 confirmed the Catholic church's worst fears for its educational rights under a Northern regime. Faced with a rapidly increasing school-aged population and insufficient school accommodation in Belfast, Ulster unionist Sir Edward Carson proposed the creation of a local authority with statutory powers to levy an education rate. In April 1919 Belfast Corporation decided to promote a bill to enable an education rate to be struck. The chief secretary, Ian Macpherson, opted for more extensive reforms and proposed to replace the semiindependent education boards with a department of education, an advisory committee, and county education committees.[1] The Catholic church objected to the abolition of the education boards, on which they had some representation, and feared that education committees would undermine the position of clerical managers. A bitter campaign ensued, the church condemning the proposed changes and unionists supporting them.

Proposals to introduce municipal reform in Belfast and Derry led to protests in both cities, supported by the local Catholic bishops.[2] In Belfast, Bishop Henry Henry and thirteen priests were among those appointed to the provisional committee of the Belfast Catholic Representation Association. This association was established to take up the cause of Catholic representation on Belfast City Council. As a result of its agitation two predominantly Catholic wards were created. This course of action was viewed unfavorably by Belfast nationalist leader Joe Devlin. Concerning these events, one scholar has commented: "The politics of the conflict were, on Devlin's side, the view that particular Catholic interests in Belfast should be pursued through a national movement, against the bishop's view that Catholic interests would be furthered within Belfast."[3] This dilemma of having to choose between short-term local and long-

---

[1]Seamus Ó Buachalla, *Education Policy in Twentieth Century Ireland* (Dublin, 1988), p. 53.
[2]"Petition read at a Public Meeting of Catholic Citizens held at St Columb's Derry, on Monday, 20th January 1896." Erskine Childers Papers, 7784/93, Trinity College, Dublin; and "A Statement of the Municipal Grievances of the Roman Catholic Ratepayers and Inhabitants of Belfast Who, according to the Census of 1891, number 70,234 out of an entire Population of 273,114, within the Parliamentary Boundary" (Printed by the Irish News Ltd.). Copy in Curran Papers, Dublin Archdiocesan Archives.
[3]Austen Morgan, "Politics, the Labour Movement and the Working Class in Belfast, 1905–1923" (Ph.D. thesis, Queen's University of Belfast, 1978), pp. 138–9.

term national goals was to face the Catholic church again in the early years of the Northern state's existence.

In times of riot, members of the church also attempted to defend Catholics. In 1886, Father John Tohill of the Diocese of Down and Connor—the diocese which included Belfast—was one of the honorary secretaries of a Catholic committee formed to look after Catholic interests during the riots and to give evidence before a commission of inquiry. Tohill's evidence referred to the treatment of Catholics "as if they were an inferior and conquered race."[4] When Belfast suffered further riots and shipyard expulsions in 1912, Tohill, now bishop of Down and Connor, became involved in relief efforts, but stressed that he wanted no political significance attached to his actions.[5] This distinction between the humanitarian and the political was to prove more difficult later.

Convinced that Catholic rights would suffer under a Northern regime, the church tried by various means to prevent the establishment of the Northern state. When the prospect of a measure of unionist establishment arose in 1916, the bishops vehemently opposed it. Four Northern bishops wrote to the press concerning the proposals.[6] Bishop Charles McHugh of Derry explained that while the bishops regarded "with feelings of the deepest regret the admission of the principle of a divided Ireland," they were even more concerned at "the perilous position in which religion and Catholic education would be placed" if the proposals were accepted.[7] Bishop Patrick McKenna of Clogher stated that "to partition Ireland would be to offer the grossest insult to the spirit of Irish nationality."[8] A conference held in Belfast on 23 June 1916 and attended by 130 priests recorded a vote in favor of the proposals. This, however, was on the understanding that the proposals would involve temporary exclusion, and would not involve a separate Northern administration.[9] When it was clarified at Westminster that these proposals would lead to permanent exclusion of the North East, John Redmond withdrew his support for the proposals and they were dropped. However, faith in the Irish Party had been lost. Father Philip O'Doherty of Carndonagh (later of Omagh)

[4]Report of the Belfast Riots Commissioners, Minutes of Evidence and Appendices 1887 [C. 4925], 507.
[5]Irish Catholic Directory (Dublin, 1913), p. 530.
[6]Derry Journal, 9 June 1916.
[7]Ibid., 21 June 1916.
[8]Ibid., 6 June 1916.
[9]Government and Ulster. Lloyd George Proposals, Belfast Convention, 23 June 1916. Gist of speeches. T 3321/2, Public Record Office of Northern Ireland, Belfast.

called for an all-Ireland unity league.[10] McHugh also sought a constitutional alternative to the Irish Party.[11] An Anti-Partition League was established with the support of many clergy and from this came the Irish Nation League, launched in Omagh in August 1916.[12] This was soon subsumed into Sinn Féin. A further attempt to prevent partition was McHugh's antipartition manifesto published in the press on 8 May 1917. This called for signatures from all those opposed to partition, but had little effect. An opportunity to influence the course of events came when the Catholic hierarchy was allotted four seats in the Irish Convention, a supposedly representative body, which met from 1917 to 1918 in a last-ditch attempt to solve the Irish Question by constitutional means. One of the episcopal representatives, Bishop Joseph MacRory of Down and Connor, wrote to the rector of the Irish College in Rome that while he had little hope in the convention, he intended to be there to oppose partition with all his heart.[13] The convention, however, failed to agree. In any case, it was not truly representative of public opinion as Sinn Féin had been allocated only five seats and had refused to participate.

The Catholic church's attempts to prevent the establishment of the Northern state failed. Partition finally became a reality with the passing of the Government of Ireland Act in December 1920. The act was generally ignored by Catholics, and the Irish Republican Army (IRA) continued to fight on for a better settlement with Britain. In the North, however, the reality of a separate state had to be confronted, at least in the short term.

For Northern Catholics, the establishment of the Northern state was all the more depressing because of the outbreak of violence in Belfast in July 1920.[14] It began with the expulsion of thousands of Catholic workers from Belfast shipyards. The Catholic cause was taken up by the church. In August the vicar general, Father Patrick Convery, together with the president of the St. Vincent de Paul Society in Belfast, issued an appeal titled, "Everyone Has the Right to Live by His Wages." The issue of justice also featured in the October 1920 statement of the Catholic hierarchy, which spoke of the "iniquity of furnishing a corner of Ulster

[10]*Derry Journal*, 7 July 1916.
[11]D. W. Miller, *Church, State and Nation in Ireland 1898–1921* (Dublin, 1973), p. 342.
[12]Ibid.
[13]MacRory to O'Riordan, 24 June 1917. Michael O'Riordan Papers, Irish College, Rome.
[14]For a discussion of the various interpretations of this violence see Henry Patterson, *Class Conflict and Sectarianism: The Protestant Working Class and the Belfast Labour Movement 1868–1920* (Belfast, 1980), chapter 6.

with a separate government, or its worst instrument, a special police force, to enable it all the more readily to trample under foot the victim of its intolerants [sic]."[15]

Few were as concerned for Catholics as Bishop MacRory of Down and Connor. He was horrified by the proposal to establish a special constabulary,[16] and wrote to Bishop Peter Amigo of Southwark, London, "Just now we are threatened with Carsonite police, most of whom would be taken from the very men whose awful bigotry has victimised our poor Catholic workers for the past ten weeks."[17] MacRory became involved in relief efforts, as his predecessor, Bishop Tohill, had done in 1912. However, MacRory had strong personal political convictions, and in publicizing the predicament of his flock, he also expressed his views on the partition question. This he clearly saw as an injustice, as is shown by the following extract from his appeal to Bishop O'Connell of Boston in December 1920:

The coming winter threatens thousands of my people with starvation. Almost ten thousand Belfast workers have been deprived of their employment simply because they are Catholics. Thousands of others, being Catholics, were the first to be dismissed owing to the prevailing slackness of work.... Fully fifty thousand Catholic victimised workers are now on the verge of starvation in my diocese, which is no longer in Ireland; not even in Ulster, for that historic province has been mutilated, but in the nameless Satrapate made up of the six amputated counties.[18]

In his pastoral letter of February 1921, MacRory criticized the British government's lack of protection of Northern Catholics in the face of continuing violence, and gave his own views on the violation of Catholic political rights. In March, responding to the prime minister's questions "Who began it? Who began shooting policemen?" MacRory said:

Who began the wrong? Who began the injustice? If they were to find the cause they could not stop where the Prime Minister would have them stop. Who refused the constitutional claim of the country, constitutionally pressed for more than forty years by four fifths of her representatives? Who permitted nineteen per cent of the population of Ireland to refuse to submit to a Dublin Parliament and now

[15]*Irish Catholic Directory* (Dublin, 1921), p. 558.
[16]The Special Constabulary was a police force established in late 1920 to deal with unrest. Many of its members had been in the Ulster Volunteer Force, and were feared and despised by Catholics.
[17]MacRory to Amigo, 28 September 1920. Peter Amigo Papers, Southwark Diocesan Archives, London.
[18]*Irish Catholic Directory* (Dublin, 1922), p. 508.

sought to compel thirty-six per cent of the Six Counties to submit to a Parliament in Belfast?

Who by all this tyranny and perfidy and denial of their rights taught their young men to distrust constitutional agitation and have recourse to physical force? If they were to find the cause of the present deplorable condition of their country they must go farther back than the last year or two and find it in the age-long denial of their unquestionable rights.[19]

As the election to the first Northern Parliament approached, Catholics decided to campaign, but to abstain from Parliament if elected. The Catholic church's education demands featured prominently in the Nationalist campaign, and a number of Unionist candidates spoke bitterly about the church's obstruction of reform measures in the past.[20] Amid fears that apathy among Catholics would affect turnout, MacRory was asked to urge voters to go to the polls. MacRory duly had a letter read at Sunday masses, in which he stated:

We need to show the world the strength of opposition to partition within the Six Counties. It is up to us to deal the insulting measure its death blow. It is a sacred duty that we should poll our fullest strength on the present occasion. More than political issues are at stake. The care of our children's education, and with it, perhaps, their eternal welfare, may depend on this election.[21]

In August Cardinal Michael Logue of Armagh declined an invitation to nominate Catholic representatives to a committee being set up to examine the education question. He stated, "Judging from the public utterances of some of the members of the Belfast Parliament and their sympathisers, I have little doubt that an attack is being organised against our schools."[22] Furthermore, his participation in the nomination process would have lent legitimacy to the Northern state. This was undesirable at a time when the IRA was negotiating with the British government on an alternative to the Government of Ireland Act. Logue had already declined an invitation to attend the opening of the Belfast Parliament. In any case, he was cynical regarding education committees. When approached by the British government to nominate a representative to education commissions in 1918, he had told one of his episcopal colleagues

---

[19]*Irish Independent,* 28 March 1921.
[20]For examples of such statements, see Mary Harris, "The Catholic Church and the Foundation of the Northern Irish State, 1912–30" (Ph.D. thesis, Cambridge University, 1992), pp. 104–6.
[21]*Northern Whig,* 23 May 1921.
[22]Logue to Londonderry, 2 September 1921. CAB 6/19, Public Record Office of Northern Ireland, Belfast.

he had "little confidence in the deliberations of Commissions, judging by the past."[23] At that time Bishop Patrick Foley of Kildare and Leighlin had also expressed wariness of becoming involved in a commission whose decisions would not be to his liking.[24] The hierarchy clearly would not allow its presence to be used to legitimize decisions it opposed.

However, the church was willing to be consulted by Sinn Féin. During the 1921 treaty negotiations Sinn Féin set up a Committee of Information on the Case of Ulster. Among the twenty-eight initially to be consulted were four Northern bishops and eight Northern priests who were asked for information on gerrymandering, on the likely effects of partition on various counties, and on education.[25] This consultation indicates a recognition of the bishops' long-standing links with politicians and the church's experience in dealing with Catholic grievances.

After the treaty there were to be further negotiations between Sinn Féin and prominent members of the church regarding protection for Northern Catholics. The Catholic clergy were all the more useful as spokespersons for Northern Catholics as Sinn Féin's organization in the North East was weak. In Belfast, Joe Devlin and the rump of the Irish Party were still very popular, and were despised by Sinn Féin. The six members of Parliament elected for Northern constituencies in 1921 included Arthur Griffith and Michael Collins, who knew little of the North and were in any case too preoccupied with Dublin politics; Eamon de Valera and Seán O'Mahony, who had voted against the treaty, and therefore were not in a position to advise the provisional government on anything; Seán Milroy, born and raised in England, and Eoin MacNeill, who was from County Antrim, but who had moved to Dublin more than a decade previously. A number of other Northern Sinn Féiners had also thrown in their lot with Dublin.[26] This left a power vacuum which was filled by Sinn Féin sympathizers within the Northern church. Bishop MacRory was the most vocal and most significant of these.

Although the treaty gave the South of Ireland greater autonomy than the Government of Ireland Act had done, it left Northern Ireland as it

[23]Logue to O'Donnell, 20 July 1918. Patrick O'Donnell Papers, Armagh Archdiocesan Archives, Armagh, Northern Ireland.

[24]Foley to O'Donnell, 24 July 1918. Patrick O'Donnell Papers, Armagh Archdiocesan Archives, Armagh, Northern Ireland.

[25]First Report of Committee of Information on the Case of Ulster to the Minister of Home Affairs, 11 October 1921. 7784/66/4, Erskine Childers Papers, Trinity College, Dublin.

[26]For example, Ernest Blythe and Patrick McGilligan.

was, but provided for the Boundary Commission to look at the border between North and South. Though they opposed partition, the bishops were prepared to support the treaty. They believed partition would be short-lived, a belief cultivated by Michael Collins. They had little time for the abstract question of sovereignty and most felt the treaty was the best that could be got at the time. MacRory was far from satisfied but felt that having been signed, the treaty could not be rejected.[27]

Nevertheless, the bishops were concerned about the position of Northern Catholics. Arthur Griffith had assured representatives of the bishops that safeguards concerning education and patronage would be written into the treaty.[28] This never happened. Griffith had also given assurances that Derry would be transferred to the Irish Free State under the Boundary Commission.[29]

The bishops were left with the problem of trying to defend the rights of Northern Catholics, especially at a time of escalating violence in Belfast. In early 1922 they maintained close links with the provisional government in Dublin, considering it the trustee of Catholic rights. Both MacRory and McHugh opposed recognition of the Northern Parliament, and it is likely that their opposition was the reason why an abstention policy prevailed, in spite of a certain degree of Catholic support for participation.[30]

MacRory made a number of visits to Collins in early 1922 and met the executive council. Over the following six months violence in Northern Ireland increased. MacRory was concerned that if Collins adopted a nonrecognition policy toward Northern Ireland, Northern Catholics

[27]*Irish Independent*, 24 December 1921. For a detailed account of episcopal reactions to the Anglo-Irish Treaty of 1921 see Harris, "The Catholic Church," pp. 112–59, and Dermot Keogh, *The Vatican, the Bishops and Irish Politics, 1919–1939* (Cambridge, England, 1986), pp. 77–100.

[28]McHugh to Byrne, 18 December 1921. Byrne Papers, Dublin Archdiocesan Archives, Dublin.

[29]McHugh to Hagan, 7 February 1922. John Hagan Papers, Irish College, Rome.

[30]In 1922 a number of Derrymen who favored Catholic MPs taking their seats in Parliament and uniting with moderate unionists consulted Bishop McHugh of Derry about the possibility of establishing a representative Catholic organization to look after Catholic interests within Northern Ireland. These plans were dropped because of McHugh's objections. Minutes of Meeting of Derry Catholics on 18 December 1924. D2738/8/3/6, Public Record Office of Northern Ireland, Belfast. A report prepared for the provisional government in Dublin in August 1922 indicated much support in the Belfast business community for recognition of the Northern Parliament, but noted that MacRory was opposed to it. Report on the North-Eastern Situation by Captain MacNaghten, 7 August 1922. S. 8998, National Archives, Dublin.

would have to fight alone. He also urged Collins to appeal to the Northern prime minister, James Craig, to have expelled Catholic workers reinstated.[31]

A further opportunity for the church to support Catholic rights arose after the signing of the second Craig-Collins Pact on 30 March 1922.[32] This pact aimed at restoring peaceful conditions in Belfast. It included proposals for three committees: a committee to discuss policing, a "conciliation" committee to investigate outrages, and a committee to oversee the distribution of relief funds. MacRory declined an invitation from the Northern minister of home affairs to participate in the police advisory committee, though he had previously been party to the drawing up of a list of names of possible candidates, including his own.[33] This committee was dogged by ill-feeling. The Belfast government felt that Catholic members were trying to extract details of police numbers and organization from the military adviser. Two Catholic members of the committee were arrested. Fathers H. J. Murray and Bernard Laverty soon became exasperated. Laverty had hoped to encourage Catholics to join the "Specials," but stated that the arrest of two members of the committee had alienated many Catholics. Murray was angered that crown forces had fired at his presbytery without explanation.[34] The problems encountered by the committee, which failed to bring Catholics into the police force, indicated the difficulty of dealing with the police question as a humanitarian issue, separate from the political and constitutional questions.

The position of Northern Catholics was debated at length at a meeting of the Northern Advisory Committee convened by Collins. Three Northern bishops and ten priests were among those who attended. MacRory contributed much to the debate. He resented the fact that Craig had refused to investigate recent murders of Catholics in Stanhope Street, for which he believed that the Special Constabulary was to blame. He was anxious to have Catholics join this force as a temporary measure, believing it would afford protection to the Catholic community. He was also anxious to avoid a breakdown in the operation of the pact, as that

---

[31]Provisional Government Minutes, 30 January 1922. G1/1, National Archives, Dublin.

[32]For a full account of the pact and its operation see Kevin Boyle, "The Tallents Report on the Craig-Collins Pact of 30 March 1922," *Irish Jurist* 12, 1 (1977): 148–75.

[33]Notes on a deputation representing the Catholics of Belfast received by Michael Collins, Arthur Griffith and William T. Cosgrave on 5 April 1922. S. 1801A, National Archives, Dublin.

[34]Notes on Conversation with "B," 21 June 1922. Stephen G. Tallents Papers, Public Record Office, London, CO 906/26.

might jeopardize the provision of £500,000 toward relief. The bishop's distrust of the Northern government was evident when he expressed fears that, while Catholics would be employed under the relief schemes, the relief projects might be located in areas where Catholics could not work in safety, and that projects in such areas would not be of long-term benefit to Catholics.[35]

Besides defending Catholic rights, the church provided interpretations of Catholic grievances, frequently presenting them as religious persecution. As violence escalated during the first half of 1922, the Belfast Catholic Protection Committee was set up with MacRory as president and Laverty as chair "to consult and advise on all matters pertaining to Catholic interests in the present crisis."[36] The committee became involved in a propaganda war with the Northern government. A number of letters were published in the press arguing that attacks on Catholics were motivated by religious bigotry and rejecting the unionist view that attacks on Catholics were politically motivated. One such refutation was that in response to a statement in the *Spectator* (London) to the effect that Sinn Féin gunmen had been imported into Belfast. The committee pointed to the absence of Sinn Féin gunmen during the attacks on Catholics in 1864 and 1872, and during the shipyard expulsions of 1886 and 1912, and concluded, "All the evidence goes to show that the original trouble is not political but religious. To be a Catholic is a crime punishable by death in Belfast."[37] While the church previously had been involved in relief efforts in times of rioting, and had provided spokespersons for the Catholic community, its publicity during the early 1920s had far more serious repercussions as the Northern state struggled for survival.

Violence abated in the summer of 1922, but the nature of legislation passed by the Northern Parliament soon gave rise to further grievances. One of the provisions of the Local Government Act of 1922 prescribed a declaration of allegiance for those in receipt of payment from local authorities. Among the groups obliged to make this declaration were the chaplains of public institutions—prisons, mental asylums, workhouses. These chaplains included some of the most politically active clergy in Northern Ireland. Many chaplains refused to make the declaration. Some continued to work, but without pay. Eventually most succumbed. This act also abolished proportional representation in local government elec-

[35]Minutes of the Proceedings of 11 April 1922. S. 1011, National Archives, Dublin.
[36]*Irish News*, 22 April 1922.
[37]*Belfast Evening Telegraph*, 6 May 1922.

tions. This required the redistribution of constituencies, and there were to be many accusations of gerrymandering.

The Local Government Act had also required that teachers in schools controlled by local authorities make a declaration of allegiance. As the Catholic church was not willing to transfer its schools to local education authorities, its teachers were exempt. The following year, however, a Promissory Oaths Act was passed requiring that teachers, among others, take an oath of allegiance. This measure affected not only lay teachers, but also priests, brothers, and nuns in the teaching profession, and was considered a serious injustice. Nevertheless, the church urged teachers to take the oath. A number of letters from priests appeared in the press justifying the taking of the oath which many, especially those who had the previous year taken their pay from Dublin rather than recognize the Northern Ministry of Education, could hardly take in sincerity. An "expert theologian" urged teachers to "trample underfoot personal feeling and political sentiment, and baulk [sic] the efforts of a narrow-minded clique whose evident purpose is to victimise our Catholic people by enforced ignorance as in the days gone by."[38] Father Robert Fullerton of Belfast described the oath as "the Test Act in slightly different form," and wrote that it need not affect teachers' consciences.[39]

Undoubtedly the most serious piece of legislation to affect the Catholic church was the Education Act of 1923. This comprehensive and ambitious measure aimed at surmounting the backward state of Northern Irish education. Provisions concerning education committees, the reorganization of primary education, and teacher training caused particular concern to the church.

Education committees were to be responsible for financial assistance to schools, the granting of official recognition to new schools, teacher appointments, provision of food to needy children, and scholarships. The church had long been opposed to the involvement of local authorities in education, fearing that such committees would undermine the position of clerical managers. Local authorities dominated by Protestants were viewed with even greater alarm and discrimination was feared. The problem was exacerbated by the Local Government Act and the gerrymandering that followed it.

There were to be three categories of primary schools. Class I schools

---

[38]*Irish Independent,* 10 November 1923.
[39]*Irish News,* 17 October 1923.

were either transferred to or provided by local authorities and were totally financed and controlled by them. This was totally unacceptable to the Catholic church. The church resented the fact that Catholics, the poorer section of the community, paid taxes for the upkeep of state schools—in fact, Protestant schools—of which they could not conscientiously avail themselves. Schools in the second category were controlled by "four-and-two" committees—four members nominated by the former manager or trustees and two by the local education committees. They would receive half of their maintenance costs and an undefined contribution toward capital expenditure. The fact that no specific proportion of costs was offered provided managers with little incentive to put their schools under such committees. The two education committee nominees were considered an irritant. This category was rejected by all but a few clerical managers.[40]

Most Catholic schools remained in the third category, and received only half their heating, lighting, and cleaning costs. The government argued that compared to the Catholics of England and the United States, Northern Irish Catholics were being treated very well indeed. The church, however, had other criteria for assessing the situation. It resented the fact that Catholics were considerably worse off than they had been before Partition, worse off than Protestants, and, of course, worse off than their coreligionists south of the border. In the Free State the government had avoided the danger of church-state clashes by restricting educational reform to the curriculum.

The Catholic church was also concerned by government proposals to provide teacher training facilities. After Partition only one of Ireland's teacher training colleges was located north of the border. Early attempts to run teacher training on an all-Ireland basis fell through because of Michael Collins's noncooperation policy, and because of the Northern ministry's dislike of the increasingly Gaelic ethos of the curriculum in Southern training colleges.[41] The Northern ministry set up its own teacher-training college at Stranmillis in Belfast, which Catholics considered unacceptable for the training of Catholic teachers.

In March 1923 the Northern bishops issued a statement outlining their objections to the education bill. They argued against the relegation of

---

[40]When capital expenditure grants of 80 percent were offered to schools under four-and-two management in 1968, the vast majority of Catholic schools transferred to that form of management. Seán N. Farren, "Culture and Education in Ireland 1920–60" (Ph.D. thesis, University of Ulster, 1989), p. 435.

[41]See Seán N. Farren, "Teacher Education: The Collapse of its All-Ireland Dimensions in 1922," *Irish Educational Studies* 7, 2 (1988): 20–34.

religion to after-school hours in state-financed schools, the disabilities faced by schools that remained under church control, and the uncertainty surrounding the finances of schools run by four-and-two committees. The bishops commented, "Certainly, if recent legislation abolishing Proportional Representation and rearranging Local Government Board areas, thereby ousting Catholics from the representation, is to be taken as an indication of what we may expect, the outlook is of the gravest character for our people." They also condemned the training of teachers in cooperation with Queen's University.[42]

The Education Act was passed regardless of the bishops' protests. In October 1923 the bishops issued another statement, this time on the "treatment of Catholics in North-East Ireland by the Six-County Parliament."[43] The bishops began, "It is doubtful whether in modern times any parallel can be found for the way in which the Catholic minority in the North of Ireland is being systematically wronged under the laws of the Northern Parliament." They went on to refer to the abolition of proportional representation, the gerrymandering of constituencies, the lack of funding for Catholic schools, and the lack of suitable teacher training facilities for male Catholic teachers. They felt particularly bitter about the imposition of an oath of allegiance, "as if to trample upon the feelings of those who have been opposed to the partition of Ireland." The bishops concluded:

This ever-advancing aggression on Catholics is a grave menace to the peace of the whole community; and, in view of what has already happened, after waiting very long in the hope of some approach to equal dealing, we consider the time has come for our people to organise openly on constitutional lines, and resolve to lie down no longer under this degrading thraldom.

They are altogether within their rights in holding parochial or other public meetings of protest.

What exactly the bishops had in mind was not at all clear. Unionists interpreted the statement as an attempt to stir up trouble. Speaking at a unionist meeting at Portadown, James Craig warned that "an awful responsibility" would rest upon "any man, or set of men who either directly or indirectly attempted to upset the peace."[44] The *Belfast Newsletter* on 22 October pointed out that Craig's statement was addressed to the bishops, who had "issued a manifesto a few days ago urging their

[42]*Irish Catholic Directory* (Dublin, 1924), pp. 602–6.
[43]Ibid., pp. 606–8.
[44]*Irish News*, 24 October 1923.

people to start an agitation against the government." A *Northern Whig* editorial referred to the "extraordinary and wholly misleading manifesto," denied that Catholics had any grievances, and stated that "the minority did not assist in establishing peace and good order."[45]

Among Catholics there was also dissatisfaction. Some felt that if Catholics had organized sooner, their position would not have deteriorated so much.[46] Armagh MP J. D. Nugent, who was also secretary of the Ancient Order of Hibernians, issued a circular warning that "the extreme section may interpret the invitation not to lie down as a covert invitation to physical force," and dismissed the idea of holding public meetings and passing resolutions as "merely idle vapour."[47]

Nevertheless, there was some willingness to follow up the bishops' proposals. A meeting of representatives from border counties was held to consider what line of action might be taken. Among those who attended were three priests who had long been interested in politics—Father Philip O'Doherty of Omagh, Dean Michael Quinn of Dungannon, and Archdeacon John Tierney of Enniskillen. It was decided to hold meetings at various centers in the border areas—Derry, Enniskillen, Omagh, Cookstown, Armagh, Newry, and Dungannon. A draft resolution was drawn up condemning the repeal of proportional representation, gerrymandering, oaths and declarations of allegiance, the transfer of reserved services (especially the post office), and the subsidizing of the Special Constabulary. The resolution also called on the Free State and the British government to implement the Boundary Commission. The meetings were held and the clergy played an important part in organizing them. The police and the Ministry of Home Affairs closely monitored the meetings and noted the role of the clergy in organizing the meetings, the tone of the speakers, and the degree of local support for the protests.[48] At these meetings the grievances mentioned were often presented in religious terms. See, for example, the following statement, which was made by Father Philip O'Doherty:

They were there as Catholics to join their voice with that of their co-religionists in the Six Counties in the resolve to lie no longer under the galling thraldom to which Belfast had subjected them. The Belfast politicians would not allow them

[45]*Northern Whig,* 15 October 1923.
[46]*Hibernian Journal,* November 1923, and *Irish News,* 13 October 1923.
[47]Copy of circular in HA 5/1854. Public Record Office of Northern Ireland, Belfast.
[48]Correspondence between District Inspector Gilfillan and the Ministry of Home Affairs. HA 5/1853, Public Record Office of Northern Ireland, Belfast.

to breathe on a soil sacred to intolerance; they might search the wide expanse of God's creation and only in Ulster with the inverted commas and in heathendom could they find a fellow for the Belfast politician; he had no country; he hated Ireland with a malignant hate and would, if he could, within twenty-four hours redden the soil of Ireland with the blood of its Catholic people. His Lilliputian Parliament was hardly two years in existence and "No Pope" or rather "To Hell with the Pope" was stamped on every line of its legislation.

A penal code was being systematically enacted and if their schemes progressed the Mass would soon be forbidden, and the priest declared a felon.[49]

These meetings were followed by a series of protests concerning political prisoners. In November Bishop MacRory sent a telegram to the *Manchester Guardian* asking for publicity for 130 men on hunger strike in Belfast Prison protesting detention without charge.[50] The bishop became embroiled in a controversy with the minister of home affairs, and rejected the minister's suggestion that there had been an improvement in the processing of prisoners. A few days later a protest meeting was held in Belfast, presided over by Archdeacon Convery and attended by fifteen other priests, including the chaplain of Belfast Prison.[51] A statement issued a week later and signed by MacRory, Convery, five Catholic MPs, and the lord mayor of Derry called for the release of the internees and described their continued detention as one more proof of the "partisan and bigoted spirit of Sir James Craig's Government."[52]

The momentum of the protests was maintained by the calling of an election to Westminster for December 1923. Catholics hoped to have two representatives elected for the border constituency of Tyrone-Fermanagh. The clergy played a significant role in chairing and speaking at election meetings in border areas, and many of the issues raised in the wake of the bishops' joint statement in October were mentioned again. A letter from Bishop McHugh read at election meetings commented, "What we may expect from the Northern Parliament when there is a question of Catholic rights and liberties we have sufficient evidence of in what has taken place during the brief period of its existence."[53] At a meeting on 2 December, Father Philip O'Doherty of Omagh protested that every act of the Northern Parliament was devised to deprive the Catholic people of their legitimate rights, that the law courts were par-

[49]*Irish Independent*, 3 November 1923.
[50]Ibid., 6 November 1923.
[51]Ibid., 8 November 1923.
[52]Ibid., 15 November 1923.
[53]Ibid., 3 December 1923.

tisan and the police force recruited on sectarian lines, and that Catholics would no longer tolerate the tyranny.[54]

Similar protests took place in 1924. In September there were renewed calls for the release of political prisoners. The tone of the protests varied. Bishop Patrick O'Donnell, coadjutor to the cardinal, avoided being politically partisan. He declared himself in sympathy with the protests "just as I was anxious for the releases in the 26 counties that were so long overdue."[55] Father O'Doherty, however, protested that the attorney general had openly proclaimed himself an Orangeman, and argued that the Catholics of the Six Counties could not expect justice with an Orangeman at the head of criminal law. Another election to Westminster in October 1924 raised issues similar to those referred to in the campaign of 1923, but the entry of (anti-treaty) Sinn Féin into the contest raised the possibility of a split Catholic vote. The Nationalists abandoned their election campaign and urged a policy of abstention.

Although the protesters railed against the government for its injustice toward Catholics, there seemed to be little hope of obtaining redress under the Northern regime.[56] In terms of achieving reform, the protests were ineffective. Their main function was to heighten Catholics' awareness of their difficulties and to rally Catholic opinion in anticipation of the Boundary Commission.

The Boundary Commission afforded the church a further opportunity to highlight the question of Catholic rights. Records of the commission's sittings in 1925 reveal that the clergy were intensely involved in preparing the cases of nationalist representatives, in organizing meetings, in submitting written evidence, and in presenting cases in person.[57] Two nationalist witnesses before the commission, Patrick Lavery and Canon McNally, were questioned as to the procedures for calling such preparatory meetings,[58] and Bishop Edward Mulhern of Dromore was questioned as to the summoning of political meetings in church.[59] The tone of the questions would suggest that the commissioners suspected undue

---

[54]*Irish News*, 3 December 1923.
[55]*Irish Independent*, 24 September 1924.
[56]An exception to this was the successful negotiation between the minister of education and O'Donnell concerning the provision of teacher training for Catholic boys. Similar negotiations between the ministry and representatives of MacRory had failed. For details see Harris, "The Catholic Church," pp. 245–56.
[57]Boundary Commission records and documents are to be found in CAB 61/1–168. Public Record Office, London.
[58]Ibid., CAB 61/120. Public Record Office, London.
[59]Ibid.

clerical influence. The written and oral evidence presented by the clergy is a catalogue of Catholic grievances. The priests spoke of the gerrymandering of constituencies, the abolition of proportional representation in local government elections, the B-Specials, and the financial difficulties facing Catholic education.

Catholics were forced to rethink their position after the collapse of the Boundary Commission, which occurred when a leak in the (London) *Morning Post* indicated that only small transfers of land from North to South were imminent, and that transfers from South to North were also envisaged. At a meeting of the heads of the Irish, Northern Irish, and British governments it was agreed that the boundary would remain as it was, and that the Irish Free State would be freed from liability for part of Britain's public debt. It was also agreed that the remaining political prisoners would be released. William Cosgrave, leader of the Dublin government, spoke highly of a new spirit of friendship that, he said, had characterized the negotiations. The Northern clergy, however, reacted angrily. Father Laurence Kiernan attended a protest meeting in Dublin where he stated that Northern Catholics had been sold into perpetuity and had been given over to their Northern masters. His clerical colleague, Father Eugene Coyle, protested that Catholics had ended up with "no country; no nation; they are simply British helots living in the Six Counties."[60] MacRory was skeptical about Cosgrave's references to a "new spirit." At a meeting of the St. Vincent de Paul Society, the bishop listed a catalogue of Catholic grievances, including the abolition of proportional representation, the gerrymandering of constituencies, and the difficulties in arranging for Catholic teacher training.[61]

Cardinal O'Donnell adopted a very different approach. Speaking in Keady in February 1926, he urged that Catholics press their case by every legitimate means, with nothing but goodwill toward their neighbors. He believed that Catholics would have the assistance of young unionists, as they already had assistance from the ranks of Labour in obtaining redress of their grievances.[62]

Between 1925 and 1927 all Nationalist MPs entered the Northern Parliament, and in 1928 the National League of the North was founded, embracing various shades of Catholic political opinion. It might have

[60]Quoted in Clare O'Halloran, *Partition and the Limits of Irish Nationalism: An Ideology under Stress* (Dublin, 1987), pp. 60–1.
[61]*Irish Catholic*, 19 December 1925.
[62]*Irish Independent*, 15 February 1926.

been expected that the reorientation of politics away from the boundary question and back toward Belfast would lead to cooler rhetoric and a more integrationist approach on the part of Belfast Catholic politicians. Belfast Catholic political thought, as expressed by the *Irish News,* had been in favor of making the best of the situation since 1922.

Nevertheless, relations between Catholics and Protestants did not improve. The Catholicism of the Nationalist politicians was emphasized by the *Irish News,* which made much of episcopal and clerical support for the National League of the North. Also divisions had begun to appear along new lines. Religion emerged as a dividing factor not only between Catholics and Unionists, but between Catholics and Labour. In January 1925 Labour put forward two candidates for the traditionally Catholic wards of Falls and Smithfield. One of the candidates, Billy McMullen, caused outrage among Catholics by defending a statement by one of his fellow Labour supporters that a recent pronouncement by the pope on socialism was merely a private expression of opinion, and that Catholics were free to take it or leave it.[63] The *Irish News* spoke of the emblem of socialism being flaunted in the streets and "the strains of the Red-International war-song borne on every wind that blows."[64] Nevertheless, McMullen was elected, and in the April elections to the Northern Irish Parliament he was again elected. For the rest of the decade Labour contested these two Catholic wards and the Nationalists fought back, with varying degrees of success, arguing that Labour could not be depended upon to support Catholic education. References were made to the need to ensure that Catholics would secure representation on local authorities so as to ensure that a few of their coreligionists would be nominated to education committees. "What father or mother amongst the Catholic people of the city would place the education of Catholic children in the hands of a socialist?" asked the *Irish News.*[65] A particularly energetic campaign was waged before the local government election of 1928. Clerical support for Catholic candidates was well publicized,[66] and Mac-Rory's letter accompanying his subscription to the election fund was published.[67] In the parliamentary election campaign of 1929 McMullen confronted the National League of the North candidate, Richard Byrne.

[63]*Irish News,* 12 January 1925.
[64]Ibid., 17 January 1925.
[65]Ibid., 14 January 1927.
[66]Ibid., 10 January 1928.
[67]Ibid., 16 January 1928.

It was a bitterly fought campaign, and the nationalists made the most of religious issues.[68] McMullen was defeated.

Catholic education rights had not totally overshadowed the rights of workers during this debate. During the 1926 campaign Alderman Byrne argued that the nationalist candidates had "supported Labour long before the Labour representatives were heard of in the Corporation or on any of the Belfast public boards."[69] During the 1929 campaign Father J. McBride argued that the Catholic church was "one of the greatest friends of Labour in the world."[70] Religion, which in the past had been a crucial differentiating factor between unionist and nationalist, now served equally as a differentiating factor between Labourite and nationalist. Catholicism and nationalism were linked more clearly than ever: the *Irish News* of 13 May 1929 reported on an election meeting which ended with the singing of "A Nation Once Again" and "Faith of Our Fathers."

An opportunity to test the National League of the North's ability to defend the church's education rights arose in the late 1920s when the Protestant churches began to campaign for amendments to the Education Act.[71] The church sent several statements to the Ministry of Education explaining its position.[72] Both the Catholic church and the laity openly recognized that the situation was now very different from that prevailing in the early 1920s. The bishops forwarded a statement of their demands to the ministry and concluded, "In the calmer atmosphere which we have now reached we trust that our claims, based as they are on elementary justice and on the principles of the natural and divine law, will be readily granted."[73] Finally a deputation led by the bishop of Derry and including four clerical managers and two other priests, as well as a number of prominent lay Catholics, visited the Ministry of Education.

Legislation was passed providing for bible instruction in state schools

[68]Michael Farrell, *Northern Ireland: The Orange State* (London, 1976), pp. 115–16.
[69]*Irish News*, 2 January 1926.
[70]Ibid., 3 January 1929.
[71]The demands were for bible instruction in any state school where the parents of not less than ten pupils demanded it, and for the appointment of ministers of religion to regional and county borough education committees. D. H. Akenson, *Education and Enmity: The Control of Schooling in Northern Ireland 1920–50* (Newton Abbot, England, 1973), pp. 99–100.
[72]Tierney to Charlemont, 6 August 1930. Joseph MacRory Papers, Armagh Archdiocesan Archives, Armagh, Northern Ireland; Finegan to Charlemont, 7 November 1929, ED/A/1/80; and Statement of the Catholic Bishops of the Six Counties on Education, February 1930. ED 31/A/1/80; Public Record Office of Northern Ireland, Belfast.
[73]Statement of the Catholic Bishops of the Six Counties on Education, February 1930. ED 32/A/1/80, Public Record Office of Northern Ireland, Belfast.

where demanded by the parents of ten or more pupils, and increasing the influence of former transferors of schools in educational administration. Catholics initially were disappointed that no concessions were made to their demands. MacRory protested against the injustice of passing "a law to meet the conscientious objection of one section of the people of the Six Counties without at the same time making an effort to meet the equally conscientious convictions of another section."[74] Craigavon finally conceded grants of 50 percent of the capital expenditure of voluntary schools. He considered this a major concession, and said he "recognised that an obligation rested on the government to go as far as possible— even to beyond what might seem justifiable on strict grounds of equity— to settle the question on a basis satisfactory to every party in the State."[75]

Catholics, however, considered the measure far from satisfactory. Joe Devlin pointed out that grants to Catholic schools had previously been refused on principle.[76] Catholics were still worse off than Protestants north or south of the border, and still worse off than they had been before Partition.

CONCLUSION

The church accurately predicted the types of threats to Catholic rights likely under a Northern state and employed several strategies to try to prevent its establishment. After the establishment of the state, leading church figures looked to Dublin as the guarantor of Catholic rights; however, the outbreak of civil war diverted Dublin's attention away from Northern Ireland. At that point the church had no means of defending Catholic rights apart from issuing protests, and assisting in the presentation of the Catholic case to the Boundary Commission. MacRory and other leading clerics looked with disfavor on recognition of the Northern state, which they presented as inherently incompatible with Catholic rights. Not all members of the Catholic hierarchy were as adamant as MacRory on this point. Patrick O'Donnell, primate from late 1924 until his death in 1927, was prepared to work within the system. But not until the Boundary Commission had met did the most politically minded

---

[74]Farren, "Culture and Education," p. 199.
[75]Ibid., p. 201.
[76]Northern Ireland, *Parliamentary Debates* (Commons), 12 (1929–30):1156.

5

The supreme law: public safety and
state security in Northern Ireland

CHARLES TOWNSHEND

Playing safe, or letting (ideally) sleeping dogs lie, is a pronounced trait
in administrative behavior. A cursory survey of British policy in Ireland
over the last century might well give the impression that it has been all
drift, "wait and see," hoping for something to turn up. The Irish problem
has occasionally been exploited cynically as a political weapon, but more
commonly Irish policy has been "bipartisan," a decorous word for vacuous. Of consistent, coherent, and above all imaginative policy there
looks to have been sadly little. Yet this impression can be misleading.
British interventions have decisively shaped the present civil crisis. The
understandable preference of British ministers for striking a pose as benign referees of a fight beyond their—or any outsider's—ken should
always be set against this history.

However much one may chafe at the burden of history, historical
development is not a ladder that can be kicked away at will, as Lord
Armstrong (see Chapter 13) and no doubt many of us would like.
(Whether any of Lord Armstrong's alternative metaphors, such as the
"map of history," "historical baggage," or even "historical hang-ups,"
is more apt is a moot point.) But what is plain is that history is important,
and two historical moments in particular need to be held in steady focus
if the structure of the present civil conflict is to be understood. The first
is the implementation of the "home rule" policy. The culminating point

CHARLES TOWNSHEND is Professor of Modern History at the University of Keele, England.
His books include *The British Campaign in Ireland 1919–1921: The Development of
Political and Military Policies; Political Violence in Ireland: Government and Resistance
Since 1848;* and *Britain's Civil Wars: Counterinsurgency in the Twentieth Century.* He is
a former Fellow of the Woodrow Wilson Center.

in the thirty-five-year history of home rule was the passage of the fourth Government of Ireland Bill in 1920. The first two bills had failed in Parliament; the third had nurtured the biggest constitutional crisis in modern British history before passing under the magic wand of the wartime party truce in September 1914 and duly disappearing. Whether or not these earlier junctures were turning points of the kind deemphasized by Roy Foster, the last of them certainly created the geopolitical structure of the "Irish Question" thereafter. It fixed the name, shape, and status of Northern Ireland, the first two of these lasting more than seventy years so far. The moment of positive intervention was followed by a scarcely less formative period, some fifty years of negative intervention. When Britain recovered direct control of Northern Ireland in 1972, it could not pick up where it had left off in 1920, much less start afresh with a blank sheet. It had to deal with the result of deliberate choices exercised during the half century of the Stormont regime.

HOME RULE

Those who refused to admit that the concept of home rule was vacuous usually admitted that it was ambiguous. Although fiscal issues and the problem of representation, as Alan J. Ward has shown, tended to dominate negotiations concerning the powers of a devolved government, they would not have been more problematic than the issue of security. The first three bills reserved the powers of war and peace and the defense of the realm in perpetuity to the imperial Parliament, which would also retain control over the armed police, the Royal Irish Constabulary (RIC), for six years. This last provision aimed to shield Dublin Castle's most loyal agents from nationalist retribution rather than to guarantee state security as such. (The whole purpose of the home rule policy was, of course, to secure internal peace and governability—"law and order"— by making an Irish parliament responsible for legitimizing law.) But the provision recognized, however reluctantly, that the maintenance of order would not be a straightforward matter after the transfer of power.

The final home rule bill was framed in the light of David Lloyd George's revealing observation that "Irish temper is an uncertainty, and dangerous forces like armies and navies are better under the control of the Imperial Parliament."[1] While the bill was coasting through the par-

[1] Notes for Caernaervon speech, October 1920. PRO CO 904 188/1; C. Townshend, *The*

liamentary process, Britain was doing dangerous things with the Irish police—things that were to mark the image of government more indelibly than the new constitutional law. The first Black and Tans were recruited at the end of 1919 and sent out to reinforce local RIC stations in March 1920. They manifested a process of perhaps semiconscious militarization (they were, after all, half-trained and half-dressed as policemen), which became a more deliberate policy after the old inspector-generalship of the RIC was topped by a new "police adviser" in May. It would be farfetched to see in this new post the foundations of an ill-omened genealogy of counterinsurgency specialists, but there is no doubt that the appointment of General H. H. Tudor had larger consequences than the government intended. In fact, Tudor was usually referred to as chief of police, a surreptitiously un-English title that indicated his determination to keep his force independent.

In the summer of 1920 the capacity of the police to enforce the law fell to a new low, far below the nadir of the most intense disturbances of the nineteenth century. The government's response was practically automatic: what had been known in nineteenth-century parlance as a "coercion bill."[2] Arthur Balfour had tried in 1887 to rationalize the odd collection of coercion laws that had been sporadically applied since the Union, codifying their cardinal points in a permanent special powers act (the Criminal Law and Procedure [Ireland] Act, commonly known as the Crimes Act) that would be adequate for all emergencies short of open war, and less contentious than temporary measures involving suspension of habeas corpus. Its most striking provision was the power of magisterial investigation, based on the experience of the special resident magistrates during the Land War. But though the Crimes Act was applied in 1917 (when special two-magistrate courts were set up in some areas) and 1918 (when sections 3 and 4 were invoked, allowing the authorities to proclaim organizations dangerous or illegal), its powers were eclipsed by the stupendous shadow of the Defence of the Realm Act (DORA). The wartime enlargement of executive horizons was reflected in the 1920 coercion bill, the Restoration of Order in Ireland Act (ROIA), which was rammed through Parliament—in instructive contrast to the Government of Ireland Act—inside the first week of August.

British Campaign in Ireland 1919–1921: The Development of Political and Military Policies (Oxford, England, 1975), p. 37.
[2]On these generally, see, e.g., C. Townshend, *Political Violence in Ireland: Government and Resistance since 1848* (Oxford, England, 1983), pp. 55–66.

ROIA was characteristic of British emergency laws in that the apparent simplicity of its provisions was followed by manifold ambiguities in their application. On the face of it the role of the army was to be decisively enlarged, through the form of "statutory martial law" familiarized by DORA. But in fact the cabinet preferred to keep military rule as a threat, and to preserve the facade of civil government. Politically this was understandable, but by the autumn of 1920 the stage was so rickety as to be a dangerous illusion. The veneer of civil authority was repeatedly splintered by the wayward actions of the Black and Tans, above all by the elite Auxiliary Division formed in July, whose military roots and manners were hardly disguised by their eclectic outfits. Police reprisals dominated the news from Ireland. For some ten months the government seemed strangely immune to the political embarrassment they might have been expected to cause. It is hard to resist the view, angrily put by the chief of the Imperial General Staff, that the cabinet connived at the illicit use of force. At the very least it courted disaster by putting ex-soldiers into situations of extreme danger and provocation under weak discipline. Covert counterterror was the order of the day.

British public opinion may well have seen counterterrorism as justified by the actions of the Irish Republican Army (IRA), and if the policy had worked its counterproductive effects might have been negated. (Though it is improbable that they would have been forgotten in Ireland.) It is not clear how close it came to success. The inner cabinet went on expecting it to work, persisting in its preference for police action even after it was driven into a declaration of martial law in southwestern Ireland at the end of 1920. As Lloyd George put it rather belatedly in June 1921, the "Irish job was a policemen's job," and "so long as it becomes a military job only it will fail."[3] The army's efforts to secure control over police operations in the martial law area were unavailing. "Unofficial" reprisals and other forms of promiscuous police violence continued and were defended by the civil authorities as necessary to sustain police morale. Conventional IRA wisdom—enshrined in Tom Barry's memoirs, *Guerilla Days in Ireland*—has it that the police terror was gaining a psychological ascendancy over the rebels as well as the people until the smashing counterstroke at Kilmichael on 28 November 1920 reversed the trend. The allegation that the Black and Tan corpses were mutilated, though hotly denied by the West Cork IRA, magnified the moral impact

[3]T. Jones, *Whitehall Diary*, ed. K. Middlemas (Oxford, England, 1971), 3:73.

of the event. Official efforts to capitalize on public revulsion against such barbarity were not successful. The republican myth of wholehearted popular support for the IRA became dangerously threadbare in 1921 as the army slowly improved its counterinsurgency techniques, but the counterterror never tore it apart.

In a form of armed struggle whose psychological dimension is recognized as decisive, the computation of inputs is notoriously erratic. Still, one outstanding miscalculation underpinned the whole of British security policy until Lord Birkenhead made his revolutionary admission on 21 June 1921 that what was going on in Ireland was "a small war." The belief that the (of course silent) majority of the Irish people was fundamentally loyal to constitutionalism and law, but was temporarily in the grip of fanatical terrorists (thugs, gunmen), was probably untestable and certainly untested, a classic instance of the comfortable appeal of unscientific, wishful thinking for even the most hard-bitten government. The crucial corollary, that the grip of the gunmen could be prized off by force without alienating the law-abiding majority, seemed so naturally self-evident that it was hardly worth demonstrating. Yet it was wrong in a way that was ominous for the whole future of colonial rule. Admittedly, the government had in the past defeated every Irish resistance movement, but it had never achieved a permanent pacification. The novel qualities of the young Sinn Féin activists were recognized in 1918 by the cabinet's weightiest Irish specialist, Walter Long, who spelled out the need for a full-blooded, gloves-off fight for control of Ireland. This his colleagues were never prepared to go through with. They let him get half way, then pulled up. By unleashing the Black and Tans, English policy went "over the precipice," in R. B. Haldane's graphic phrase, and—some would say—took English law with it.[4]

It would be hard to overstate the severity of the policy-making crisis of 1920–21. Only the steady erosion of the old English concern with civil liberties and the heavy overhang of the war emergency blunted its impact. English amnesia can be as destructive as Irish mnemotechny. The extent of earlier misconceptions led to an astonishing collapse of confidence in May 1921 when the cabinet realized that its application of force would have no measurable impact on Sinn Féin's capacity to win the first general election held under the Government of Ireland Act. At that

[4]For Haldane's "two precipices," see C. Townshend, "Military Force and Civil Authority in the United Kingdom, 1914–1921," *Journal of British Studies* 28, 3 (1989): 267.

point the home rule policy was effectively paralyzed, because the imagined majority for whom it had been designed no longer had a political voice.

BELFAST RULE

Alan J. Ward rightly draws attention to the irony of the fact that home rule has only operated in the one place that was most bitterly opposed to it. But in terms of its salient objectives—"peace, order, and good government"—the Northern subset of home rule was radically different from the original. Home rule was intended to achieve peace by resolving antagonisms, but its *raison d'être* in Northern Ireland was to maintain them. In fact, the territory which was to bear that title was administratively segregated in advance of the 1921 elections to the Northern Ireland Parliament, indeed in advance of the home rule act itself. The first giant stride down this path was taken to secure public order. On 2 September 1920, Sir James Craig warned the cabinet that "the loyalists were losing faith in the government's determination to protect them, and were threatening an immediate recourse to arms which would precipitate civil war." He called for the appointment of a separate police chief for the Six Counties, whose first task would be to organize a supplementary special constabulary, armed and trained "on military lines." The plain justification for this—invoked in the formation of reactionary militias elsewhere in Europe as well—was that it could keep explosive forces under some sort of regular control. But order was purchased at an obvious political price. The new special constabulary was to be recruited through the surviving organizational machinery of the Ulster Volunteer Force ("as was done for raising the 36th [Ulster] Division," Craig pointedly reminded the cabinet, though the few surviving Liberal ministers will not have forgotten why the UVF had originally been created). Thus the implicit fact of Partition became practically explicit. The cabinet made an effort to minimize the cost. John McColgan points out a small but telling detail in the minutes of the decision to begin enrollment of "well-disposed persons" into a special constabulary: "In Ulster," printed in the first draft, was hastily amended to "in Ireland."[5] The illusion of wholeness hardly disguised the fact that only in Ulster would well-disposed persons dare to enroll, though the impulse to preserve the illusion later reappeared

---

[5] J. McColgan, *British Policy and the Irish Administration 1920–22* (London, 1983), pp. 26–7.

in attempts to encourage proportional Catholic membership in the Royal Ulster Constabulary and, ultimately, the Ulster Defence Regiment.

On the same day, 8 September 1920, a separate under secretaryship "for the six counties of the north-east of Ireland" was established. Sir Ernest Clark was not such a glittering star in the Whitehall galaxy as the head of the Dublin administration, Sir John Anderson, but Clark became Anderson's equal in Ireland. ("Another little king" was the gloomy view of an exponent of unified command.) His outlook shifted in response to the force of Ulster attitudes. At first his reaction was wholly English: He found Craig, Wilfrid Spender, and other unionist leaders "full of grievances," painting "a picture of deathly peril which threatened all loyalists. At the time I failed to sympathise with them and indeed hardly understood what they were talking about, so widely did the conditions they described differ from my notions and previous experience of an 'ordered government.' "[6] Eventually, though, Clark understood "how the love of the province could grow in the heart of one becoming associated with it." Without the benefit of such association, the British were not inclined to love Ulster, but they were happy to do the next best thing: leave it be.

Leave it be they did for fifty years. Ward remarks that there were no serious conflicts between London and Belfast over representation or finance, partly because the unionist government was not making any demands for larger powers, and partly because it was in a weak position. It is true that as long as Northern Ireland "did not trespass upon the restrictive provisions of the Government of Ireland Act," the imperial Parliament would not involve itself by overriding the legislative authority of the Northern Ireland Parliament. But as suggested earlier, there is a kind of negative intervention that may be less dramatic but no less deliberate than positive intervention. The first and final test case in Westminster-Belfast relations arose when the Northern Ireland government brought in the Local Government Bill on 31 May 1922. This bill began the dismantling of the minority protection built into the Government of Ireland Act through the device of proportional representation. It was, at least in retrospect, the most important provision of the act, and has shaped the whole political structure of the twenty-six-county state. The six-county state, however, regarded it as un-British and, more important, dangerous. Thus it was to be abolished, first in local elections, and finally in elections to the Northern Ireland Parliament.

[6]Autobiographical notes, Clark MSS, PRONI D 1022, q. McColgan, *British Policy*, p. 30.

Early in July the bill, which had passed unopposed, was sent to the lord lieutenant to receive the royal assent. It was withheld, however, until 11 September on the urging of the Free State provisional government. Michael Collins wrote passionately to Winston Churchill on 9 August:

Do you not see, or have His Majesty's advisers not disclosed, the true meaning of all this? ... It is a matter involving the political submergence of our people in the North-East, an attempt to defeat the obligations of His Majesty's Government contained in the Treaty and finally that everywhere, innocent though it looks or has been made to look to people outside this country, it is designed in Malice.[7]

British officials took substantially the same view. Assistant Under Secretary Sir Alfred Cope sent a long and reasoned rebuttal of the unionist arguments to Lionel Curtis, and Sir Francis Greer, the Irish Office parliamentary draftsman, although rejecting Collins's farfetched contention that the bill would affect the boundary question, accepted that it "does affect Imperial interests." The problem was that the system of representation had not been expressly excluded from the jurisdiction of the parliaments under the Government of Ireland Act, and reserving the bill at this point would, Greer held, "be justifiable only in the hope or expectation that it might lead to some settlement."[8] Thus the British were impaled on a dilemma: if they pushed the unionist government to the point of resignation, it would be reelected, and they would either have to climb down or reimpose direct rule. Clearly they had no expectation, or even any hope, of "some settlement," and resigned themselves to accepting the inevitability of a virtual one-party state. This *non possumus* was to be reiterated in the 1930s in response to official complaints from Eamon de Valera's government about discrimination and gerrymandering in Northern Ireland. The Home Office returned in 1938 to the conclusion that "it is of course obvious that Northern Ireland is, and must be, a Protestant 'state,' otherwise it would not have come into being and would certainly not continue to exist."[9]

Though discrimination in employment and housing and the gerrymandering of constituencies were pervasive and corrosive mechanisms of Protestant dominance, they were in many ways diffuse and surprisingly hard to quantify. Modern academic analysts have been almost as baffled

[7]PRO HO 45 13371/463565, q. P. Buckland, "Who Governed Northern Ireland? The Royal Assent and the Local Government Bill 1922," *Irish Jurist* 15 (1980): 330–1.
[8]Ibid., pp. 335–6.
[9]C. Townshend, "Northern Ireland," in R. J. Vincent (ed.), *Foreign Policy and Human Rights: Issues and Responses* (Cambridge, England, 1986), p. 124.

as the British government in the 1930s.[10] However, one symbol of the unionist state, announcing its determination to preserve public safety, was unambiguous. The Civil Authorities (Special Powers) Act, passed on 7 April 1922, gave power "to take all such steps and issue all such orders as may be necessary for preserving the peace and maintaining order." Collins threatened that the Free State would be driven to take counter-measures, but the British government made no move to dispute the act at this time.[11] One reason was that it was portrayed by the Northern Ireland government as a lineal descendant of the British Restoration of Order Act, though in fact its whole tenor was markedly different; it was not designed to involve the military authorities in the administration of justice, it did not establish courts martial, and its powers were much more vaguely defined. Indeed it was rightly criticized in the Northern Ireland Parliament by G. B. Hanna as being too long, because "one section would have been sufficient: 'The Home Secretary [actually minister for home affairs] shall have power to do whatever he likes.' "[12] But the Free State, threatened with full-blown civil war, was also moving toward an equally far-reaching public safety law, and was to enact several draconian measures over the next twenty years. The apparent reasonableness of the Special Powers Act (always referred to by its parenthetic title) was but-tressed by the fact that it was a twelve-month law.

After the first twelve months, however, the act was renewed, and renewed again annually until 1928, when it was extended for five years. Finally, in 1933, it was made permanent. Thus was instituted what the National Council for Civil Liberties called "a permanent machine of dictatorship."[13] One of its most characteristic and perhaps most invidious provisions was section 2(4):

If any person does any act of such a nature as to be calculated to be prejudicial to the preservation of the peace or maintenance of order in Northern Ireland and not specifically provided for in the regulations, he shall be deemed to be guilty of an offence against the regulations.

---

[10]See J. Whyte, "How Much Discrimination Was There under the Unionist Regime, 1921–68?" in T. Gallagher and J. O'Connell (eds.), *Contemporary Irish Studies* (Manchester, 1983), pp. 1–35.
[11]CP 3884, CAB 24 134, 21 March 1922.
[12]D. Harkness, *Northern Ireland Since 1920* (Dublin, 1983), p. 30.
[13]National Council for Civil Liberties, *Report of a Commission of Inquiry Appointed to Examine the Purpose and Effect of the Civil Authorities (Special Powers) Acts (Northern Ireland) 1922 and 1933* (London, 1936), pp. 38–40.

Section 5 permitted courts to order whipping in addition to any sentence imposed for offenses against the 1883 Explosive Substances Act, the 1920 Firearms Act, the 1916 Larceny Act, or for arson or malicious damage. Regulations authorized, among other things, the imposition of curfew, the closure of licensed premises, the restriction of public meetings, the requisitioning of land or vehicles, and the prohibition of the collection of information about the police, possession of unlawful documents, or membership of unlawful associations. The 1934 edition of the *Regulations and Orders* ran to thirty-two pages.

To Protestants the Special Powers Act was a necessary and reasonable defense against the enemies of the state. To Catholics it was a mark of their perpetual subordination, oppressive on the (admittedly few) occasions when it was applied, and insulting in its very existence at all times. These differing perceptions, which deepened sectarian cleavage, had their roots deep in a history of communal conflict that is beyond the scope of this essay. It is worth noting that the simple loyalist chain of perceptions—Catholic/disloyal/dangerous to state/excluded from power—was recognized by "enlightened" unionists as being circular. Lord Dufferin told the Dominions Office in 1938 that many Protestants were "uneasy about the attitude of their government which had the effect of perpetuating a division which a more enlightened policy might close"—that is, treating Catholics as "a part of the nation to be incorporated" rather than as "a minority to be kept under."[14] Such natural adherents to the "British way" might have expected to get more concrete support from London, whose larger interests they plainly represented, than its resignation permitted.

DIRECT RULE

When the eleventh-hour attempt by enlightened unionists to generate an atmosphere of incorporation in the 1960s broke down, the apparatus of government came apart with surprising speed. Within four months of Prime Minister Terence O'Neill's resignation in April 1969, British troops were sent into the streets of the Catholic areas of Londonderry (14 August) and Belfast (15 August). This was a desperate recourse, and though the British government was to labor erratically for the next two decades to prove that it was not quite the last, the weight of historical experience

[14] PRO DO35 893 X.II/123, 251.

was stacked against every effort. Again as in 1920, policy was underpinned by one crucial proposition: that eradicating or at least controlling
political violence would create sufficient space for constitutional dialogue.
Tom Wilson points out that the policy framework was vitiated by the
fact that "the main British parties preferred to delude themselves with
the belief that they could somehow limit their commitment to Northern
Ireland," producing a "half-hearted policy of not wanting to stay without
feeling able to go."[15] But Wilson concedes that "initially there was an
exaggerated but understandable belief in the contribution to peace that
could be made by social and political reform." That belief was nowhere
more understandable than in relation to the police force, whose instability
had triggered the process of reintervention. British complaisance had
fostered a situation so bad as to create an illusion of hope.

The 1969 Hunt Committee report on the reform of the Royal Ulster
Constabulary (RUC) was suffused with the hope that "normalization"
was possible and would be effective. The norm was of course that of the
English local police. The idea lay in the tradition of liberal imperial police
doctrines such as those of Arthur Young in Malaya or the warning of
Charles Wickham (himself inspector general of the RUC) against the
militarization of the police in Palestine in 1946: "An armored car per-
forms no useful police function." But however attractive or well-attuned
to British political culture such doctrines were, they ran into daunting
problems in practice. The very impulse to normality, as in Lloyd George's
insistence that the "Irish job was a policemen's job," repeatedly pushed
the police into dangerous situations at or beyond the limits of their
capacity. Unless the benign influence of "normal" policing reduced the
danger very quickly, militarization was an inevitable response. The sudden disarmament of the RUC failed to pull off this chancy trick.[16]

The rearming of the RUC stands as a poignant symbol of the fundamental dilemma of internal security. This was recognized in a typically
unassertive article by George Boyce in the midst of the present conflict
as lying in the tension and perhaps in the contradiction between the
"security" and the "due process" approaches to maintaining order. The
emphasis on the salience of visible adherence to law in the contest for
public allegiance reaches far back into British colonial history, and was

---

[15]T. Wilson, *Ulster: Conflict and Consent* (Oxford, 1989), p. 164.
[16]D. G. Boyce, " 'Normal Policing': Public Order in Northern Ireland since Partition,"
Éire-Ireland 14 (1979):35–52; J. D. Brewer et al., *The Police, Public Order and the State*
(London, 1988), pp. 50–51.

carved in stone by Sir Robert Thompson's account of the Malayan war.[17] Since the beginning of the Northern Ireland conflict it has been most fiercely expounded by Kevin Boyle.[18] The core of the "due process" argument is that every departure from strict legality undermines the legitimacy of government, and plays into the hands of its opponents in the long run, however useful such deviations may seem at the time. The problem is that, even if this argument is correct, it does not supply a means of regaining legitimacy—merely of preventing further erosion. Clear analysis of terms is very important here. If it is a question of *maintaining* order, the case for strict legalism is overwhelming. If, despite a natural official preference for using the rhetoric of the "maintenance" of order, the project is in fact the *restoration* of order, the issue is quite different. And if "restoration" is an official euphemism for *imposing* order, or what in colonial parlance was formerly labeled *pacification,* it is meaningless to appeal for legitimation to any established public culture of law.

Boyce concluded judiciously but discouragingly (for government) that "to use a 'due process of law' response requires a supportive public opinion in the first place."[19] Hence where, as in some areas of Northern Ireland, the project is at least to restore and even, it must be said, in some respects to impose law and order, a government must find it agonizingly difficult to cleave to the path of due process. The RUC was rearmed for the same basic reason that the RIC was militarized in 1920: to protect the lives and (one should perhaps say "or") sustain the morale of the police. Likewise the abandonment of jury trial, which Boyle and others see as the most corrosive degradation of traditional legal standards, was a response to the fact that witnesses and juries were directly intimidated. This is one straightforward meaning of the term *security,* but its wider significance lies in the capacity of the term to shroud a cumulative sequence of departures from strict legalism in the name of public safety. The Diplock (nonjury) courts were in fact designed as an improvement on the ad hoc arrangements under which internment had been enforced since 1971, and followed Thompson's principles: he did not after all say that the law could not be changed, only that it should be published.

---

[17]R. G. K. Thompson, *Defeating Communist Insurgency* (London, 1966); R. G. K. Thompson, "Regular Armies and Insurgency," in R. Haycock (ed.), *Regular Armies and Insurgency* (London, 1979), p. 10.

[18]Most substantially in K. Boyle, T. Hadden, and P. Hillyard, *Law and State: The Case of Northern Ireland* (London, 1975).

[19]Boyce, "Normal Policing," p. 47.

Juryless trial was seen by government not as a departure from due process, but a redefinition of it.[20]

As always in face of armed resistance, the first task of those responsible for internal security in Northern Ireland was to evaluate the nature of the threat. I have argued elsewhere that liberal-democratic governments are especially ill-equipped to make this assessment accurately.[21] The kind of optimism observed in the 1919–21 period is likely to inform all policy and even to short-circuit recognition of the need for analysis. In Britain the belief in automatic public repudiation of political violence had become very deeply ingrained by 1970. British consensus was rooted in the capacity of constitutionalism to contain dissent. The remarkable if not magical success story of the British police system in the nineteenth century was a function of the coercive force of the nation (not, in English thought, the state). It had not been paralleled in Ireland. While the RIC had seldom been, in its quotidian interface with the people, the "army of occupation" against which nationalists fulminated, it had never derived its authority from the English kind of contract. The representative character of the RUC was quite different: complete in respect to one community, negative in respect to the other. Any attempted reforms in the 1970s would have had to deal with a cultural legacy that none of the principal actors was likely to understand.

The assessment of the threat posed by the renascent IRA in the 1970s was culturally conditioned. Loyalists took the view that had so bemused Sir Ernest Clark in 1920, and of course it was not just a view of the IRA but a view of the "nationalist" threat in general, which had caused them to see the civil rights campaign as a stalking horse for republicanism. The British government was disposed to see the IRA not as a characteristic but as a deviant form of nationalism and to look for ways of prizing it off the main body of moderate nationalists; hence the notion that the force of the state could be applied impartially, as between two warring factions, in the interest of an abstract idea of law. But this intention was unrecognizable at street level where the British Army's function was seen by both sides as prejudicial to their interests. The "pig in the middle" in this case (the armored personnel carrier floodlit by petrol-bomb flames, which has decked every visual image of the Northern conflict) could

---

[20]Merlyn Rees, "Terrorism in Ireland and Britain's Response," *Terrorism* 5 (1981): 83–8.

[21]C. Townshend, *Britain's Civil Wars: Counterinsurgency in the Twentieth Century* (London, 1986), pp. 13–23.

never catch the ball or join one of the sides.[22] The shifting of aim from the eradication of terrorism to some sort of containment was driven by this limitation. Amid the new technology of riot control, probably the most poignant symbol of the gap between intention and performance has been the "baton round," the rubber bullet that represents the authorities' best attempt to give a police function to service weapons.

As in 1919–21, the government was not prepared to pay the price of a full-blown war against terrorism. Not only has there been no declaration of martial law at any time or place during the crisis, there has been no declaration of a state of emergency in any of the sophisticated hybrid forms such as were used in colonial conflicts in Palestine or Malaya, or the domestic form created by the Emergency Powers Acts. Since 1973 the legal framework for security operations has been the Northern Ireland (Emergency Provisions) Act, which replaced the Special Powers Act, supplemented by the Prevention of Terrorism Act of 1974. Fine-tuning has been applied to both, notably via the Amending Act of 1975 (which followed the report of the Gardiner Committee) and the Emergency Provisions Act of 1987. Legal commentators continue to remark on the weakness of parliamentary scrutiny of powers exercised under these acts, a criticism which has been made of all delegating legislation since the Defence of the Realm Act.[23] There appears to be little political or public curiosity about the definition of the confrontation or the powers taken to deal with it. Though the words "civil war" have from time to time been used by the press, they have been confined to headlines and not subjected to analysis. Margaret Thatcher caused a minor stir by using the unadorned word "war," but hastily qualified it as an attempt to describe the delusions of the republicans. Since words like "the troubles" and "imbroglio" have lapsed into desuetude, preference has been given to "conflict" and, of course, "crisis." Promiscuously applied, these terms indicate nothing of the actual intensity of violence, or of perceptions of threat to individuals or state.

The usage which seems best to have expressed (or least to have traduced) the meaning given to the confrontation by its participants is "paramilitary." This is itself profoundly ambiguous, but it plainly indicates a refusal to accept the official designation "terrorist," and concedes a

---

[22]D. Hamill, *Pig in the Middle: The Army in Northern Ireland 1969–1984* (London, 1985), is a notably honest portrayal of the army's bafflement.

[23]G. Hogan and C. Walker, *Political Violence and the Law in Ireland* (Manchester, 1989), part II.1.

degree of legitimacy to some violent organizations. Academics have gone on to write about "paramilitarism" (though none to my knowledge has consciously related this perplexing concept to the more familiar "militarism"), "paramilitants," and "parapolitical" activity. If we have parapolitics, can we have parawar? Soldiers, following General Kitson's acute work, have leaned to "low-intensity operations," but this term is too long as well as too technical for general use (and is in any case open to criticism on technical grounds). What, one may ask, is wrong with "rebellion," which conveys not only the precise legal standing of the conflict, but also the evaluation placed on it by all sides?

The answer seems to be that even "rebellion" is regarded by government as conceding too much legitimacy to opponents whose means (if not aims) are branded as wholly illegitimate. The movement away from the tacit recognition of the IRA through the "political status" of detainees and occasional moves toward direct negotiation, and into a rigidly enunciated policy of "criminalization," attests to official determination to minimize discussion of such issues. Likewise the oddly named policy of Ulsterization is more a confession of failure than a path to the kind of success envisaged in the 1970s: a damage-limitation device to disguise the significance of a military presence that has gone on at least twenty times longer than the first military commander said it would. The underlying logic is contained in some version of the formula, "an acceptable level of violence."[24] This is not and never can be a war; therefore—in British legal terms—it must be peace.

There is an important truth in this which many ministers over the last twenty years have been hesitant to grasp: that government, even without consensus, has immense power to lay down rules.[25] All that is required is a certain fixity of purpose, and the 1985 Anglo-Irish Agreement was the most striking evidence of this in many years. Public security is in large (though sadly unmeasurable) part a product of confidence, and government is not without power to break into the vicious spiral of terrorist demoralization. The root problem has always been how a government designed for a consensus system should manage another system producing an unacceptable level of violence. The answer seems to be that

[24]R. Weitzer, "Contested Order: The Struggle over British Security Policy in Northern Ireland," *Comparative Politics* 19 (1987): 293–5.

[25]See, e.g., B. Crick, "The Concept of Consent and the Anglo-Irish Agreement," in C. Townshend (ed.), *Consensus in Ireland: Approaches and Recessions* (Oxford, England, 1988), pp. 110–27.

it must either modify its instinctual insistence that *any* political violence is unacceptable, or abrogate its constitution—as in wartime—in favor of some kind of military administration. The latter course has never been seriously entertained because it runs so sharply against the grain of British political culture, but it may be less dangerous to liberty, in the end, than the pragmatic alternative. Thinking about the possibility of martial law in November 1920, Sir John Anderson worried about "the enormous difficulties of getting back to Civil Gov[ernmen]t after the Army *pur et simple* have killed or cured the situation."[26] Yet it would be hard to argue that the alternative devised by the civil power at that time was either morally or politically superior.

Analogous doubts must assail anyone trying to evaluate the British campaign of the 1980s. The avoidance of a formal state of emergency seems to have led inexorably to the covert reshaping of the rules. The alleged "shoot to kill policy," above all, fixed an unwonted degree of public attention on the elements of the security forces that the authorities are most concerned to shield from public scrutiny. After the very odd affair of the inquiry whose head, Deputy Chief Constable John Stalker, was first denied access to RUC records and later suspended from duty in connection with charges still unresolved, there came the refusal "in the national interest" to publish the findings eventually completed by Chief Constable Colin Sampson or to initiate any prosecutions.[27] Whether or not the decision was technically correct, the blurring of the distinction between public and state security has left a justifiable disquiet. Whose safety is the supreme law? An event such as the shooting near Lurgan, Co. Armagh, on 11 November 1982, when no less than 109 rounds were fired at the car in which three IRA men were killed, does seem to call for public explanation. No doubt the government was compelled, in assessing the report, to weigh the credibility and legitimacy of its forces against their physical and psychological security. The outcome of that assessment tells its own story.

[26]Diary of Mark Sturgis, 30 November 1920. PRO 30 59/3.
[27]The inquiry up to September 1985 in a way has been put in the public record in the first part of J. Stalker, *Stalker* (London, 1988); for the case generally, see P. Taylor, *Stalker: The Search for the Truth* (London, 1987).

Part II

The politics of social and political division

6

Dynamics of social and political change in Northern Ireland

JOHN WHYTE

To use the term *dynamics* in relation to Northern Ireland may seem infelicitous. There are few situations anywhere in the world that appear more static. A narrow majority of Protestants faces a large minority of Catholics. Many Catholics are deeply dissatisfied with their position of inferiority; many Protestants are deeply fearful of being forced into a united Ireland in which their values would be disregarded. Internal divisions in each camp increase the immobility: If moderates were prepared to compromise, they could be undercut by more extreme elements within their own communities. A campaign of violence by sections of both communities helps freeze the situation. Their violence is sufficient to keep bitterness in the other community alive; the security measures their campaigns provoke help maintain support for them in their own communities.

Changes are occurring underneath the frozen surface, however. The difficulty is not that changes are not happening but that different changes push in different directions, so that the overall balance remains much as ever. I shall illustrate the point by discussing, first, changes that seem to be weakening the position of the unionists and, second, changes that seem to be maintaining the status quo.

The first way in which the position of unionists within Northern Ireland is weakening is that the proportion of Catholics in the population is slowly rising. It was estimated even by a cautious observer to have

JOHN WHYTE was Professor of Politics at University College, Dublin, and at Queen's University, Belfast. His publications include *Church and State in Modern Ireland, 1923–79; Catholics in Western Democracies: A Study in Political Behaviour;* and *Interpreting Northern Ireland.*

reached 40 percent by 1986,[1] and others might put the figure higher. True, the latest projection suggests, with the Catholic birthrate dropping toward the Protestant one, that the increase will decelerate and eventually cease.[2] It is also true that not all Catholics vote nationalist or want a united Ireland—although a 1990 article reports that the proportion of Catholics voting for nationalist parties is rising.[3] But even if the population eventually levels off at around 45 percent Catholic to 55 percent Protestant, and even if not all Catholics are nationalist, this means that the nationalist minority will be far too large to be coerced, and will be in a position at least to force a compromise. The situation that existed in the first forty years of the Northern Ireland state, whereby the unionists could use their two-to-one majority to dominate the nationalists, will not recur.

Second, the economic position of the unionist population is weaker than it used to be. In the early days of the troubles, the unionists had a fallback position to which they could retreat as a last resort if the British abandoned them. This was to move to independence. An independent Northern Ireland would have been poorer than Northern Ireland as part of the United Kingdom, but it might not have been any poorer than the Republic. Its economy had some strengths. An energetic policy of attracting foreign investment had considerable success in the 1960s, and Northern Ireland had become a major center of, for instance, the synthetic-fiber industry. Industrial output continued to grow until 1974.[4] However, since then a series of economic hammer blows has struck the region. The synthetic-fiber industry has been shattered by foreign competition. Other industries have gone to the wall. Unemployment has burgeoned. Outside investment has almost dried up. The decline in industry was, for a time, masked by a rise in public-sector jobs, but that too has leveled off. The region is kept going only by massive subventions from Great Britain. In one book Northern Ireland is described as a workhouse economy, because "like a typical workhouse, it is supported by taxes levied on the external community, while providing very little in

---

[1]Paul Compton, "Population," in R. H. Buchanan and B. M. Walker (eds.), *Province, City and People: Belfast and Its Region* (Antrim, Northern Ireland, 1987), p. 246.
[2]Paul Compton and John Coward, *Fertility and Family Planning in Northern Ireland* (Aldershot, England, 1989), pp. 214–15.
[3]Brendan O'Leary, "More Green, Fewer Orange," *Fortnight* 282 (February 1990): 13.
[4]Bob Rowthorn and Naomi Wayne, *Northern Ireland: The Political Economy of Conflict* (Cambridge, England, 1988), p. 79.

return."[5] Independence now, if outside support were not obtained, would produce a catastrophic decline in the standard of living. Money is not everything, and there may be many in the unionist camp who would prefer an independent state, no matter what the deprivation, to joining a united Ireland. But the willingness of all unionists to make the necessary sacrifices is more open to question. Meanwhile the Republic, despite serious difficulties such as high unemployment and a huge national debt, has a fundamentally sounder economy. Exports are booming, and there is a favorable balance of payments. If independence were to come to Northern Ireland now, the standard of living might be well below that of the Republic.

Third, the Anglo-Irish Agreement of 1985 exposed the unionists' lack of political clout. The agreement was bitterly unpopular among them, and they tried many methods of pressuring the British government into abandoning it—mass demonstrations, boycotts of public bodies, and the forcing of by-elections to Parliament, among others. None of them worked, and the unionists have now retreated to asking for a temporary suspension of the working of the agreement as their precondition for entering negotiations. Unionists have a problem in their dealings with the British government that the nationalists do not have. They want to remain within the United Kingdom, but if they take their opposition to British policy too far, they may simply provoke a British withdrawal.

One feature of the post-agreement situation was that the public sector remained loyal to its British employers. It was noted at the time of the agreement that the Royal Ulster Constabulary, despite enormous pressure from the people among whom its members lived, stood firm against loyalist demonstrations. It is less often noted that the Northern Ireland civil service, a substantial majority of whose members are Protestant, continued to work, and that judges, most of whom are Protestant, handed down a number of judgments declaring illegal various attempts by union-

[5]Ibid., pp. 96–7. There have been a number of recent surveys of the Northern Ireland economy. Rowthorn and Wayne's is the gloomiest, but the others are hardly less bleak. See David Canning, Barry Moore, and John Rhodes, "Economic Growth in Northern Ireland: Problems and Prospects," in Paul Teague (ed.), *Beyond the Rhetoric: Politics, the Economy and Social Policy in Northern Ireland* (London, 1987), pp. 211–35; Kieran A. Kennedy, Thomas Giblin, and Deirdre McHugh, *The Economic Development of Ireland in the Twentieth Century* (London and New York, 1988); Graham Gudgin, "Prospects for the Northern Ireland Economy: The Role of Economic Research," in Richard Jenkins (ed.), *Northern Ireland: Studies in Social and Economic Life* (Aldershot, England, 1989), pp. 69–84.

ist-dominated local authorities to protest against the Anglo-Irish Agreement by refusing to carry out their statutory duties.[6] It is likely that most of these Protestant policemen, civil servants, and judges shared the gut reactions of their community; but the traditions of their respective services, as well as concern for their salaries and pension rights, acted as a restraint upon them.

In recent years some unionists have attempted to improve their position by seeking to persuade the principal British political parties to organize in Northern Ireland. They argue that if these parties were competing for votes in the region they would pay more attention to the actual wishes of the people there (meaning, implicitly, the unionist majority). They also argue that if people in Northern Ireland had a chance to vote for Labour or the Conservatives, two parties with no religious affiliations, the politics of Northern Ireland would become less sectarian.[7] They have had a certain amount of success. The Conservatives were persuaded to organize in Northern Ireland, and have already put up candidates in some local elections. However, the impact seems likely to be limited. The Labour Party is unlikely to follow the Conservatives' lead. The Conservative Party is committed by international treaty to the Anglo-Irish Agreement, and it will take more than a few party members in Northern Ireland to induce it to reverse its policy. After all, Scotland has many more seats in Parliament than Northern Ireland (seventy-two compared to seventeen), but that has not stopped the Conservative government from pursuing policies that have cost it most of its representation in Scotland.

Fourth, the British Labour Party is now committed to seeking a united Ireland by consent. Irish unity has been formal party policy since 1981.[8] In 1988, the party's spokespersons on Northern Ireland issued a document that spelled out in some detail how they proposed to nudge Northern Ireland toward unity with the Republic. For instance, Labour proposed to harmonize the economies of the two parts of Ireland; unify the railway system and even the currencies; harmonize the two social welfare systems, company law, and criminal law; and possibly provide

[6]Kathy Sinclair, "A View of Recent Legal Decisions in Northern Ireland Affecting Local Authorities," *Local Government Studies* 12, 5 (September–October 1986): 25–35; M. Connolly and C. Knox, "Recent Political Difficulties of Local Government in Northern Ireland," *Policy and Politics* 16 (1988): 89–97.
[7]For the arguments of the electoral integrationists see Arthur Aughey, *Under Siege: Ulster Unionism and the Anglo-Irish Agreement* (Belfast, 1989), pp. 132–67.
[8]Geoffrey Bell, *Troublesome Business: The Labour Party and the Irish Question* (London, 1982), p. 148.

an all-Ireland policing structure. A promise was made that Northern Ireland would continue to receive financial support until the benefits of unification were realized. It was stated that this program would proceed "even in the face of sustained opposition from some sections of the community."[9]

A few years ago Labour's statement might not have seemed much of a threat, for it was open to question if the party would ever win a general election again. Labour's defeat in three successive general elections (1979, 1983, 1987), its noisy internal squabbles, its commitment to policies such as unilateral disarmament that were unpopular with the British electorate, and the serious challenge being mounted to its position as leading opposition party by the Liberal–Social Democratic Party Alliance, all gave the impression that it might be in terminal decline. But since 1987 Labour has improved its position considerably. Its internal disputes have died away, its front-benchers look increasingly competent, the Alliance has collapsed as a credible alternative, and the Conservatives are saddled with some deeply unpopular policies. Therefore, despite its surprise defeat in the 1992 general election, the likelihood of a Labour government at some point in the 1990s is now much greater.

One might deduce from the above that all the nationalists have to do is to sit tight and wait for a united Ireland to fall into their laps. A Labour government will work for it, and the unionists are now too weakened, demographically, economically, and politically, to withstand the pressure.

However, it would be foolish for nationalists to be too sure of success, for there are also countervailing trends at work. In the first place, Labour may not return to power, or if it does, it may not stick to its current pro–united-Ireland line. There has always been a minority in the Labour Party with united-Ireland sympathies. In 1971 it included the party leader himself, Harold Wilson, who proposed in Parliament a plan to move by stages to Irish unity.[10] But in office, the limits of the feasible have reasserted themselves, and in practice Labour governments, faced with the adamant opposition of unionists to any kind of united Ireland, have proved as committed to the union as Conservative ones. Indeed it was a Labour government that first gave the guarantee that Northern Ireland would not cease to be part of the United Kingdom without its consent,

---

[9]Kevin McNamara MP, Jim Marshall MP, and Marjorie Mowlam MP, "Towards a United Ireland. Reform and Harmonisation: A Dual Strategy for Irish Unification" (London, 1988), photocopied document.
[10]Bell, *Troublesome Business*, p. 116.

in 1949,[11] and it was a Labour secretary of state for Northern Ireland, Roy Mason (in office from 1976 to 1979) who is still remembered by unionists as the most friendly to their position of all the secretaries of state who have served since the office was established in 1972. On the other hand, it was Conservatives who delivered the most damaging blows to the unionist position: the suspension of the Northern Ireland government and Parliament in 1972, and the signing of the Anglo-Irish Agreement in 1985. There were signs of caution even in Labour's 1988 policy document. Although it argued for a policy of fostering a united Ireland, the party was not prepared to use coercion to do so. It seemed genuinely doubtful of the morality of forcing out of the United Kingdom a population that wishes to remain within it: "Any democratic government should accept that where a change in sovereignty was in prospect which would affect directly the interests and citizenship of a part of its population, those thus affected should have a determining say in the question."[12] Under that scenario unionists would have only to remain firm, refuse all blandishments to join a united Ireland, and wait until the Conservatives return to power.

Second, it is far from certain that the Republic could take on the economic burden of coping with Northern Ireland. Ironically, the extent of this burden was first quantified by a body set up to develop the case for Irish unity—the New Ireland Forum of 1983–84. The forum comprised representatives of the main constitutional nationalist parties north and south of the border. It commissioned a number of research reports, one of which was conducted by a leading economic consulting firm, Davy Kelleher McCarthy Ltd., to study the economic consequences of Irish unity. The study was deeply pessimistic about the effects of uniting Ireland unless massive aid were received from Britain or elsewhere. It noted that by the early 1980s the United Kingdom subvention provided 25–30 percent of the Northern Ireland population's disposable income.[13] For the Republic, whose economy is only about double the size of Northern Ireland's, to replace a subvention of this size was beyond its power, and

---

[11]Under the terms of the Ireland Act of 1949, Northern Ireland would not cease to be part of the United Kingdom without the consent of the Northern Ireland Parliament. The disappearance of that Parliament in 1972 rendered the commitment inoperative. Under the terms of the Northern Ireland Constitution Act of 1973, Northern Ireland would not cease to be part of the United Kingdom without the consent of the majority of its people voting in a referendum.

[12]McNamara, Marshall, and Mowlam, "Towards a United Ireland," para. 16.

[13]New Ireland Forum, *The Macroeconomic Consequences of Integrated Economic Policy, Planning and Co-ordination in Ireland* (Dublin, 1984), p. 11.

any attempt to do so would lead to "exploding and unsustainable deficits."[14] These conclusions applied whether the arrangements envisaged were unitary or federal. Only if Northern Ireland came under joint authority, which would entail a continuing British presence and British subvention, would the results be less drastic.[15] It is true that, since this report appeared in 1984, the economic position of the Republic has improved—but not by enough to enable it to take on lightly the burden of a decrepit Northern Ireland. It is interesting to note that a later writer, Bob Rowthorn, who personally favors a united Ireland, still considers it impossible for the Republic to incorporate Northern Ireland unless it receives financial help from outside.[16]

Third, it is far from clear how strongly the people of the Republic actually want reunification with the North. The troubles have brought home the possible consequences of unity. There are the economic penalties just noted. There is the evident determination of the unionists to oppose even the slightest hint of a rapprochement with the Republic. The possibility exists that in a united Ireland Protestant paramilitaries would be as much of a burden to the Irish security forces as the Irish Republican Army (IRA) now is to the British. There is even the unlikable character of many Northern nationalists, those stubborn people from whose ranks comes a determined paramilitary force, the IRA, committed to overthrowing the Southern regime as well as the Northern. Finally, there is the fact that the Republic has developed institutions that suit it comfortably within its present boundaries, and that the absorption of 1.5 million Northerners could have unpalatable effects. As the Irish political scientist Tom Garvin has put it:

If such an offer [of a united Ireland] were to be seriously and publicly made by the British government . . . it would have devastating, and possibly destabilising effects on the Republic. . . . The structure of the Dublin state is predicated on the unspoken assumption of indefinite continuance of partition, as is its party system. Furthermore, the Republic has developed a corporate identity of its own that sudden reunification would threaten; an analogy would be requiring the United States to absorb Mexico.[17]

[14]Ibid., p. 87.
[15]Ibid., p. 117.
[16]Bob Rowthorn, "Northern Ireland: An Economy in Crisis," in Teague (ed.), *Beyond the Rhetoric*, p. 131.
[17]Tom Garvin, "The North and the Rest: The Politics of the Republic of Ireland," in Charles Townshend (ed.), *Consensus in Ireland: Approaches and Recessions* (Oxford, England, 1988), p. 109.

The evidence for saying that the people of the Republic are now ambivalent toward unification comes from opinion polls, which have been analyzed by a number of authors,[18] whose conclusions are substantially similar. All agree that, in principle, the ideal of reunification retains majority support in the Republic, but a much smaller proportion of the population is prepared to suffer any serious inconvenience to help that to happen. Three surveys, in 1978, 1980, and 1984, asked if people would be prepared to pay more taxes in order to achieve unity. All three showed a majority against.[19] Other surveys have shown that Northern Ireland comes low on the list when electors in the Republic are asked what they consider the most important political issues.[20] The political scientist Peter Mair sums up the attitude of voters in the Republic as follows: "Unity would be nice. But if it's going to cost money, or result in violence, or disrupt the moral and social equilibrium, then it's not worth it."[21] The contrast with the two Germanies is glaring. There, West Germany willingly took on the burden of the decrepit East German economy. But there is one big difference: The West Germans knew that the East Germans actually wanted to be united with them.

The lack of interest in the Republic in placating Northern opinion was shown in two referenda during the 1980s. In the first (1983), the existing legal prohibition of abortion was strengthened by making abortion not just illegal but unconstitutional. In the second (1986), a proposal to introduce a limited form of divorce was rejected. In both cases, the Protestant churches supported the "liberal" side—that is, they opposed the entrenching of the ban on abortion in the constitution, and they favored the end of the constitutional ban on divorce. (Divorce has been legal in Northern Ireland since 1939.) In both cases, the Catholic hierarchy (although respecting the rights of those who conscientiously differed) supported the "conservative" side, and in both cases the conservative side was victorious by a margin of two to one. In neither

---

[18]Ibid., pp. 106–9; Richard Rose, Ian McAllister, and Peter Mair, *Is There a Concurring Majority about Northern Ireland?*, Studies in Public Policy No. 22 (Glasgow, 1978); Conor Cruise O'Brien, *Neighbours: The Ewart-Biggs Memorial Lectures 1978–1979* (London, 1980), pp. 19–34; Padraig O'Malley, *The Uncivil Wars: Ireland Today* (Belfast, 1983), pp. 80–4; W. Harvey Cox, "Who Wants a United Ireland?" *Government and Opposition* 20, 1 (Winter 1985): 29–47; Peter Mair, "Breaking the Nationalist Mould: The Irish Republic and the Anglo-Irish Agreement," in Teague (ed.), *Beyond the Rhetoric*, pp. 81–110.
[19]Mair, "Breaking the Nationalist Mould," p. 91.
[20]O'Malley, *The Uncivil Wars*, p. 84; Cox, "Who Wants a United Ireland?" p. 35.
[21]Mair, "Breaking the Nationalist Mould," p. 105.

case did the prospect that the outcome might affect Northern Protestant attitudes toward the Republic cut much ice with the electorate. Indeed, the then Taoiseach, Garret FitzGerald, admitted that to make the repercussions on Northern Ireland an issue would have been "counterproductive."[22]

Fourth, the attitudes of Northern Catholics are also uncertain. The fact that the bulk of them vote for two parties—the Social Democratic and Labour Party (SDLP) and Sinn Féin—which, whatever their disagreements about methods, both seek some form of Irish unity, might seem to suggest a clear commitment to a united Ireland. However, other evidence indicates a more complex picture. Survey data suggest that many Catholics would be prepared to settle for a solution falling far short of a united Ireland. Generally the most favored solution among them has been power-sharing within a Northern Ireland which remains basically part of the United Kingdom.[23]

True, surveys of attitudes in Northern Ireland must be used carefully. There are grounds for believing that interviewees offer opinions more moderate than those they really hold. The best evidence for this comes from comparing party support as measured by attitude surveys with party support as tested in elections. The Alliance Party, which is in the middle of the spectrum of opinion, consistently does better in polls than it does in elections; Sinn Féin, on the extreme nationalist wing of opinion, consistently does better in elections than it does in polls. However, the differences are only a few percent. Attitude surveys can be taken as at least a rough guide to public opinion, and they have shown repeatedly that Northern Catholics are far from unanimous in their support of a united Ireland—much less unanimous than Protestants are in their opposition to it. Perhaps this is not surprising. Northern Catholics, as well as Northern Protestants, are likely to be aware of the economic costs of reunification. Some of the other features of the Republic that repel Northern Protestants could also be repugnant to Northern Catholics. For instance, the influence of the Catholic church in Southern life would not necessarily be attractive to all Northerners of Catholic background.

The economic position of Northern Catholics also may be slowly

---

[22]G. W. Hogan, "Law and Religion: Church-State Relations in Ireland from Independence to the Present Day," *American Journal of Comparative Law* 35, 1 (Winter 1987): 96, note 114.

[23]For an analysis of the survey data see my book, *Interpreting Northern Ireland* (Oxford, England, 1990).

improving although this is not a subject on which it is easy to find hard evidence. The baseline used for most comparisons is the census of 1971, which was the first since before Partition to cross-tabulate by religion and occupation. It showed a substantial degree of economic disadvantage among Catholics relative to Protestants.[24] Because the 1971 census is relatively recent, it does not leave much space for tracing subsequent developments. The next census, in 1981, was flawed by the refusal of thousands to answer the religion question, and by the refusal of thousands more to fill in the census form at all. Since then, there has been only fragmentary evidence, of which the most important is provided by the Continuous Household Survey, in operation since 1983. These data indicate that in one respect the position of Catholics has not improved at all. The census of 1971 showed that the unemployment rate among Catholic men was 2.5 times the rate for Protestant men; in the late 1980s, despite massive increases in unemployment in Protestant areas, the gap remained unchanged.[25] However, for those Catholics who did have jobs, or at least for some of them, the situation did seem to be slowly improving. One researcher, basing his findings on data from the Continuous Household Survey of 1983–85, found that a higher percentage of Catholics than Protestants were employed in some nonmanual and skilled manual occupations.[26] The Northern Ireland civil service has found that among civil servants under age thirty-five, Catholics are overrepresented in proportion to their population.[27] One may perhaps expect an acceleration in the improvement of the Catholics' economic situation as recent government measures take effect. The Fair Employment Agency, founded in 1976 to promote equality of opportunity between religious groups, was replaced by the Fair Employment Commission with more extensive powers. A "Making Belfast Work" campaign was launched, targeted on the

[24]Edmund A. Aunger, "Religion and Occupational Class in Northern Ireland," *Economic and Social Review* 7, 1 (October 1975): 1–18.
[25]*PPRU Monitor* 1/89 (April 1989): 11, using data from the Continuous Household Survey for 1985–87. (The *PPRU Monitor* is the bulletin of the Northern Ireland government's Policy Planning and Research Unit.)
[26]David J. Smith, *Equality and Inequality in Northern Ireland. Part 1: Employment and Unemployment,* Policy Studies Institute Occasional Paper No. 39 (London, 1987), p. 61.
[27]Derived from *Equal Opportunities in the Northern Ireland Civil Service: Third Report of the Equal Opportunities Unit* (Belfast, 1989), tables 1.16, 2.22, 2.49, and 6.50. Tables 1.16 and 6.50 show that, overall, Catholics are employed in the civil service almost exactly in proportion to their strength in the working population. Tables 2.22 and 2.49 show that Catholics in the civil service are overrepresented in the age groups under thirty-five.

most deprived areas of the city, which has made some inroads into the unemployment in Catholic West Belfast. It is difficult to judge how much political effect these economic changes will have. Political attitudes are not simply a product of economic conditions, and doubtless many nationalists will remain nationalist no matter how much money the British government pumps into Northern Ireland. But if an economic convergence between Catholic and Protestant does take place, at the very least it will do the status quo no harm, and may serve instead to increase the legitimacy among Catholics of the Northern Ireland state.

A fifth factor in the equation is the activity of the IRA. From the IRA's own point of view, its campaign has not been without success. It played a major part in bringing down Stormont. It has kept Irish unity on the map. It helps sustain mutual suspicions between the British and Irish. The great majority of episodes that have exacerbated these suspicions in recent years have been connected with security. These include the Stalker affair, the Guildford Four and the Birmingham Six, the row over the leaking of documents on republican suspects from the security forces to Protestant paramilitaries, and the refusals to extradite republican suspects from the Republic. None of these would have happened if it had not been for the IRA's activities. Finally, the IRA can claim it has strengthened the hand even of constitutional nationalists. As Gerry Adams, president of Sinn Féin, has put it, "the political leverage of the SDLP . . . has been unwittingly enhanced by the armed struggle of the IRA."[28] Indeed, unionists sometimes suspect that constitutional nationalists, while publicly deploring the IRA campaign, are secretly not unhappy with it because it strengthens their own bargaining position.

In other ways the campaign has been counterproductive, however. It embitters unionists. It alienates moderate nationalists, who feel that a united Ireland brought about by such means would not be worth having. Perhaps most important of all is its impact on opinion in Great Britain. Keeping Northern Ireland within the United Kingdom is not a major issue in British politics. Indeed, all the survey evidence suggests that a majority in Great Britain would be prepared to abandon Northern Ireland.[29] But the one snag to doing so is that it would be seen as giving

[28]Gerry Adams, *A Pathway to Peace* (Cork and Dublin, 1988), p. 58.
[29]For examples, see Rose, McAllister, and Mair, *Is There a Concurring Majority?* pp. 27–9; Roger Jowell and Colin Airey (eds.), *British Social Attitudes: The 1984 Report* (Aldershot, England, 1984), p. 33; W. Harvey Cox, "Public Opinion and the Anglo-Irish Agreement," *Government and Opposition* 22, 3 (Summer 1987): 348–51. A survey reported in *The Observer*, 31 December 1989, found that there was substantially more

way to violence. The IRA is caught in a bind—only by continuing its campaign can it keep consideration of Irish unity on the agenda, but that very campaign also provides a motive for making unity impossible. Even a Labour government might find it difficult to work for Irish unity if it seemed to share an objective with the IRA. Since the IRA's campaign seems likely to continue, I would consider it an additional reason for supposing that Irish nationalism will not be totally victorious.

A sixth factor operating against Irish unity is the policy of the Conservatives, which seems to be to retain Northern Ireland within the United Kingdom, but to make sufficiently extensive concessions to the Catholic community to reconcile most of them to that situation. This policy was first articulated in a discussion paper of 1972, which laid down that: (1) Northern Ireland would remain part of the United Kingdom so long as a majority of its people desired, and (2) two important concessions would be made to the nationalist minority—first, any regional institutions must "seek a much wider consensus than has hitherto existed,"[30] and second, there must be some kind of "Irish dimension," that is, a link between the two parts of Ireland.[31] The policy was reaffirmed in the Anglo-Irish Agreement, which (a) stated that any change in the status of Northern Ireland would come about only with the consent of its people, (b) provided an Irish dimension in the form of an intergovernmental conference and secretariat, and (c) envisaged devolved government on "a basis which would secure widespread acceptance throughout the community."[32]

This Conservative Party policy has three possible outcomes. The first is that it may actually succeed. There are formidable difficulties, but on both sides of the divide in Northern Ireland there is a realization that the present situation is unsatisfactory, and that some compromise is necessary to attain a settlement. Some observers see hope in the second rank of politicians on both sides, who have never had a chance to fulfill their political ambitions and who might be prepared to go further than their leaders toward compromising to secure an autonomous government in Northern Ireland. The second possibility is that negotiations peter out, and that the status quo—that is, direct rule—continues. The third possibility is that, following the failure of negotiations, the Conservatives

---

support in Britain for staying in the Falkland Islands (53 percent of those questioned) than in Northern Ireland (36 percent).
[30]*The Future of Northern Ireland: A Paper for Discussion* (London, 1972), para. 79(d).
[31]Ibid., paras. 77–8.
[32]*Anglo-Irish Agreement 1985* (Dublin, 1985), Article 4(b).

would alter their policy. There has long been a strand of opinion in the Conservative Party that favors the abandonment of efforts to restore autonomy in Northern Ireland, and the integration of the region into the United Kingdom. As already noted, this strand has had some success recently, with the Conservative Party, for the first time, contesting elections in Northern Ireland. I do not expect this strand to grow much stronger, because it runs counter to the mainstream Conservative analysis, which is that Northern Ireland is in crucial ways different from the rest of the United Kingdom and therefore needs special institutions, but if there is a change in Conservative policy it is likely to be in this integrationist direction rather than in the direction of encouraging a united Ireland. The full name of the party after all is the "Conservative *and Unionist* Party."

I have so far listed changes that are weakening the unionist position, and changes that seem to be working the other way. For completeness's sake, I must also mention a cluster of changes in Northern Ireland that do not point clearly in any direction. In some ways the two communities, or parts of them, are moving closer. The proportion of mixed Protestant-Catholic marriages, though very low, is rising. A large-scale survey in 1983 found that, whereas only 1 percent of marriages dating from 1943–47 were mixed, the proportion rose fairly steadily through succeeding cohorts until in the most recent (1978–82) it was 10 percent.[33] A program screened by Ulster Television on 19 March 1990 reported that in the Catholic Diocese of Down and Connor (which includes Belfast and much of eastern Northern Ireland), one in five marriages that according to church records took place during 1988 was mixed. There is a growing movement too toward integrated education. By 1990 there were two integrated secondary schools and eight integrated primary schools in Northern Ireland, and the government promised increased support for such schools. However, they reach less than 1 percent of the school-going population. The vast majority of schoolchildren go to schools that are de facto either Catholic or Protestant. On the other side of the coin, there are signs that residential segregation is increasing. One piece of research has found that in the intercensal period 1971–81, areas with Catholic majorities became more Catholic, while on the whole areas with Protestant majorities became more Protestant.[34]

---

[33]Compton and Coward, *Fertility and Family Planning*, p. 186.
[34]Paul Compton and John F. Power, "Estimates of the Religious Composition of Northern Ireland Local Government Districts in 1981 and Change in the Geographical Pattern of

There is another area in which change is undoubtedly occurring, but in which it is difficult to assess the implications. This is the movement toward European unity. In a few years' time one can expect the border between North and South in Ireland to mean less in practical terms than it does now. Tax rates will converge, customs clearance will become a formality, and businesspeople from continental Europe will become much more in evidence. Because it will make less practical difference on which side of the border one lives, unionists may become less hostile to joining a united Ireland, or nationalists less hostile to remaining in the United Kingdom. Another possibility, however, is that there will be little impact on either community. National loyalties are not simply a product of economic issues, and may remain capable of arousing intense emotions even when the practical consequences of belonging to one unit rather than another are no longer great.

In conclusion, then, it is reasonable to speak of Northern Ireland as being "dynamic" rather than "static." All sorts of changes are going on—political, demographic, and economic. The wider context in which both the United Kingdom and the Republic of Ireland operate is changing too. The trouble is that the changes work in different directions, and largely cancel each other out. This conclusion is pessimistic, but it is not un-realistic. There are other conflicts around the world that seem stalemated: Cyprus, Lebanon, Sudan. In all these countries the current situation is unsatisfactory to all the contending parties, but it is not the worst con-ceivable. They hold on to what advantages they have, lest in the course of bargaining they are forced to lose even more than they have lost already. One must accept the possibility that the same is true in Northern Ireland.

Religious Composition between 1971 and 1981," *Economic and Social Review* 17, 2 (Spring 1986): 101.

7

Dynamics of social and political change in the Irish Republic

JOSEPH LEE

The Irish Republic finds itself in the throes of rapid social change in the 1990s. Indeed, change has been occurring so rapidly for the past generation, at least by inherited standards, that it has seemed to many to be careering out of control, provoking gloomy prognostications about the collapse of traditional society and prompting intense concern about the nature of Irish identity.[1]

Population movements are perhaps the most striking indicator of social change. Between 1841 and 1926, the population of the twenty-six counties that constitute the Irish Republic fell from more than 6.5 million to 2.97 million—a unique demographic experience for the world of the time. Having hovered at that level for twenty-five years, the population decreased from 2.96 million in 1951 to 2.82 million in 1961. Then it recovered to a peak of 3.54 million by 1987—reversing the trend of more than a century—only to fall, however slightly, to 3.50 million in 1990.[2]

Population decline since the Great Famine of 1845–50 had been intimately related to emigration movements. Emigration continued to exert a major influence on the changing demographic contours after 1960. Net emigration rates fell from 14.1 per 1,000, the highest of the century, between 1951 and 1961, to 4.6 between 1961 and 1971. This turned

JOSEPH LEE is Professor of Modern History, Head of Department, and Director of the Degree Programme in European Studies, University College, Cork. His many publications include *The Modernisation of Irish Society 1848–1918* and *Ireland 1912–1985: Politics and Society*.

[1]J. J. Lee, *Ireland 1912–1985: Politics and Society* (Cambridge, England, 1989), pp. 658–87.
[2]National Economic and Social Council, Report No. 90, *The Economic and Social Implications of Emigration* (Dublin, 1991), table 2.1, p. 48.

into a net immigration rate of 3.2 between 1971 and 1981. But this trend was not sustained. The tide turned again, with a net outward rate of 4.1 from 1981 to 1986 and 9.6 between 1986 and 1990. In absolute terms, the average of 34,000 emigrants a year between 1986 and 1990 was the highest for any five-year period of the century except during the 1950s.[3]

However important the role of emigration, it has not been the only contributory factor to changing demographic contours. Between 1961 and 1981 the average age at marriage for both sexes fell significantly. But this did not lead directly to the baby boom that might have been anticipated on the basis of inherited fecundity rates. On the contrary, total birth rates remained virtually constant between 1961 and 1981. This in turn reflected the collision of countervailing forces. The impact of the lower age at marriage was reinforced by an increase in the marriage rate, from 5 to 7, over the twenty years. For more than a century Ireland had an exceptionally low marriage rate. As this changed spectacularly after 1960, the combined impact of the earlier marriage age and the increase in the marriage rate was just about compensated for, over this twenty-year period, by a dramatic drop in completed family size. Family planning swept through Ireland in those decades. The perception of its impact was delayed by the contrary impact of the age/rate developments, so that the birth rate remained relatively high by Western European standards even while the average number of children per completed family was rapidly falling.[4]

The change in reproductive behavior began to become clearer in the 1980s. Age at marriage began to creep upward again, and the marriage rate began to fall once more, as the trend of the previous twenty years went into reverse. Completed family size continued to fall. Without the compensatory impact of the age/rate factors, birth rate edged downward. The result was that the number of babies born in 1990 was only half the number that would have been born on the basis of the reproduction regime of 1980. The number of births would have been even smaller but for the sharp rise, from 6 percent to 12 percent, in "illegitimate" births during the decade. By 1990 only remnants remained of what many had come to consider immutable Irish patterns of marital behavior. It is

---

[3]Ibid., table 2.4, p. 53.
[4]F. Kennedy, *Family, Economy and Government in Ireland,* ESRI Paper 143 (Dublin, 1989), ch. 2, esp. pp. 32–3; R. Breen et al., *Understanding Contemporary Ireland* (Dublin, 1990), ch. 5; M. A. Busteed, *Voting Behaviour in the Republic of Ireland* (Oxford, England, 1990), p. 178.

doubtful if so rapid a rate of behavioral change has been recorded in any other Western country, except perhaps in wartime.

Such abrupt and sweeping changes at the mass level reflected powerful underlying influences. Economic change was presumably the single most important current coursing through Irish society. In contrast to most of Western Europe, the 1950s was a depressed decade in Ireland, with an annual average growth rate of just 1 percent. This shifted abruptly to a 4-percent annual average rate during the 1960s. The correspondingly spectacular impact on expectations and behavior was reflected in the rising marriage rate and the falling age at marriage.

The rapid shifts in emigration rates directly reflect economic conditions in Ireland itself and, to some extent, in Britain. The sharp fall during the 1960s, from a gross total of about 500,000 in the 1950s to perhaps 150,000 in the 1960s, seems to have been a direct response to improved Irish economic prospects. The 1970s reveals a more complex pattern. About 176,000 migrants left Ireland. But there was a net immigration of 104,000. It seems that the 280,000 inflow consisted mainly of Irish migrants of an earlier generation who returned from Britain, often with their children. As the British economy lurched through the 1970s, an Ireland that still appeared to be on a sustained upward trend proved more attractive for many who had earlier emigrated to Britain, but now chose to return to rear their children in Ireland.

This trend had already begun to change in 1979. It is likely that emigration would have been higher between then and 1983, as the Irish economy slithered into a protracted recession, but for the continuing difficulties in Britain. As Ireland remained in depression until the late 1980s, and Britain recovered, emigration resumed after 1983, with the result that the total gross outflow for the decade was, the 1950s always excepted, the highest of the century. Ironically enough, emigration sharply declined between 1990 and 1992 as Britain succumbed once more to recession and the sluggishness of the Southeast in general and of the building industry there in particular, discouraging many potential emigrants from venturing along the beaten path.

Four notable features characterized the emigration of the 1980s, all reflecting, directly or indirectly, economic influences. First, net female emigration was less than three-quarters of male emigration. Historically, the numbers of female and male emigrants were roughly equal, taking one decade with another. Had the normal pattern persisted, the already low female ratio of the 1970s would have been balanced by a rise during the 1980s. The contrary was the case. Never had the proportion of female emigrants fallen so low in peacetime as during the 1980s. This in turn probably reflected the changing sex ratio of the labor force. Although females still accounted in 1988 for only a third of the total work force, the total number of males at work had fallen by 33,000 between 1971 and 1988, whereas the total number of females had increased by 75,000.[5] This modest but cumulative shift reflected, on the demand side, the expansion of the more female-friendly service sector compared with the more male-orientated manufacturing and agricultural sectors. On the supply side, changing attitudes toward work outside the home among wives, 23 percent of whom featured in the labor force in 1990 compared to 5 percent in 1960, and rising education levels for girls as well as boys, augmented the female labor supply.

The second notable feature, the substantial increase in the proportion of better-educated emigrants, also reflected in part the improved access to education, which saw the proportion of sixteen-year-olds in full-time education rise from 38 percent in 1965–66 to 90 percent in 1989–90.[6] Although employment opportunities for graduates were distinctly better than for nongraduates in Ireland itself, a rising proportion of graduates, about 30 percent in 1990, emigrated.[7] Thus, although the proportion of nineteen-year-olds in full-time education had risen from 10 percent to 28 percent between 1965–66 and 1989–90, job opportunities, even during what was considered a boom period in Ireland, fell far short of the graduate labor supply.

Indeed, the four years 1987–90 were unique in Irish economic history in that emigration reached extraordinary heights by historical standards during what was officially deemed a boom period. Emigration had hitherto invariably fallen during recovery periods. The emigration of the 1950s had occurred during a depression. The recovery of the 1960s had led to a rapid fall in emigration. But the recovery from the long depression of the 1980s did not produce a similar result. That was scarcely surprising, in that the "boom" never managed to reduce unemployment below 13 percent. Indeed, but for emigration, unemployment would have hovered around 20 percent, perhaps even higher.

[5]NESC, *The Economic and Social Implications of Emigration*, table 3.1, p. 68.
[6]Department of Education, *Education for a Changing World* (Dublin, June 1992), statistical appendix.
[7]John Sheehan, "The Economic Relevance of Irish Education: An Emerging Debate," *Irish Banking Review* (Autumn 1992), fig. 5, p. 40.

The third distinctive feature of the 1980s was that migration rates became more or less nationalized. Whereas earlier in the century there had been a notable east-west gradient in emigration, with eastern levels distinctly lower than western ones, by the 1980s the rates had more or less leveled out across the country. They were leveling off at a high rate, of course, and, west of the Shannon River in particular, individual communities could become moribund. While emigration rates rose in Dublin also,[8] the impact on metropolitan localities tended to be shrouded by the general density of population.

Return migration, which had exceeded emigration in the 1970s, remained high in the 1980s. But it was now of a rather different type. It no longer reflected depression in Britain, at least until the very end of the decade. It did not therefore consist to the same extent of more mature emigrants returning to Ireland with families. Now it seemed to be more a return of younger emigrants who had heard of job opportunities back home, at least again until 1990, when many were obliged to return home by the collapse of the building industry in England's Southeast.

Migration movements therefore continue to reflect economic changes intimately. But now the developments are more complex, more differentiated, more subtle. The type of generalization that sufficed to explain mass movements in earlier decades can no longer satisfy.

The changing nature of family life reflects two further factors less directly connected with economic experience. The reception of British television in the East of Ireland from the late 1950s and the inauguration of an Irish television service in 1961, now massively reinforced by access to a whole range of British and satellite stations, has enabled television to play an influential role in both articulating and molding opinion. While a wide variety of views has been expressed on television programs, notably on the phenomenally successful "Late Late Show" hosted by an extraordinarily accomplished broadcaster, Gay Byrne, the very expression of a variety of views has itself been revolutionary. There was little scope for variety in the orthodox consensus concerning "family values" of the preceding century.

Apart from opinions influenced by the articulation of specific views, it can hardly be doubted that the life-styles portrayed in the vast majority of imported "soaps," and in most other programs presented on British or satellite television, show little respect for "traditional family values."

[8]NESC, *The Economic and Social Implications of Emigration*, pp. 75ff.

It may be that television would not have exerted so insidious an influence on the rising generation if Ireland had remained as poor as it was in the 1950s. Irish society had always had a strong materialistic impulse to it, as is inevitably the case with pre-industrial societies. That impulse, however, was essentially utilitarian, not hedonistic. But the relatively rapid rise in per capita income over the past thirty years has fostered a receptivity toward the hedonist values widely portrayed on television that makes them a reference point for the behavior of many.

It is difficult to identify the precise influence of television for a number of reasons, not least the fact that the launching of Radio Telefís Éireann more or less coincided with the convening of the Second Vatican Council in 1962. The consequences of the council can be endlessly debated. Would the sharp fall in vocations have occurred, or occurred so rapidly, but for the impact of the Vatican Council? Perhaps not. On the other hand, the church might have failed to attract some of its most idealistic subsequent adherents. It is probable that a rising standard of living, improving access to education, and the changing content of education, as well as the spread of television, would in any case have fostered a great deal more individual judgment.

But the Vatican Council undoubtedly facilitated the sharp shift from an obey/command, authority/deference type of relationship between clergy and laity in areas of sexual morality. As this relationship had long depended on the perceived self-interest of the laity it was, indeed, likely to change as the weight of the agricultural sector in the economy declined and the nature of self-interest changed. As Ireland became increasingly urbanized, self-interest expressed itself in new ways. It did not become, insofar as the historian can judge these essentially unmeasurable things, any more intense. But it did express itself in new forms. It now dictated a different response from the traditional one—traditional meaning something that had lasted roughly a century. The strong farmer ethos that came to dominate Irish society after the Famine normally required that one son should inherit the farm, and one daughter marry into a neighboring farm. The rest of the children had to be kept celibate until they emigrated. The church's teaching on celibacy before marriage (in effect, before emigration) naturally appealed to this mentality. It carried much less conviction in a primarily urban society, whose needs became increasingly different.

The response to Pope Paul VI's 1968 encyclical, *Humanae Vitae*, which reaffirmed the Catholic church's ban on artificial contraception, revealed

just how little authority the church now enjoyed in that particular area.[9]
The rapid decline in completed family size indicates that a substantial
number, probably a large majority, of younger couples are now consciously practicing birth control, presumably primarily by the means
condemned in official church teaching. The laity has always been selective
in choosing which doctrines to obey or ignore. What is revolutionary is
that it is now, for the first time, choosing to ignore church teaching in
the area of contraception.

As it was illegal, under legislation dating from 1935, to import con-
traceptive devices, tension arose between the law and reality. Politicians
on all sides played the issue with the customary combination of calculation and conscience, leading to a series of compromises and shuffles as
they sought to square the various circles involved, often reluctantly because of the danger of offending some interest, but obliged at times to
respond to Supreme Court rulings that found the 1935 legislation unconstitutional. The details can be left for connoisseurs of political gym-
nasts striking various poses, some more aesthetically alluring than others
(including some even following their consciences). The end result was
that by 1990 contraceptives, having been illegal in 1972, were legally
available to everybody over age eighteen.

The issue of contraception, although controversial enough at times,
roused nothing like the degree of public dispute that two other issues,
divorce and abortion, were to provoke in the 1980s.

The 1983 abortion referendum, in particular, convulsed the body politic. The origins were instructive. The constitution of 1937 designates
the Supreme Court as the final interpreter of the document. For the first
twenty-five years or so after its adoption, relatively few constitutional
cases were taken. From the early 1960s, however, the Supreme Court
played an increasingly active role in constitutional affairs, consciously
emulating the United States Supreme Court and looking increasingly to
American rather than English judicial styles, if not necessarily judicial
decisions. During the 1970s these decisions clearly moved in the direction
of protecting the privacy of the individual against the claims of the state,
not least in the area of contraception.

It was in response to this Supreme Court "privatizing" activity that a
number of Catholic laity founded the Society for the Protection of Unborn

---

[9]For a general survey see Busteed, *Voting Behaviour*, ch. 6; J. H. Whyte, *Church and State
in Modern Ireland 1923–1979*, 2nd ed. (Dublin, 1980), pp. 413–16.

Children (SPUC) in 1980 and, launching a Pro-Life Amendment Campaign (PLAC), agitated to have an amendment prohibiting abortion inserted in the constitution. In a finely balanced electoral situation, they found the main party leaders receptive. SPUC deemed it essential to have an explicit clause in the constitution banning abortion, because of its fear that the Supreme Court could interpret the constitution to permit abortion under some implied natural-rights judgment of a type that the court had increasingly favored during the 1970s.

Following intense political maneuvering, an amendment purporting to prevent abortion was approved in a referendum in 1983 by a two-to-one majority in a turnout of 53.7 percent.[10]

This result contained some surprises. First, the turnout was remarkably low for an issue that the Catholic hierarchy, while acknowledging the right of Catholics—who constituted 97 percent of the population—to vote according to their conscience, had declared to be of fundamental importance. Perhaps many assumed the proposal would be automatically carried, and therefore felt their vote would not really matter. Or it may be that people who opposed abortion nevertheless believed the prohibition ought not to be included in the constitution, either because it was seen to impose the values of one church, or because it was felt it would offend Protestants in Northern Ireland, whom people in the Republic were simultaneously insisting would be entitled to freedom of conscience in a united Ireland. Some may have been offended by the phraseology: "The state acknowledges the right to life of the unborn and, with due regard to the equal right to life of the mother, guarantees in its laws to respect and, as far as practicable, by its laws to defend and vindicate that right." Some may have felt that the mother ought to have a greater, others a lesser, right to life. Perhaps many were genuinely undecided. It is impossible to know.

It is possible to know that the longer-term outcome was far different from what SPUC had intended. In the sensational "X" case in January 1992, the attorney general sought to prevent a fourteen-year-old girl ("X") from leaving the country with her parents to procure an abortion in England, after an alleged rape. The High Court upheld the attorney general's demand for an injunction. But the Supreme Court overruled the High Court decision, interpreting the 1983 constitutional amendment

---

[10]Busteed, *Voting Behaviour*, ch. 6; G. FitzGerald, *All in a Life* (Dublin, 1991), pp. 416–17, 440–4.

as justification for defending the mother's right to life on the grounds that the fourteen-year-old girl was potentially suicidal. This ruling left the Republic, at least on paper, with one of the most potentially permissive abortion laws in the world. To the layperson, at any rate, "potentially suicidal" was a potentially highly elastic category. This was the precise opposite of what SPUC had intended.

SPUC could not claim, however, that it had not been warned. During the 1983 debate warnings had been issued by, among others, Attorney General Peter Sutherland and a young barrister, Mary Robinson, who had foreseen possible scenarios of this type. Their fears were derided at the time. It added to the irony that the same Mary Robinson was elected president of Ireland by popular vote in 1990.

The Supreme Court ruling in the X case unleashed a variety of responses that ranged the whole spectrum from abortion on demand to no abortion. Opinion polls are even more difficult to interpret on an issue as sensitive as this than on most others. For what they may be worth, however, the polls conducted in the first half of 1992 seemed to suggest that, while the majority of the population rejected abortion on demand, and indeed detested the idea of abortion in principle, a substantial proportion, perhaps a majority, accepted the idea of abortion in cases of rape or incest. A large majority purported to accept a right to travel for an abortion and a right to information about abortion services abroad.

This public response, more differentiated than previously, meant that it would be extremely difficult for the government to find a new wording, as demanded by a rejuvenated SPUC, that could be guaranteed a majority in the referendum that the Taoiseach, Albert Reynolds, promised for autumn 1992. The potential for a vicious campaign, reminiscent of and perhaps exceeding in unsavoriness the 1983 campaign, was considerable. But the outcome was more uncertain. Much would depend on the precise phraseology presented to the people.

Intimations of the potential for conflict could be detected in some of the tactics adopted during the campaign concerning the Maastricht Treaty, which was put to a referendum on 18 June 1992. What, the uninitiated might wonder, has Maastricht got to do with abortion? The answer is that in order to ensure that no European court could foist abortion on Ireland, the Irish government succeeded in having a protocol inserted in December 1991 to the effect that nothing in the treaty would override the Irish constitution in this area. Within a mere two months the Supreme Court ruling on the X case transformed the situation. The

Irish constitution now contained, at least on paper, a highly permissive abortion law.

Those who had been instrumental in having the protocol incorporated into the treaty now swung frantically in the opposite direction, demanding that it be excised or renegotiated to make it clear that it meant the opposite to what it might now be taken to mean. The other member states refused to renegotiate, on the grounds that, as the treaty contained something unpalatable for every country, the whole package would unravel if an individual member were permitted to begin renegotiation. In any event, SPUC waged a fierce anti-Maastricht campaign. This left it in an improbable if entirely understandable alliance with the pro-abortion-rights lobby, which also opposed Maastricht on the grounds that Protocol 17 might soon be reinterpreted, in the light of a referendum promised by the Taoiseach, to mean more or less what it was originally intended to mean.

The electorate said, at least in the precise context of the Maastricht referendum, a plague on both your houses, by recording a 69 percent-to-31 percent vote in favor of the treaty. This was not, it must be stressed, a vote on abortion. The electorate largely accepted the government's assurance that abortion was not an issue, and that voting on Maastricht on the basis of its presumed implications for abortion was mindless.

In addition to the abortion referendum of 1983, the Republic also conducted a divorce referendum in 1986. In contrast to the abortion measure, which involved inserting a new clause in the constitution, the divorce referendum proposed to remove an existing prohibition and replace it with a more permissive phraseology. The 1937 constitution explicitly forbade divorce, whereas it did not mention abortion. However, the proposal to introduce divorce, in however limited a form, was opposed by nearly the same proportion—63.5 percent in a turnout of 60.8 percent—as had supported the ban on abortion. As the geographical distribution of the two votes was very similar, the natural inference seemed to be that there were two more or less separate constituencies in the country on matters presumed to relate to sexual morality. However, this may not be entirely the case. The votes possibly conceal, or at least blur, more complex issues.[11]

In contrast to public opinion on abortion, opinion polls suggested a

---

[11]J. Coakley, "Moral Consensus in a Secularising Society: The Irish Divorce Referendum of 1986," *Western European Politics* 10, 2 (April 1987): 293–4.

clear majority in favor of some form of limited access to divorce at the time that Garret FitzGerald's government initiated the proposal in 1986.[12] It was in the course of a two-month campaign that this majority was not only whittled away, but transformed into a clear minority. Moral considerations doubtless influenced part of the change in voting intentions. The Catholic hierarchy pronounced strongly against divorce, while again conceding the right of the individual to vote according to conscience. The anti-divorce forces had much the better of the debate, on both tactical and substantive issues. But it also seems clear that the precise terms of the divorce proposal, and especially the provisions for property arrangements, which many felt might discriminate against women, may have turned a good deal of opinion against it.

Ironically, and again in complete contrast to views on abortion, opinion polls taken shortly after the referendum recorded a reversion to the earlier prereferendum results, registering a substantial majority in favor of divorce in principle. Nevertheless, no political party was eager to resume the campaign until harder evidence became available of a decisive shift in public opinion.

A number of women's groups strongly supported the divorce proposal. But an even higher majority of women than of men appear to have voted against the amendment. This reveals something of the complexity of the role, or rather roles, of women. Some spokespersons for women obviously did not speak for women on some issues. However, they may have spoken for the majority on other issues. The gradual rise into prominence of "women's issues," or, more generally, of the role of women in society, has perhaps been the single most significant social development of the past generation in Ireland. Although agonizingly slow in some respects, the tendency was irreversible and, however convoluted the process, it ensured that increasing attention would be paid to women's perspectives on public affairs. The election of Mary Robinson as president in 1990, even if largely symbolic in one sense, was nevertheless symbolic in a manner that could scarcely have been contemplated a decade before. Both her election and the distinction with which she immediately began to discharge her responsibilities fostered a particular sense of pride among Irish women.[13]

Excited though the immediate protagonists and the media could be-

---

[12]FitzGerald, *All in a Life*, p. 630.
[13]For various viewpoints see The Council for the Status of Women, *Leadership and Women: From Participation to Partnership* (Dublin, 1991).

come about conflicts over sexual morality, it would be wrong to convey the impression that these dominate public discourse in the Republic. Economic issues remain far more central to the daily concern of most citizens. For instance, the Maastricht campaign focused almost entirely on the presumed economic benefits of the treaty. Of course, a number of persons are more concerned about Northern Ireland than about divorce or abortion.

Perhaps the most striking feature of the political response to the dramatic social changes of the past generation is simply the stability of the party political system. The individual parties and the system as a whole have displayed remarkable resilience in the light of changing circumstances. It is not that the internal history of the parties has been untroubled. Quite the contrary. Fianna Fáil, the lynchpin of the system, has been wracked for more than twenty years by bitter leadership struggles revolving largely around the personality of Charles Haughey.

Haughey, the thrusting young Turk of the 1960s, found himself out in the cold when his party leader and Taoiseach, Jack Lynch, dismissed him from the cabinet in 1970, following allegations that he had illegally sanctioned, while minister for finance, the importation of arms for the Irish Republican Army (IRA) campaign in Northern Ireland, where conflict had erupted once more. A jury acquitted Haughey. Combining tenacity and energy, charm and cunning, he gradually clawed his way back until he finally won the leadership, after Lynch resigned in 1979, following a bruising leadership battle against George Colley, Lynch's preferred successor.

Under Haughey's leadership, Fianna Fáil remained bitterly factionalized. Haughey survived no fewer than three challenges to his leadership. Eventually he forced the most tenacious of his critics, Desmond O'Malley, out of the party in 1985. But O'Malley established a new party, the Progressive Democrats, whose support Haughey would ironically find himself needing after the general election of June 1989, when he failed to win an absolute majority. To secure O'Malley's support Haughey had to jettison a "core value" of Fianna Fáil to which it had clung since its foundation in 1926—that it would never enter into a coalition government. Fianna Fáil was seized by further convulsions when Haughey succumbed to pressure from O'Malley to dismiss his Tánaiste (deputy prime minister), an old stalwart, Brian Lenihan—even as the latter was campaigning as the party's candidate in the presidential election of 1990—

when Lenihan found himself trapped in a web of contradictory recollections about disputed events a decade earlier.

The tensions continued throughout 1991, culminating in a further futile challenge to the leadership by Albert Reynolds, a one-time Haughey supporter, now a disillusioned minister for finance. Haughey appeared to have seen off yet one more challenge, dismissing Reynolds and his most forthright supporters from the government in November. But in January 1992 Haughey faced further accusations from another former supporter and sometime minister for justice, Seán Doherty, concerning the extent of his knowledge of phone-tapping allegations a decade previously. Haughey was finally forced to resign.

When Reynolds won the leadership contest by an overwhelming majority, he made a nearly clean sweep of Haughey's cabinet, relegating to the back benches long-established ministers whose resentment would no doubt continue to fester and who would be ready to pounce if fortunes should change once more.

The spectacular internal feuding in Fianna Fáil served to divert attention from the fact that other parties also experienced unprecedented internal instability over much of the period. Between 1987 and 1992, Fine Gael had three leaders—Garret FitzGerald, who resigned his leadership position immediately following the defeat of his government in the general election of 1987; Alan Dukes, who won the succession contest, only to be forced out within three years; and John Bruton.

The Labour leader, Michael O'Leary, not only resigned the leadership in 1982, but resigned from the party and joined Fine Gael. His successor, Dick Spring, tenaciously clung to the leadership in the face of repeated attempts to undermine his authority by those regarding themselves as more "socialist." Spring has now consolidated his authority, but only after a protracted guerrilla conflict. A more doctrinaire left-wing group, the Workers Party, underwent various revisions of nomenclature as it sought to wriggle free from its association with either militant republicanism or with communism. Eventually, in 1992, all but one of its Dáil members resigned from the party to establish a new political party, Democratic Left.

A casual glance at the internal history of the parties would therefore suggest that they were all in frequent turmoil throughout much of the period. It is then all the more striking how the party system itself has remained so stable. Numerous reasons might be adduced for this, including a number of accidental events. But the most important factor was probably the managerial skills of the party leaders, and the commitment of party members and the electorate at large both to the idea of party and, for the most part, to the inherited parties.

The fact that citizens of the Republic tend to take political stability for granted is itself the finest tribute that can be paid to the managerial skills of the party leaders. They operate within an electoral system, proportional representation with the single transferable vote in multimember constituencies, that might have been designed to achieve maximum instability. The system not only pits party against party, but even more emphatically pits party members against their colleagues in the ceaseless prowl for votes. What is striking in the circumstances is not that parties are sometimes riven by faction, but how effectively the party leaders manage to keep factional interests under control within the unifying embrace of the party.

The challenge is probably most daunting within Fianna Fáil, a catchall party that has historically sought to transcend virtually every sectional division in society by mobilizing nationalism as the ideological bonding agent. This worked effectively between 1926 and 1969, when nationalism could be employed for largely rhetorical purposes. But the appeal to nationalism became a double-edged sword after 1969, when Northern Ireland erupted.

Much of Fianna Fáil's subsequent trauma revolved around the desperate search for an escape route from the implications of its own rhetoric. Lynch sought to reposition the rhetoric of republican defiance to edge it closer to the reality of close cooperation with Britain in trying to quarantine the Northern Ireland problem. Haughey sought to convey the impression that he remained loyal to the party's republican roots and would stand foursquare on the claim for historic rights rather than furtively cooperate with Britain to frustrate legitimate republican demands. Despite some delicate ballet-dancing with Margaret Thatcher in 1980, it was not until he returned to office in 1987 that Haughey, having vehemently denounced in the meantime the Anglo-Irish Agreement negotiated by Garret FitzGerald which recognized the Republic's right to a voice in certain Northern Ireland affairs, apparently felt secure enough to resist his republican wing and to implement the agreement.

In a little-noticed remark, Haughey had already jettisoned the inherited Fianna Fáil position that the unity of Ireland could be accomplished only within the confines of the existing 1937 constitution. This constitution, devised by the legendary founder of Fianna Fáil, Eamon de Valera, was one of the main creative achievements of independent Ireland. In political terms it incorporated the principles of liberal democracy. Some of its social clauses inevitably closely reflected prevailing Catholic doctrine, the dominant ethos of the society of the time. Had it confined itself to a jurisdictional claim on the Twenty-Six Counties only, few could have questioned its representative nature. But it also claimed, in Article 2, jurisdiction over Northern Ireland, even while hastening to disavow, in Article 3, any intention of immediately implementing that jurisdiction. It therefore claimed to be a constitution for North as well as South, despite the very different ethos of Protestant society in the North, especially in the area of sexual morality. In fact, de Valera boasted that his constitution had been devised so that it could be immediately extended to the North once unification was achieved.

Seán Lemass, de Valera's successor, had indeed accepted that this could not be the case. He himself established a committee on the constitution shortly before his own resignation in 1966. He served on the committee and signed its report in 1967, but now as an ordinary backbencher. That report recommended various amendments to the constitution to take account of changing realities, not least in the area of divorce. But the report was immediately pigeonholed. The only concession made to the facts of Northern life was an amendment in 1972 that eliminated a clause recognizing the special position of the Catholic church. In practice, this was purely symbolic. It is true that Northern Protestants had criticized it as meaning something. When it was removed they rightly said it had meant nothing. But Fianna Fáil drew the conclusion that if that was to be the unionist response, then there was no point in further amending the constitution to take account of alleged unionist grievances about its tone or content. Haughey's admission in 1984 that an entirely new constitution would be needed in the event of unification signaled a major change in Fianna Fáil attitudes.

Ironically, this *bouleversement* by Haughey was largely ignored. It occurred in the immediate aftermath of the furore following the publication of the report of the New Ireland Forum. The forum, which met in Dublin for over a year, included representatives of all the main constitutional nationalist parties in Ireland, North and South. It was convened under intense pressure from John Hume, the leader of constitutional nationalism in the North, who insisted in the immediate aftermath of the highly emotive "H-block" prison hunger strikes that constitutional nationalist Ireland had to spell out a specific ideal for the future if the electoral basis of constitutional nationalism in the North was not to be eroded by growing sympathy for Sinn Féin.

The forum report identified a unitary state as its agreed ideal, but immediately went on to dilute this by indicating that other alternatives, including joint authority (British and Irish), a federal arrangement, or indeed any other conceivable possibility could also form the basis for some sort of agreement. Haughey hijacked the subsequent press conference by insisting that the unitary state was the only option he took seriously.[14] This, perhaps naturally enough, commanded the headlines and allowed the media to focus on points of dispute between the signatories to the report. Haughey's almost incidental admission that a unitary state would require an entirely new constitution went largely unnoticed in the media scramble to cover the fracas.

The recognition that the traditional Dublin attitude toward unification was simplistic to the point of infantilism was an indication of how far even the type of nationalist opinion usually associated with Fianna Fáil had come. The widespread assumption that unification would simply mean the incorporation of the North into the existing Southern way of life, with no changes required in institutions or in attitudes, could no longer survive the brutal evidence of more than a decade of internal conflict in the North. Only the least discerning observers could now support the view that unionists were merely misguided nationalists waiting to be rescued from the consequences of their misunderstanding of their own true natures, requiring only unification for the scales to drop from their eyes and for them to rejoice in their liberation from their own false consciousness. Nevertheless, Haughey's concession could be located within the general political philosophy of Fianna Fáil. It was, after all, a cherished self-image that Fianna Fáil was the party of reality. And the constitution would be "on the table" only in the context of agreement on unity, when everything could be "on the table." The prize was so great that nothing was "non-negotiable." Haughey could isolate possible critics within Fianna Fáil, or outside it, by charging them with only conditional commitment to that ultimate aspiration of Irish nationalism, a "nation once again."

Haughey could also make the commitment to a revised constitution in the confident expectation that a unitary state lay sufficiently far in the

---

[14]FitzGerald, *All in a Life*, pp. 492–3.

future that he would never have to negotiate such a revised constitution. More dangerous from a Dublin point of view, and from that of Fianna Fáil in particular, was the possibility of piecemeal bargaining. If Ulster unionists demanded the amendment of specific clauses in the Republic's constitution as a condition for entering into negotiations on the future of Northern Ireland, then what should Dublin's response be? In particular, if unionists demanded the revision of Articles 2 and 3 of the constitution, which contained the jurisdictional claim on Northern Ireland, how should Dublin respond?

The issue was highly delicate in ideological terms and in terms of practical politics. For one thing, no Dublin government could be confident of the result of a referendum on either a simple abolition of Articles 2 and 3, or on an amendment. Much might depend on the specific wording. In any case, the issue would be likely to be hugely divisive in the South. The least desirable situation for Dublin would be to be maneuvered into a position where Articles 2 and 3 could be isolated and made the focal point of unionist assault. The obvious Dublin retort would be to argue that if Articles 2 and 3 were to be discussed, it could only be in the context of all territorial claims in Ireland—including the British territorial claim to Northern Ireland, and not least to those parts of Northern Ireland with a nationalist majority, whose representatives had resisted incorporation into a Northern state, imposed by British violence, in 1920. This is indeed the scenario that began to emerge in the course of the protracted Brooke-Mayhew talks in 1991–92.

The Northern Ireland imbroglio has not only had some influence on the party politics of the Republic. It has also contributed to what is loosely called "revisionism" in terms of the self-image of the South. The Provisional IRA claims to be doing nothing more than pursuing the historic struggle for independence to its logical conclusion. It claims lineal descent from generations of freedom fighters, and more specifically from the rebels of Easter 1916, hitherto virtually canonized in the official rhetoric of the Republic.

There have been two broad responses to this. The first is to reject the claim, generally on two grounds. First, it is still widely believed that the struggle for independence had an explicit mandate from the general election of 1918, and the 1916 rebellion an implicit mandate from numerous election results in favor of home rule, defined as the maximum amount of independence that Ireland could secure from Britain. It is true that the leading advocates of home rule sought to achieve it by constitutional means. But they repeated regularly that the only reason they did so was because rebellion stood no earthly chance of success. They accepted the legitimacy of rebellion, rejecting only its practicality. In contrast, the IRA today has no electoral mandate for seeking a united Ireland through the use of violence against Ulster unionists who, recalcitrant though they may be, are still regarded as fellow Irish. Second, it is argued that the 1916 rebels fought a clean fight, and did not inflict wanton injury on the civilian population. Many therefore find repugnant the idea that the bestiality of the Provisional IRA could be associated with the tradition of honorable republican rebellion.

On the other hand, at least some seem to accept the validity of the Provisional IRA claim that it is indeed the legitimate successor to the Volunteers of 1916 and to the IRA in the War of Independence. They insist that the rebels of 1916–21 were therefore no better than the Provisional IRA, and should be condemned. Provisional IRA atrocities thus became a weapon in the attempt to revise Irish history through condemning by association long-venerated national heroes.

Much of this revisionism has seeped into historical and journalistic writing in the past twenty years. A lively industry has developed in some media and academic circles in seeking ways of discrediting Irish nationalist views of Irish history.[15] It can hardly be said that revisionism has been entirely successful. But it has achieved a degree of success in undermining nationalist self-confidence and in fostering a more defensive intellectual atmosphere. The extremely muted 1991 commemoration of the seventy-fifth anniversary of Easter 1916 eloquently reflected the loss of nerve of the leadership of nationalist Ireland, even though it occurred when Charles Haughey, who strove to project himself as the spirit of the nation, was still Taoiseach.

This loss of nerve has disturbing implications not only for the purely political performance, but for the economic and social performance of the Republic. The Taoiseach who presided over the economic surge of the early 1960s, Seán Lemass, always considered nationalism a crucial motivating factor in persuading the public to think in terms of a national interest and to impose even some limited restraint on its own predatory

[15]The issue of historical revisionism can be pursued in R. Foster, "We Are All Revisionists Now," *The Irish Review* 1 (1986); D. Fennell, "Against Revisionism," *The Irish Review* 4 (Spring 1988); B. Bradshaw, "Nationalism and Historical Scholarship in Modern Ireland," *Irish Historical Studies* 104 (November 1989); M. Laffan, "Insular Attitudes: The Revisionists and Their Critics," in M. Ní Dhonnchadha and T. Dorgan (eds.), *Revising the Rising* (Derry, Northern Ireland, 1991).

private interests in the context of some concept of a common good.[16] This may have been naive even at the time, although it can be argued that many of the more prominent public figures, both in politics and in the public sector of the economy, did indeed drive themselves in the interests of what they perceived as the common good. As confidence in national ideas waned, however, public commitment of this type became harder to discern. There is now widespread public distrust of the motives of politicians and of many in the public sector of the economy, as well as in the private sector. This distrust was reinforced by a flood of revelations in 1991–92 about the nature of business practices and of relations between business and government, which the public widely perceives rightly or wrongly to cast grave doubt on the integrity of many of those involved.

The loss of confidence is perhaps even more noticeable at a more general intellectual level. Expectations of economic performance have declined. This may seem a sweeping assertion at a time when we are assured that, if only we pursue austere fiscal policies, prospects have never looked brighter. But the historic expectation was that economic performance would translate into national performance, as measured by the unemployment and emigration statistics. For instance, it was an axiom of nationalist faith that Ireland could support a significantly higher population, and that emigration and unemployment—allegedly largely the result of English misgovernment—would vanish once Ireland achieved self-government. These opinions persisted, even in the face of evidence to the contrary, into the 1970s. The rhetoric of Lemass in the 1950s and 1960s, and even the more sober appraisal by T. K. Whitaker, the gifted secretary of the Department of Finance who wrote a historic report on the economic potential of the country in 1958, were still committed to the assumption that economic performance could be sufficiently improved to stem the tide of emigration and unemployment, and to reverse the population drain.

Gradually, in the course of the 1970s, and more emphatically during the 1980s, population growth came to be seen more as a problem than as a solution. Politicians lamented that a rate of growth higher than the European Community average imposed impossible demands on job creation. The rise in population from 2.8 million in 1961 to 3.6 million by the mid-1980s was seen as a major cause of the economic stagnation of

[16]Lee, *Ireland 1912–1985*, p. 401.

the first half of that decade. Ireland was, objectively, still one of the most sparsely populated countries in Western Europe, and probably the most sparsely populated in terms of inhabitable area. But that meant nothing to this mentality. If the Irish economy was languishing during the first half of the 1980s, whereas that of the Organization for Economic Co-operation and Development generally was expanding, this must be due to insupportable population pressure. The easy assumptions of an earlier generation that Ireland could support four or five times its then-population—a population level that would bring it broadly abreast of average Western European densities—now vanished as the lunacies of incorrigible day-dreamers. The optimum population for the Republic was now believed to be less than 3.5 million, or roughly its population around 1900.

Two conclusions followed inexorably from this cast of mind. Emigration, far from being a symptom of national failure, had been a blessing. One calculation suggested that, in the absence of emigration since the Great Famine, the population of the Republic would now be about 14 million. Given that the Republic could not support 3.5 million at a standard of living even two-thirds that of the EC average, and that it was incapable of generating jobs to achieve anything remotely approaching full employment with a population of that size, the conclusion followed that the bulk of the 10 million surplus residents would be unemployed. The Irish economy would simply not be capable of supporting a population density of that scale. It was, for this cast of mind, thoroughly unsporting of Northern Ireland to have double the population density of the South. The North may have had an industrial head start on the South seventy years before, but those days had long passed. Nevertheless, despite having no obvious advantages, it was able to support a population density that was twice that of the Republic.

As emigration was now to be seen as a good thing, public opinion had to be weaned from its inherited assumption that emigration somehow represented national failure. Ireland's membership in the EC proved convenient from this point of view. Migration within the EC could now be considered as merely a form of internal migration. Emigration to EC countries was therefore no longer emigration, but simply a type of local movement. It has become fashionable to question the difference between moving from Ireland to Germany and moving from, say, North Dakota to California.

The analogy reveals much about the national self-image of those addicted to this type of thinking. It clearly assumes that sovereignty does not really matter in economic affairs. Self-government means no more than statehood in the United States. Since national governments within the EC still in fact enjoy, at least on paper, far more control over their domestic economic policies than do state governments in the United States, this implies that such control of policy can make effectively little difference to, and therefore bear little responsibility for, the quality of national economic performance.

The argument tends to overlook the fact that emigration in Irish circumstances has been regularly related to population decline. It has been, in net terms, almost entirely an outward movement, except for the decade of the 1970s. The population of American states has not actually fallen over a long period as a result of migration. The psychological consequences are therefore likely to be very different, to say nothing about size of the domestic market and other factors. Local or regional economic difficulties do not damage the self-image of America. Local emigration does not induce a psychology of defeatism. Neither of these considerations applies in the Irish case.

The analogy therefore fails on economic, demographic, and psychological grounds. It is striking that advocates of this analogy themselves often reject its political implications. When emigrants have sought the right to vote in Irish elections, they have met a frosty reception. The moment they seek the right to express an opinion on the affairs of the country, they find they are no longer internal migrants, but now revert very firmly to being emigrants. The North Dakota/California analogy suddenly loses its attractiveness for many of its proponents. The candid disclosure by the Irish foreign minister and deputy prime minister to a New York audience in 1987 that "we can't all live on a small island" nicely captures both the sense of fatalistic resignation and the acceptable level of analytical rigor for those of this defeatist disposition.[17]

The concept of overpopulation, so useful in revising attitudes toward emigration, has been if anything even more effective in reconciling the public to the highest recorded unemployment level in the OECD. In 1992 official unemployment was hovering around 20 percent. There was, no doubt, some activity in the black market, not least because of the punitive incidence of taxation. But the black market was not the major reason

---

[17]For a more detailed critique see J. J. Lee, "Emigration: A Contemporary Perspective," in R. Kearney (ed.), *Migrations: The Irish at Home and Abroad* (Dublin, 1990), pp. 33–44.

for unemployment. It was simply the lack of jobs, at least according to market criteria, deriving in turn largely from the inability of indigenous Irish industry to win a larger market share in the rest of the EC or to compete more effectively on the home market. Indeed, the official figures significantly understated the incapacity of the economy to create jobs for the potential labor force. Net emigration had accounted for at least 150,000 potential workers since 1986. In addition, the proportion of working wives in Ireland fell far below the OECD average. It was still "only" 23 percent in 1992, less than half that of other industrialized capitalist countries. Had the Irish rate reached the average, far more than another 100,000 workers would have been recorded as seeking employment. The real deficit in job creation, in relation to potential demand, was not 20 percent, but more than 30 percent.

To the unimaginative, these data might seem an index of economic failure. But the prevalent mind-set in policy-making circles found no difficulty in coping with the potential reflection on the effectiveness of their regime. The technique adopted was to divorce the concept of the economy from the concept of the country. In effect, this meant that employment must no longer be venerated as the principal criterion of economic performance. By 1992 this object had been largely achieved as far as public relations was concerned. Economic commentator after economic commentator, and editorial writer after editorial writer, continued to assure the public that the economy was really performing very well. Was not its growth rate impressive compared to the EC average? Were not the economic "fundamentals" sound? The inflation rate was one of the lowest in the OECD, the exchequer borrowing requirement had been brought firmly under control from its exorbitant levels only five years before, and the national debt, although still very high by EC standards, had been significantly reduced from its astronomical levels of the mid-1980s.

All this was indeed true. Policy-makers did deserve immense credit for the manner in which they had brought the public finances under control, sometimes in the face of intense public opposition, especially after 1987. The problem was that sound "fundamentals" were not delivering jobs. And despite the energy devoted to persuading the public that employment was not a fundamental, but only an incidental, of economic activity, many of the public remained uneasy about this thought process.

The unease derived from three sources. First, many had been taught that employment was itself a fundamental criterion of economic performance. They found it difficult to believe that the fundamentals were sound if anything from one-fifth to one-third of the potential work force was unemployed. Second, the residual force of traditional patriotism, although much diminished, still claimed some adherents. This had historically insisted that large-scale unemployment was incompatible with "the national interest." Third, and probably most effective, was fear. The nearly 300,000 unemployed people in 1992 were located largely in working-class quarters on the outskirts of Dublin, Cork, and Limerick. They were sustained in apathy through relatively generous welfare payments, or through drink and drugs. The drug culture, literally and metaphorically, had hitherto been largely successful in reducing indignation to apathy.

As long as unemployment remained a problem for the unemployed, it did not threaten the social fabric. But at what level would it become a social problem for the employed? As long as the problems could be bottled up in working-class areas, they impinged little on the majority of those in safe jobs, particularly in the sheltered sector, safe from market pressures. But supposing it might spill over to upset the tranquil atmosphere of the more salubrious suburbs? Supposing even that the tax burden on the sheltered sectors were to increase as a result of the necessity of paying out more in welfare because of rising unemployment? The danger began to become real during 1992 that unemployment could no longer be effectively isolated from the world closest to the concern of the official mind.

A second realization began to permeate the public mind in the summer of 1992. Hitherto, politicians had been persuaded that the main reason unemployment proved so intractable was the surplus labor supply deriving from the baby boom of the 1970s. They could hardly be blamed for that. Did not Ireland have the fastest rate of population growth of any OECD member state in the 1980s? But closer scrutiny revealed that, due to emigration, the actual increase in labor supply on the Irish market between 1981 and 1989 had been not the fastest, as the politicians never tired of proclaiming, but in fact the slowest in the whole of the OECD.[18] The argument could be pursued at ever more recondite levels. But at the level at which politicians choose to operate, the most basic excuse of all began to lose credibility.

Public discussion of the issue of the historic "twin evils" of emigration

---

[18]P. Tansey, *Sunday Tribune*, 16 August 1992, C.4.

and unemployment therefore took an instructive turn in the 1980s. Hitherto, in accordance with the nationalist gospel, the elimination of both these "evils" had loomed alongside the achievement of national unity and the restoration of the Irish language as the major national goals. Failure to achieve these objectives was regarded as national failure, calling for renewed efforts generation after generation. By the 1980s, at least part of the official mind came to strike on a different approach. The failure to achieve the economic goals was not really a failure at all. Either the "evils" were no longer evils, or their existence was not an Irish responsibility, but was due to factors entirely beyond national control. Therefore no sense of failure should attach to their continued existence. Renewed effort was not required, because all that was humanly possible was already being done.

From this perspective, Ireland was in fact a very successful economy. Where were the "fundamentals" sounder? One should not flagellate oneself for nonexistent failure. If the inherited standards of aspiration were proving unattainable, the answer lay more in redefining standards than in improving the performance, which was already deemed generally satisfactory. Thus is explained one of the more intriguing mind-sets to emerge in contemporary Ireland—the complacency, not to say the condescension, of much of the official mind in the face of criticism.

But it would be misleading to end on an entirely censorious note. Ireland today is throbbing with talent. The individual abilities of Irish men and, increasingly, of Irish women, have never had greater opportunity to realize their potential. Precisely because society is in so many ways in flux, because of the dramatic demographic changes, and because of wider access to education than ever before, the quality of Ireland's performance will depend to a disproportionate extent on the quality of national leadership. Even though the office of president is a largely symbolic one, a people capable of electing Mary Robinson president in 1990 should not be dismissed as incapable of responding to the excitement of new challenges. The 1990s could, of course, be a decade of missed opportunities. But the opportunities are there to be seized.

8

<hr/>

New forces for positive change in Ireland

ENDA McDONAGH

The dynamics of social and political change suggest that in any society there are some powerful forces that, if discerned, could be harnessed or at least modified to attain a certain desired result—in this case, let us assume, peace with justice in Northern Ireland. That there are social forces that analysts and leaders must seek to understand and manage is a sufficient first account of the challenge to any society. It is the further accounts that test the skills of analyst and leader. It is widely agreed that there are forces in at least four fields at work in relation to the Northern Ireland question: the political, the economic, the cultural, and the religious. Most subdivisions can be addressed under at least one of these four headings, although one might make even finer distinctions, between the ethnic and the political and cultural, for example. As a theologian, I have to look at the other three areas, not least because the four are so intertwined that the religious cannot be understood in isolation from the others.

A 1990 book and several earlier articles by John Whyte (see Bibliography) survey the dominant interpretations of Northern Ireland that have emerged over the last twenty years. They adopt one or other of these four fields on its own or in combination with others as the key to understanding the situation.

One last preliminary point must be made, concerning the vexed question of language. Social divisions always carry a language penalty. One result of social division is that people are unable to agree on how to

ENDA McDONAGH is Professor of Moral Theology, St. Patrick's College, Maynooth, Ireland. A Catholic priest with firsthand parochial experience in Ireland, he has written many books, including *Roman Catholics and Unity* and *Social Ethics and the Christian*.

describe it. What happened seventy years go, a division/partition of Ireland or of the United Kingdom? And so with any proposed solution. Should an agreement between the governments of the United Kingdom and the Republic of Ireland be described, as it usually is, as the Anglo-Irish Agreement? Even such seemingly neutral phrases as the goals of peace with justice or of justice and peace may reveal which side the speaker is on. This is not at all peculiar to this dispute. Language and politics are everywhere interladen, as Arabs and Israelis or blacks and whites in South Africa or North America would readily agree. Sensitivity is therefore required, but paralysis must not be allowed to supervene. If the language difficulty cannot be resolved until the political difficulty is, language is still an essential instrument in the search for solutions. But it must be used sensitively, allowing participants to choose their own language in the search for an agreed vocabulary on the way to an agreed solution. In this way language becomes an instrument of liberation rather than of oppression or paralysis. In this context I will discuss Northern Ireland as a British-Irish problem. In doing so I do not wish to get involved in any complex allocation of blame for the past, but instead to recognize where responsibility lies for the present and the future.

POLITICAL, ECONOMIC, AND CULTURAL DYNAMICS

This attempt to examine briefly three such distinct if interrelated forces as political, economic, and cultural dynamics may claim in aid previous presentations, and in partial justification the interrelation between my own particular concern, religion, and these three. I will look at changes in context and in content of the operation of these three forces, defining as I go along context and content. Brevity demands selectivity, which inevitably includes bias. Pray it be instructive and constructive bias! All British and Irish problems are affected by the changing European context. The years of "the troubles" have fairly closely coincided with British and Irish involvement in Europe. Increasing economic and political integration will continue to influence relations between the islands and between the two parts of Ireland. I will attend to just a couple of these influences.

Sovereignty has been a key concept, symbol, some would say shibboleth, in the debate about united Ireland and United Kingdom. Sovereignty, like nostalgia, is not what it used to be. The self-governing autonomy of a particular country no longer operates in practice. That is being increasingly recognized in theory, in principle, in national law, and in constitutions. Resistance to easy transfer of power from London or Dublin to Brussels or Strasbourg continues, and so it should. Easy transfer is unlikely to make for the best transfer. Yet to insist that full national sovereignty can be maintained in the House of Commons, for example, while one continues to be an effective member of the European Community, is at best self-deception. As the force of this change in principle and in practice is borne in upon nationalists and unionists, their perception of our political divisions and needs will begin to change. How long that will take to yield results at the polls is impossible to predict.

The economic impact of all this may be perceived more quickly. What that impact may be in the peripheral regions of Britain and Ireland not even the economists dare project. For all my political and cultural commitment to Europe I remain very wary of the economic effects of European integration on the western and northern parts of the island of Ireland, for example, or on Scotland and Wales. Offshore islands have a long history of providing workers and tourist facilities for more populous, powerful, and prosperous mainlands. At least, there is a serious economic battle to be fought, and Europe's Atlantic offshore islands or their more deprived areas should combine their forces. In that changing economic context much will depend on people seeing beyond the old political-economic horizons in organized pursuit of their fair share of European prosperity. Transcending national sovereignty is only one aspect of the European integration project. Indeed if that first one is not to end in destructive centralization, the transfer downward to the regions must proceed with equal speed and effectiveness. The economic and political implications of this could be enormous, particularly for heavily centralized countries with very deprived marginal regions such as Britain and Ireland. As a Mayoman from the West of Ireland I sometimes think that the division between East and West in Ireland is more deep-seated and more destructive politically and economically than that between North and South. No doubt there are many people in Scotland, Wales, and Northern England who harbor similar feelings in regard to London and the Southeast. An effective regional policy could empower these marginalized peoples. Such a policy might have to breach some of the conventional political borders, or at least encourage alliances across these borders.

European consciousness has been enhanced for all by the collapse of the Communist regimes in Eastern Europe. This changing situation may also affect Irish concerns, not however by invoking naively the coming down of the Berlin Wall and the reuniting of Germany as a prescriptive model. The lessons are more complex and ambiguous. The grand vision of a Europe from the Atlantic to the Urals flourishing in unity and diversity sets our petty problems in perspective and encourages a larger vision for our peoples. What may be delivered on the ground is more disputable. The peoples of Eastern Europe, with their economic and political needs, their ethnic and emotional ties to the West, and their historical and moral claims on it, will be in sharp competition for jobs and investment with the less developed regions in the West—another reason for greater British-Irish and North-South economic cooperation. More ambiguously the emerging ethnic and religious divisions in Eastern Europe, and their increasing recourse to armed force, might drive leaders and people here to despair of a stable, just, and peaceful solution to our own difficulties and settle for "an acceptable level of violence." However, a successful resolution of the Northern Ireland problem could offer encouragement and perhaps insight to people struggling with the revival of old animosities and divisions. Britain, Ireland, and Northern Ireland have much to offer in influencing Europe, not just much to receive in being changed by it. The changing and being changed will be positive and enhancing insofar as people have the insight to discriminate and the determination to succeed.

The general cultural ambience in which all Irish people, and indeed in which all British people live, is Anglo-American. Our clothes, food, language, what is generally described as life-style, bespeak this. Above all our television, radio, and newspapers reflect it. Of course there are degrees of influence and variations of reflection or expression. The Irish and British electronic media are more akin to each other than either is to the American. Irish social relations are more akin to American in their informality than they are to British in their formality. But all such generalizations need endless qualification. There are local and historical influences that distinguish, sometimes sharply, how the shared language of English is used in the three countries and within these countries as well. A further cultural difference with obvious implications relates to religion. Britain and the United States have been in important senses Protestant countries while Ireland has been a predominantly Catholic country. The qualifications positively scream for attention. How Catholic a country has Ireland been for much of its history, given the long exclusion of Catholics from any participation in power? How Catholic is Ireland now, with increasing secularization and declining episcopal influence? How

Protestant are the United States and Britain with their increasing multiculturalism and the spread of Islam and Eastern religions? How religious are they in the face of secularization? One cannot help noticing that, despite the strict separation of church and state in the United States and the formal establishment of the Church of England, the public presence of religion is more evident in the United States. It is in some senses a much less secularized society than British society if no less materialist. Which of these models, if either, will prevail in Ireland is difficult to say. The cultural context is still heavily influenced by religion, but in its higher reaches often by rejection or transcendence of formal religion in search of spiritual insight and nourishment.

The intense cultural activity that in its highly visible and popular folk forms characterizes Irish society today creates the usual mixture of complexity and ambiguity as far as our difficulties are concerned. Yet it is worth noting the number of good poets and playwrights originating in Northern Ireland and on both sides of the traditional divide. How far they and the growing number of musicians and painters influence the dynamics of that society and in what direction cannot yet be said. The life and the interaction between the diverse personalities and movements, not easily confined to any one tradition, are destined to gradually erode the stereotyping in Ireland, Britain, and perhaps the United States.

One last item of political, economic, and cultural significance that might be overlooked in examining the dynamics of change is the women's movement. Women were, for a long time, not evident much in the conventional political or economic fora; the isolated instance of Margaret Thatcher as prime minister of the United Kingdom only proved the rule. The disappointments associated with the Peace Women in Northern Ireland and their Peace Movement obscured the continuing work for reconciliation between peoples pursued by many women's groups throughout the island. The election of Mary Robinson in 1990 as president of the Republic, however, had an impact, and the women's movement may transform structures and attitudes in and between these islands. To do that it needs courage and encouragement from the mostly male power-holders, who are, however, likely to be fearful of the outcome. At least that is my impression of those male-dominated social institutions, the churches, of which I can speak with more authority.

The contexts of which I write are not somehow external to the fabric of society in these islands but woven in and through them. Yet it is useful to balance this discussion by attending more explicitly to certain features internal to that society or more correctly to those societies. The features may be external and visible ones such as leaders, structures, and movements, or more internal but no less influential ones such as aspirations and attitudes. The external and internal interact and may mutually shape one another.

Leaders carry a responsibility to shape society. In our democratic societies, political leaders are peculiarly accountable and so are easily credited or discredited. Without seeking to call our political leaders to account here, I wish to remark on how they changed as they came to address Northern Ireland and British-Irish relations. All four British prime ministers who had to deal with the question in recent times, Harold Wilson, Edward Heath, James Callaghan, and Margaret Thatcher, changed significantly in attitude and policy, but not just from a state of ignorance to a state of some knowledge. Irish Taoisigh, Jack Lynch, Liam Cosgrave, Garret FitzGerald, and Charles Haughey, also changed in attitude and policy, and not just from ignorance or prejudice about the unionists. Leaders internal to Northern Ireland, unionist, nationalist, Alliance, and even Sinn Féin—Provisional and Official—have all changed, some of them several times, over the last twenty years. I emphasize this point not to belabor the poor politicians once more, this time on the charge of inconsistency, but to look beyond the more usual charge of intransigence. Clearly they have not all changed enough. But they have all changed and some have managed to influence their constituencies to change also. Not all change is for the better. Discernment is also required. The capacity of politicians engaged with this issue to change themselves and to change the people they represent is crucial to the hopes of peace and justice. Such leaders have the possibility of organizing or reorganizing movements and structures, aspirations and attitudes in ways which are convergent rather than divergent, which enable coexistence to emerge, perhaps move to collaboration, and even finally translate into a genuine community of peace and justice.

RELIGION AND THE CHURCHES

Leadership in pursuit of peace and justice is not solely the responsibility of the politicians. In a democratic culture, such pursuits are the responsibility of all citizens. People with roles other than the immediately political may have to make particular contributions. This could apply to academics, trade unionists, businesspeople, and a whole range of professionals and others who have the opportunity and the skill to contribute to mutual understanding and cooperation between unionist and nationalist and between British and Irish. A number of effective voluntary organizations like the Irish Association, Co-operation North, and the British-Irish Association have engaged the skill and energy of a great many ordinary citizens in promoting such understanding and cooperation.

In a narrow legal sense, because Ireland does not have an established church, the Irish churches belong among the nonpolitical voluntary organizations. In historical status and social influence they are much more. How that translates or should translate into influence in helping to solve our problem is deeply disputed. I follow the line that religious allegiance has contributed to the historic and hostile divisions without accepting that it is the only or necessarily the main contributor. Because they contributed to the division and continue to exert important influence in the divided society, churches and church leaders have a responsibility to contribute to the solution. This is all the more urgent in view of their beliefs that peace and justice are intended by the God of Jesus Christ for all. While the foregoing is generally agreed, further interpretation and application can be bitterly disputed within, between, and beyond the churches. It is not possible then to speak for all the churches or perhaps officially for any. Here it may be most useful to follow the earlier model and look at forces for change in the context in which the churches have to work and in the internal lives of the churches themselves.

The context of Europe, West and East, with the political and economic ramifications already discussed, will seriously affect the churches. Ian Paisley–type reaction to the Treaty of Rome may be irrelevant, but the European Court's ruling on the Republic's inherited law against homosexuality has found echoes among church leaders north and south of the border, Protestant and Catholic. More profoundly, integration into a largely secularized Europe will present a new set of challenges to the Irish churches. These challenges will be all the more pointed if hostile divisions with a strong religious mix persist, in the light of how Europe's own religious wars contributed to its subsequent secularization in the eighteenth and nineteenth centuries. How the role of religion in Eastern Europe will develop and how it may influence the West is difficult to say. The original natural delight at the liberation and restoration of religion in the East must be tempered by awareness of the eagerness of Eastern Europeans to join the capitalist consumer society whose regard for religion frequently reduces it to yet another consumer good, a brand of celestial comforter.

More frightening is the spread of religious fundamentalism in the East and West. Although at present the more obvious and frightening kinds seem to be Islamic in origin, there are fundamentalist Christians and Jews, Hindus and Sikhs as well. The fundamentalism we see is basically antihuman and in that sense opposed to the great religions in their authentic life. It is not always easy to demonstrate that to a fundamentalist, and it is cold comfort to someone threatened by him or her. There have been religious fundamentalists in Ireland and there still are. Separated from political causes, they have not been so threatening. The present rise of fundamentalism in the wider world and the movement toward more closed and conservative views among many church leaders, Protestant, Catholic, and Orthodox, might make our situation more serious.

Such developments at least partially muffle the impact of that liberating context for Catholics known as the Second Vatican Council. Despite some muffling it empowers Catholics, lay and clerical, to contribute to a society that is genuinely free and tolerant, just and egalitarian, fraternal (sororal) and peaceful. For biblical Christians the promotion of such a society would correspond to the partial and temporal promotion of the Kingdom of God. The ecumenical movement in which Catholics became active partners through the Vatican Council provides a similar impetus for other Christians. How dynamic is all this in Britain, Ireland, and Northern Ireland? Not as dynamic as it needs to be, but with considerable energy still.

How does that fresh source of social energy, the women's movement, fit into this ecclesiastical picture? Awkwardly at best. A great deal of the real and the best work in all the churches is done by women, but they are by and large excluded from decision-making and accompanying leadership roles. If that is not remedied soon, many potential leaders will desert the official churches. If it is, the renewal may be really radical, and the contribution by the churches to peace with justice in Ireland will be really significant. The Church of England Synod voted in 1992 to allow the ordination of women priests.

Meanwhile, there is much the churches can and should do to realize their own essential engagement with the cause of peace and justice. The more obvious would include a much clearer commitment to joint education of adults and children, of laity and clergy, from the different traditions. This would include, but not be confined to, what are called integrated schools, which may not be always practical or appropriate. It would be particularly desirable in regard to clerical education. Mixed marriages should be seen as a Christian opportunity rather than as a threat, and special pastoral programs should be developed in every diocese. More thought by the churches must be given to how individual freedom, justice, and solidarity in society may be developed in Irish circumstances. Politicians seldom have the time or inclination for such consideration, and academics from the regular disciplines do not often see it as their remit. The churches could encourage theologians and philosophers to work with people in other disciplines and with social activists in this field. The Irish Theological Association and other related professional bodies have done some work of this kind. In this activity the tradition of liberal Christianity with its concern for freedom and that of the more recent liberationist Christianity with its concern for justice and peace could combine to the benefit of church and society. New forces for positive change could well be released.

9

The institutional churches and the process of reconciliation in Northern Ireland: recent progress in Presbyterian–Roman Catholic relations

JOSIAH HORTON BEEMAN and ROBERT MAHONY

Because the Catholic church is the largest of the world's Christian denominations, movements within it or adopted by it seem usually to have a disproportionate impact on public perceptions in general. Thus the ecumenical movement is frequently understood to have gained its momentum from the efforts of Pope John XXIII to bring *aggiornamento* to the Catholic church in the early 1960s and from the Second Vatican Council he called, which concretized those efforts. In fact the ecumenical movement was by that time well on its way among the Protestant churches, both internationally and within a number of individual countries, its successes marked by cooperation in biblical translations, by the union or reunion of denominations within particular nations, and by the establishment of such bodies as the National Council of Churches (NCC) in the United States and the World Council of Churches. In Ireland during the 1960s, a landmark of ecumenism similarly derived from a Protestant initiative, as the Corrymeela Community was begun in 1965 at Ballycastle, County Antrim, by the Reverend Ray Davey, a minister of the Presbyterian church in Ireland. A prisoner of war in Germany during

JOSIAH HORTON BEEMAN is President of Beeman and Associates, Washington, D.C. Former Chair of the General Assembly Council of the Presbyterian Church (USA), he is a member of the Northern Ireland Working Group of the Presbyterian Church and of the Interchurch Committee on Northern Ireland.

ROBERT MAHONY is Director of the Center for Irish Studies at the Catholic University of America, Washington, D.C., and a member of the delegation of the U.S. Catholic Conference to the Interchurch Committee on Northern Ireland.

World War II, Davey envisioned Corrymeela as a means by which committed Christians of all denominations throughout Europe could explore the process of reconciliation.

Ecumenical activities with a specifically Irish brief were decidedly less significant in the 1960s, however, even as the movement in Western Europe and North America seemed to evolve in concert with the accelerating pace of secular change, and despite the enormous economic and political progress Ireland witnessed in that decade. The slow beginnings of the movement may be attributed in good part to the unusual strength of denominational identity among both Protestants and Catholics in Ireland, rooted in the country's troubled history, combined with the doctrinal and social conservatism of the major churches. But these were also factors in the resurgence of heated sectarian animosities in Northern Ireland from the mid-1960s, as intercommunal conflict began to take shape. Coinciding with the early stages of the conflict, even as its sectarian features were setting firmly around 1970, ecumenism began to make noteworthy progress.

In 1970, for instance, the Irish School of Ecumenics was established in Dublin. Conceived by Father Michael Hurley, an Irish Jesuit then lecturing at the Gregorian University in Rome, the idea for the school was adopted enthusiastically by both Catholic and Protestant church leaders in Ireland. The school began classes in autumn 1970 with Hurley as its first director, and research into the theological and practical aspects of ecumenism as its principal objective. The further aim of promoting the ecumenical movement throughout Ireland evolved as a consequence of its teaching and research programs. Also in the early 1970s an important initiative emerged from the Irish Council of Churches, representing the non-Catholic Christian denominations. This was a proposal that high-ranking Protestant and Catholic authorities meet to discuss the question of mixed marriages and other practical matters dividing the churches. The Catholic archbishop of Armagh and primate of all Ireland at the time, William Cardinal Conway, suggested in response that the discussion include the whole range of divisive issues: scriptural, doctrinal, and pastoral, as well as practical. This suggestion met with broad approval, and starting in 1973 a conference of experts on such issues has met yearly at Ballymascanlon, County Louth, near the border between the Republic and Northern Ireland, with working parties on specific areas meeting more frequently and reporting to the annual conference.[1]

[1]For an account of the inception, organization, and proceedings of the Ballymascanlon

While academic ecumenism and interchurch dialogue were thus being institutionalized, the ongoing conflict in Northern Ireland prompted the first major American effort under ecumenical auspices to assist the work of reconciliation there on the ground. Father David Bowman, an American Jesuit who was shortly to become a liaison officer for the NCC in the United States, had visited Northern Ireland in August 1971. There he witnessed the trauma of the large-scale internment operation imposed that month, mainly upon the Catholic population, by the Northern Ireland government. After giving an account to the NCC in New York, Bowman returned to Northern Ireland in January 1972 with Father Donald Campion, the editor of the influential Jesuit magazine *America,* and the Reverend Wesley Baker of the United Presbyterian Church in the United States. Their experiences and widespread discussions with clergy and laypersons over the week leading up to "Bloody Sunday" (30 January 1972) convinced them to organize Colleagues from American Churches as an unofficial American interchurch approach to the conflict. Over the rest of the decade, Colleagues from American Churches provided volunteers from the United States to the Corrymeela Community and to newer, neighborhood-based reconciliation projects in Belfast and Derry.[2]

Many such projects, involving committed Christians of both communities in Northern Ireland, sprang up in the 1970s in response to the conflict. A number of these were short-lived, but one in particular, the Peace People, attracted international attention and in 1976 won its founders, Betty Williams (a Protestant) and Mairéad Corrigan (a Catholic), the Nobel Prize for Peace. In America, media accounts of their work acquainted many with the activities being undertaken at the grassroots level to mitigate the effects of violence in Northern Ireland, but these accounts also misled many Americans and others into regarding such efforts as the long-sought key to solving the Northern question. As the problem persisted, therefore, most lost interest. A few Americans and others from outside Ireland have continued to volunteer to work with the Peace People and other community-based groups, and the gradual recognition that reconciliation proceeds at best incrementally has drawn some international financial support for these efforts, though hardly at the levels achieved by the Peace People in the late 1970s.

Conference in its early years, see Cahal B. Daly and A. S. Worrall, *Ballymascanlon: A Venture in Inter-Church Dialogue* (Belfast and Dublin, 1978).
[2]Lynne Shivers and David Bowman, *More than the Troubles: A Common Sense View of the Northern Ireland Conflict* (Philadelphia, 1984), pp. 9–15.

A significant impediment to a renewal of widespread American interest in reconciliation efforts was apparent in the extent to which American Catholics and Protestants differed in terms of identification with their Irish coreligionists. Concern about the Northern Ireland situation was more common, from the very beginning of the current "troubles," among American Catholics, especially those of Irish heritage who were often instinctively sympathetic toward their coreligionists in Northern Ireland. Moreover, they remained the basis of a constituency of concern as the troubles wore on, whether favoring the Irish republican cause, a constitutional settlement, or the movement for reconciliation. However, few American Protestants, even those of "Scots-Irish," or Ulster, extraction, took much notice of the situation beyond the common presentation of it in the media as a long-standing quarrel between Protestants and Catholics. Most perceived it as archaic and unsolvable, taking place in a part of the world to which they had only the most attenuated links. Some, indeed, were drawn by the publicity given the Reverend Ian Paisley, the only Protestant leader most Americans recognized, to consider Protestants in Northern Ireland collectively as extremists and therefore ultimately blameworthy for the conflict.[3] Only a concerted and sustained movement to inform American Protestants about the cross-community work of reconciliation in Northern Ireland would appreciably broaden support in the United States for these efforts.

Nonetheless, during the 1980s American Protestants as well as Catholics, at both grassroots and institutional levels, became more responsive to other means of addressing the Northern Ireland problem. Projects to bring children of both communities, usually in mixed Protestant-Catholic pairs, to the United States for holidays with American families were initiated in the 1970s and blossomed in the following decade under a variety of auspices. These projects exposed the visiting Northern children to the values of a more pluralistic culture and demonstrated the possibilities of cross-community interpersonal relationships, which have often been maintained and built upon as the visitors matured at home. Another

---

[3]Such impressions are hardly confined to the United States. Somewhat more circumspectly, a 1988 publication of the Project of the Churches on Human Rights and Responsibilities in the United Kingdom and the Republic of Ireland locates the dynamic that "fuels conflicts and erects barriers" in Northern Ireland in "the theology and doctrine advocated by ultra-Protestant sects, drawing their strength from a narrow interpretation of Christianity, yet finding resonances within the main Protestant Churches." See Sydney D. Bailey (ed.), *Human Rights and Responsibilities in Britain and Ireland: A Christian Perspective* (London, 1988), pp. 148–9.

American initiative, the campaign for the MacBride Principles, had a more institutional orientation. The idea for a set of guidelines on fair employment for American companies with subsidiaries in Northern Ireland originated in the office of the comptroller of New York City, Harrison Goldin, in late 1983. The notion was embraced by the Irish National Caucus, a Washington-based lobby headed by Father Seán MacManus, with whom the set of guidelines were formulated. Closely modeled on the Sullivan Principles on hiring by U.S. companies in South Africa, which had been promoted successfully by American church and investor groups, the guidelines for Northern Ireland essentially called for American-style affirmative action to increase employment among Catholics, long victimized by job discrimination in Northern Ireland. They were endorsed by, and with his permission named for, Seán MacBride, a founder-member of Amnesty International and winner of the Nobel and Lenin peace prizes.[4] Designed especially to appeal to Americans, the principles have been adopted since the mid-1980s in a variety of formats by a number of state legislatures and city councils with funds invested in American companies having Northern Ireland subsidiaries; they have also been endorsed by some American church groups, including a number of Catholic religious orders and a few Protestant organizations, most prominent among them the Episcopal Church.[5]

In the situation of fairly static overall employment that obtains in Northern Ireland, however, the MacBride Principles are vague about expanding the total number employed as a means of achieving the desired proportion of Catholics and Protestants in jobs. For this reason, and because the MacBride campaign seemed to many in Ireland likely to discourage future investment in Northern Ireland by American corporations, the principles were opposed by the British government and most of the Northern Ireland political parties, including the Social Democratic and Labour Party, which represents the majority of the Catholic electorate, as well as by the Irish Protestant churches. Sinn Féin, the political wing of the Irish republican movement, endorsed the principles. The Irish Episcopal Conference, composed of the country's Catholic bishops, took no formal position on the MacBride Principles.

Among American Protestant bodies, the Committee on Mission Re-

[4]Niall O'Dowd, "Behind the MacBride Principles," *Irish America* (November–December 1985), pp. 15–17.
[5]See, e.g., Resolution No. D-057a, *Journal of the 1988 General Convention of the Episcopal Church* (New York, 1988), p. 691.

sponsibility through Investment (MRTI) of the Presbyterian Church
(USA)—the denomination reuniting, in 1983, the former United Pres-
byterian Church in the United States and the Presbyterian Church of the
United States—supported the principles in the early years of the cam-
paign. Following strong representations from the Presbyterian Church in
Ireland, however, the American church decided to reassess its position.
The MRTI committee accordingly appointed a delegation to travel to
Ireland in August 1987 "to investigate job discrimination and the
MacBride Principles as a remedy."[6] After meetings with more than fifty
people with a wide range of viewpoints, the delegation prepared a report
to the full committee, which adopted it on 25 September 1987. The
"MRTI report" presented a sensitive overview of the issues and perceptions to which the well-attested fact of job discrimination had given rise,
indicating the persistent and complex nature of the problem and com-
mending the MacBride Principles for addressing it substantively. But the
report distinguished sharply between the principles and the campaign for
their adoption. The campaign had certainly prodded the British government to combat discrimination more forcefully, and new legislation to
this effect was now forthcoming. Otherwise, however, advocates of the
principles had gained few followers in Ireland, North or South, apart
from Sinn Féin, and had for a variety of reasons estranged even moderate
Protestant opinion in Northern Ireland, whose support would be necessary to the success of fair-employment measures. Thus the MRTI report
concluded with a reluctant recommendation against a renewed endorse-
ment of the MacBride Principles. It thus averted a rift with the Presbyterian Church in Ireland, taking into account action on the part of the
Irish church against job discrimination and encouraging its members to
become "effective advocates" for fair employment.[7] Other American
Protestant bodies, in endorsing the MacBride Principles, had not heeded
the opposition of their Irish coreligionists; the U.S. Presbyterians, by
contrast, had chosen to work with theirs.

In the first instance, this meant strengthening the links between the
American and Irish Presbyterian churches, and especially extending those
links as much as possible beyond the leadership to congregations and
clergy. An opportunity to do this and more soon presented itself. In

[6]Committee on Mission Responsibility through Investment, "Northern Ireland and the
  MacBride Principles" (unpublished document available from the committee, and herein-
  after referred to as the "MRTI report"), p. 1.
[7]Ibid., p. 13.

October 1987 the authors of this chapter met with Canon Michael Hamilton of the Washington Episcopal Cathedral to consider how best to attempt an American ecumenical approach to the Northern Ireland situation. Each of us independently had long been concerned about the issue, and had concluded that the constituency of concern for it in America was too narrow, especially among Protestants. We decided together that information about the continuing process of reconciliation would not only be an effective means of broadening that concern, but if disseminated under American ecumenical auspices, would also balance the ecumenical nature of that process in Northern Ireland itself. We agreed also that the vehicle should be an American speaking tour by a Protestant-Catholic pair of activists involved in the reconciliation movement, preferably clergy, in order to emphasize the affirmation of the movement by the Irish institutional churches. Two such involved clergy from Belfast accepted the invitation: the Reverend Sam Burch, a Methodist minister who directed the Cornerstone Community, a neighborhood reconciliation center in West Belfast, and Father Gerry Reynolds, a priest with the Redemptionist monastery in the area. Burch and Reynolds regularly visited the families of victims of violence from both communities, and almost always they were welcomed; it was likely that their poignant account of their experiences would make a lasting impression on American audiences.

Their April 1988 speaking tour was indeed successful. It was sponsored by the Center for Irish Studies at the Catholic University of America in Washington with the aid of the three organizers, institutional funding from Washington Episcopal Cathedral, Catholic University, and the Presbyterian Church (USA), and the assistance of the national office of the United Methodist Church and the U.S. Catholic Conference. The two clergy spoke to congregations and interchurch and university audiences in major cities as "A Ministry of Reconciliation." They drew enough interest to encourage the organizers to plan a similar tour for the next year; in the interval their invitation to the members of a Presbyterian congregation in Washington to visit Belfast brought an informal interchurch group from the Washington suburbs to Northern Ireland in November 1988. This group met with religious leaders, reconciliation activists, community organizers, and politicians, a number of whom have maintained and developed their connections with further developments such as a U.S.-Northern Ireland seminarian exchange program. The group's experience and response to it encouraged the authors, who were included, to consider other group visits even as they prepared for a second Northern Ireland clergy tour of American cities. This second tour took place in April 1989 and was followed by two more that year and annually since. Most involved Presbyterian and Catholic clergy, including on one occasion a nun from Belfast, and another tour included both the Catholic and the Church of Ireland bishops of Derry, Doctors Edward Daly and James Mehaffey. As the series progressed, the U.S. Catholic Conference took a larger role in organizing the speaking tours, while the initial funding by the Presbyterian Church (USA) continued with supplements, mainly from Catholic sources.

The growing interest of the U.S. Catholic Conference led us both to formulate, and Josiah Beeman to propose, the idea of an interchurch committee—embracing the institutions of the American and Irish Presbyterian and Catholic churches—to endorse and support reconciliation efforts, including the speaking tours in America and group visits to Northern Ireland, and also to assist efforts for economic development. No joint body with so pronounced an institutional foundation and character had previously been established to treat Northern Ireland issues. It was understood that the proposed committee would avoid matters of doctrine and constitutional aspects of the problem and instead would concentrate on the practicalities of publicizing and advocating the process of reconciliation by, in particular, promoting community-based economic-development projects in areas of high unemployment. Even with this focus on the practical, the notion of an institutionally composed Catholic-Protestant committee entailed considerable discussion within and among the staffs of the Irish and American bishops' conferences and the two Presbyterian churches. None of the bodies opposed the objectives put forward for the committee, as it was generally recognized that, whether Northern Ireland ultimately remained part of the United Kingdom or became united with the Republic of Ireland, the Protestant and Catholic people living there had to be encouraged to cooperate peacefully in nonpolitical respects and that to achieve this, religious mistrust would have to be reduced and the economic standing of the two communities brought to relative parity. Yet while the church leaders in Ireland individually had often endorsed both reconciliation and economic development, it was a different matter to promote them jointly and practically. At length, in spring 1990, the four bodies agreed that the interchurch committee be established, with representatives nominated by the U.S. Catholic Conference, the Irish Episcopal Conference, the Church and Government

Committee of the General Assembly of the Presbyterian Church in Ireland, and the Northern Ireland Working Group of the Presbyterian Church (USA).

Meanwhile, even as plans developed for further clergy tours in America, ground was laid for a project to bring American clergy and lay leaders to Ireland, North and South, in summer 1990 to learn firsthand about the dynamics of conflict and reconciliation. This "Irish Summer Institute" was intended to be an annual event lasting two weeks, beginning in mid-August with an orientation session of three days organized by the Irish School of Ecumenics in Dublin. Thereafter seminars, workshops, and visits to reconciliation centers both urban and rural would take place in Belfast, Derry, and other towns in Northern Ireland, with a visit included to Ramelton, County Donegal, the home of Francis Mackemie, organizer of the first American presbytery of the Presbyterian Church in the eighteenth century. The institute was sponsored by the Presbyterian Church (USA), the Center for Irish Studies at Catholic University, and a number of theological seminaries. It drew more than thirty participants from throughout the United States, both Catholic and Protestant.

The Interchurch Committee on Northern Ireland convened for the first time in Belfast on 15 September 1990, with Josiah Beeman as its chair. The committee agreed to sponsor the American speaking tours as a continuing project and determined to seek out other projects through which to promote economic development. The committee has met annually since, undertaking cosponsorship of the Irish Summer Institute and, as of 1992, facilitating grants and investments from U.S. Presbyterian sources totaling nearly $900,000 (and leveraging another $625,000 from international funding bodies) to assist cross-community development projects. Moreover, between formal meetings, the delegations maintain contact with each other, sharing information and concerns about further plans and issues.

Fundamental to all these projects is the understanding that Americans, whether individually or institutionally, have only a limited part to play in facilitating the progress of reconciliation in Northern Ireland. But promoting that progress and thereby helping to advance it is an activity in which Americans can be useful. Institutional cooperation, moreover, is valuable not only in lending weight to this effort, but in preserving Christianity from the discredit that arises from the frequent description of the troubles in Protestant-Catholic terms. There are inescapably religious dimensions to the conflict, but religion is a misleading metaphor

if used to characterize it as a whole, however intertwined religious identification has become with the historical, political, economic, and cultural
issues also involved. Joint action by institutional bodies is always deliberate and usually slow, yet those bodies provide a surer foundation than
most for a positive approach to the problem of Northern Ireland. Furthermore, the effectiveness of the Christian churches in Northern Ireland—like that of many institutions—is ultimately threatened by the
conflict and its terms. By working together to reduce those tensions they
can address, these churches undertake a task conducive to their own
viability as institutions, and one that is truly Christian.

10

The cultural issue in Northern Ireland, 1965–1991

TERENCE BROWN

Until very recent times the cultural issue played no part in the public life of Northern Ireland and little part in the social life of the province. For official purposes the province (or six-ninths of a province) was a peripheral region of the United Kingdom and could be expected to exhibit an indigenous culture only to the extent that, for example, the Northeast of England might be said to do so. In the fifty years in which it held hegemonic power in the region, the ruling Unionist Party had no cultural policy whatsoever other than, through its Department of Education, maintaining a curriculum of indisputably British complexion in the primary and secondary schools. Indeed, it is possible that such Unionist ministers who over the years thought about such matters at all with any degree of sophistication would have prided themselves on the degree to which the cultural question was kept off the public agenda; for that meant that the Catholic minority, who as Irish nationalists might have been expected to raise the issue, were content to transmit Irish cultural self-awareness and teach the Irish language in a social ghetto without any sense that these would pose a fundamental threat to the viability of the state. That the unionist and largely Protestant community raised no questions of a cultural kind, readily acquiescing to or in fact welcoming a British focus in the educational curriculum, could be read as a distinguishing characteristic that set it apart from the population of the Free

TERENCE BROWN is Associate Professor of English at Trinity College, Dublin. He has written *Ireland: A Social and Cultural History*; *The Whole Protestant Community: The Making of an Historical Myth*; and *Ireland's Literature: Selected Essays*.

State and Republic, where the cultural question was frequently aired and was often an object of anxious debate.

The Southern state of course had good reason to be anxious about cultural matters in a way which the Northern semistate had not. It had been a central tenet of the cultural nationalism that had served as an adjunct to the political nationalism of the independence movement that Ireland possessed a distinctive Irish-language-based culture and that separatism was intimately bound up with cultural aspirations. Unionism, although it occasionally made propagandist play with such formulations as the Protestant idea of liberty and the British way of life, had no essential reason to foster or valorize a distinctive culture in the North of the country as some kind of justification for the political decisions that had been made in the 1920s. Rather, unionism was content to identify in complacent fashion the similarities between Northern Irish cultural formations and those "across the water" on the British "mainland" with which it was happy to remain in political union. The Southern state by contrast considered the Irish language and Gaelic tradition crucial to its existence and was accordingly much embarrassed because the process of anglicization, which had been set in motion in the years following the Famine of the 1840s, was not significantly affected by the establishment of an independent Irish legislature in 1922 and by the declaration of a republic in 1948–49. So cultural life in Southern Ireland since independence has been marked by much debate about Irish identity, by earnest efforts to forge distinctive Irish modes in literature, drama, music, painting, and sculpture, and by an implicit assumption that a national consciousness must find expression in the arts as in social forms. In the North no such concerns nor any similar preoccupations disturbed the even tenor of a provincial cultural life, which for almost four decades was content to languish as a peculiarly supine cultural region of some ideal and essentially illusory conception of a British Isles culture, where local color could be admitted (in Orange bands and a homely accent, for instance), but nothing encouraged suggestive of authentic and creative cultural distinctiveness.

There were some in the first four decades of Irish independence who were less than happy with this state of affairs in Northern Ireland, which in the same period enjoyed a kind of semi-independence. There were some who had come to adult consciousness before Partition who could not easily accept that the Six Counties should be cut off from the cultural capital of the island, Dublin, which had once been the second city of the British Empire and which contained the country's major libraries, museums, and art galleries, as well as its oldest university. But these were an extremely small minority, mavericks like Denis Ireland, the Presbyterian bourgeois (his family were in linen, the staple of Protestant prosperity and respectability in the first half of the century) who served in the Irish Senate and who in his brief essay, "A Journey into the Protestant Mind," lamented late in life that:

from the recesses of the once brilliant Ulster Protestant mind nothing emerges but an empty clanging of gates against ghosts that no longer exist. The Ulster Protestant power to floodlight a political scene by clarity of thought...has now been paralysed by sheer negation, by a refusal to face the founding of the united states of Ireland.[1]

Others, while they felt no particular compulsion to look to Dublin or the rest of Ireland, were not content to see life in Northern Ireland as simply a provincial version of English culture. In the early 1940s a group of poets associated with the short-lived periodical *Lagan* and with the longer-lasting *Rann* sought to develop the concept of regionalism, then in the air, to Ulster conditions. Foremost among these was the poet John Hewitt (1907–87). In the 1940s his message about the ideal cultural unit ("In a word the region, an area of a size and a significance we could hold in our hearts") fell on stony ground. However, the cultural program he developed at that time was later to meet with greater enthusiasm and is still reckoned a valuable contribution to Northern Irish self-understanding:

The Ulster writer must, if he is not to be satisfied in remaining "one of the big fish in the little pond," seek out and secure some recognition outside his native place. But the English language is the speech of millions. There is no limit to its potential audience. Yet I believe this had better not be achieved by choosing materials outside and beyond those presented by his native environment. He must be a *rooted* man, must carry the native tang of his idiom like the native dust on his sleeve; otherwise he is an airy internationalist, thistledown, a twig in a stream.[2]

Since the mid-1960s Northern Ireland has experienced something of a renaissance in the arts. For example, the annual Belfast Festival, which began hesitantly in 1964 as the Queen's University Festival, is now second

---

[1] Denis Ireland, "A Journey into the Protestant Mind," in *From the Jungle of Belfast* (Belfast, 1973), p. 175.
[2] John Hewitt, "The Bitter Gourd: Some Problems of the Ulster Writer," in Tom Clyde (ed.), *Ancestral Voices: The Selected Prose of John Hewitt* (Belfast, 1987), p. 115.

only to the Edinburgh Festival in the British Isles in the range and quality of its offerings. A lively and well-endowed Arts Council supports artistic endeavor in many fields. The Ulster Folk Museum, formally opened in 1964, is now one of the foremost examples of such institutions in the world and attracts visitors and specialists in the study of material culture from many countries. The Ulster Museum, long neglected, has since the 1960s seen redevelopment of its interior and the consolidation of a collection of Irish and modern art, as well as natural history holdings, industrial archaeological exhibits, and geological remains, which rank it as perhaps the most innovative and well-stocked museum in the United Kingdom outside London. Historical research has been stimulated by the funds available to the Public Record Office, and such local assets as the Linenhall Library in Belfast, with its collections by eighteenth-century weaver poets and its archive of publications relating to the political disturbances of the last twenty years, have, through the simple dedication of inspired individuals, established a priceless cultural resource. The Lyric Players, with their origins in amateur enthusiasm, developed in the same period into a local theater of real distinction in a handsome Laganside facility. And the BBC, in the production of radio and television features on local literary and artistic matters, has made its contribution to raising Northern Irish consciousness to an awareness of the cultural vitality of the province in the last two decades.

It was in literature and most especially in poetry that Ulster first began to stir itself from artistic sleep in the mid-1960s. A short-lived if impressively handsome periodical of the period, *The Northern Review,* grasped at the straws in the wind in its first issue in 1965. It editorialized:

The signs are that we are breaking out of our long-standing cultural deep-freeze. ... The second issue will be primarily devoted to a group of young Irish writers who we feel represent an important and long-awaited revival of our literary tradition. Among this group Michael Longley and Derek Mahon recently shared the E. E. Gregory Award, Seamus Heaney has published extensively in the New Statesman and the Listener, while Stewart Parker, now lecturing in the United States, has had several of his poems broadcast on American radio.[3]

These of course soon became names to conjure with and each of them is now reckoned a major voice in contemporary Irish letters. In 1965 their work, along with slim collections by Seamus Deane and James Simmons, appeared in pamphlet form in the Festival Publications series

[3]"Editorial: Mainly for Irish Readers," *The Northern Review* 1, 1 (Spring 1965): 3.

associated with the Queen's University Festival, and a local poetic movement seemed at hand. The 1968 founding of a literary periodical, *The
Honest Ulsterman*, by the poet James Simmons, was to give the bur-
geoning poetic activity in the North a focus it had not had since the days
of *Lagan* and *Rann*. It was the outbreak of "the troubles" in the same
year that fortuitously gave a certain public visibility in journalistic terms
to Simmons's magazine that its predecessors had never enjoyed in less
interesting times. The magazine in its early days even advertised itself as
the handbook for a revolution, though its radicalism was more of the
sixties international student variety than anything more locally or na-
tionally inspired. But the magazine survived and, having passed through
several editorial hands, remains a lively outlet for poetry and literary
criticism in the province.

In 1971 the Arts Council (itself established in 1962) was encouraged
by artistic quickening in the North to issue a publication entitled *Causeway: The Arts in Ulster* under the editorship of the poet Michael Longley,
who had recently been appointed the council's literature officer. The
volume ranged over artistic endeavor in the province from poetry to
architecture, jazz to traditional Irish music. In his introduction Longley
adverted to an earlier similar work edited by Sam Hanna Bell, Nessa
Robb, and John Hewitt in 1951, but declared that he intended his volume
to be more comprehensive, suggesting that there was more to be comprehensive about and that the understanding of what constituted artistic
activity had broadened in the interval. He also indicated in a significant
fashion that he chose to include an "essay on the origins and aims of the
Ulster Folk Museum" because he believed it to be "a significant product
of the *new desire to know and understand our cultural roots*"[4] (italics
added). The note struck here by Longley, that the arts are a way to
comprehend a cultural inheritance and are indeed part of it, was also
new and suggested that "the troubles" had stimulated a self-consciousness
about the social and cultural formations of a society that was enduring
seismic shocks.

In the 1970s such embryonic cultural self-awareness was in the first
instance directed by literary critics toward the phenomenon of the Ulster
poetic revival itself. This was customarily accounted for as the product
of an educational transformation wrought by the extension to Northern
Ireland in 1947 of the British Butler Act of 1944, which had created the

---

[4]Michael Longley, "Introduction," *Causeway: The Arts in Ulster* (Belfast, 1971), p. 7.

opportunity for universal secondary education and for university education for all who could benefit from it. The same processes that were reckoned to have educated a cohort of young people who involved themselves in the civil rights movement of the late 1960s were seen to have thrown up a newly educated, ambitious group of young men from Catholic and poor Protestant backgrounds, who could not, without British support, have enjoyed the privileges of humane university education. In 1979 the first full-scale anthology to give recognition to their work, edited by the poet Frank Ormsby under the title *Poets from the North of Ireland*, popularized this cultural thesis.[5]

What the thesis implied, however, whatever its sociological accuracy, was that culture was an effect of upward mobility. It suggested, moreover, that cultural life was something that, however much it had roots in a native place or local loyalties, was somehow free or could be free from the contagion of the local quarrel. It allowed the cultural questions that Michael Longley had tentatively raised in 1971, in relation to the Ulster Folk Museum in particular, to remain largely undiscussed in relation to literature, since poetry was deemed, or seemed, to occupy some "neutral" aesthetic zone, the reserve of the upwardly mobile, even where it permitted the atrocious realities of Ulster experience in the period to register upon it. It is perhaps not surprising therefore that in the 1970s no self-conscious body of culturally based literary criticism emerged in Northern Ireland, even though it could have had the artistic achievements of a number of remarkably gifted young poets as grist to its theoretical mill. The culturally concerned reflections on what had occurred poetically north of the border that did get written tended in the 1970s (with the notable exception of some of the writings of Queen's University lecturer Edna Longley) to be the concern of critics and writers associated with the Dublin-edited *The Crane Bag*.

Where cultural matters were being addressed in systematic fashion in the 1970s was in the field of the human sciences. Michael Longley had recognized in 1971 that the establishment of the Ulster Folk Museum was founded upon a concern for cultural particularism. He was no doubt aware that the distinguished human geographer Estyn Evans was the "onlie begetter" of that imaginative enterprise. It was Evans too who was a major influence in establishing an Institute of Irish Studies at

---

[5] See also my *Northern Voices: Poets from Ulster* (Dublin, 1975), and "Poets and Culture: Seamus Heaney, Derek Mahon, and Tom Paulin," in Alan J. Ward (ed.), *Northern Ireland: Living with the Crisis* (New York, 1987), pp. 155–71.

Queen's University that took for granted an interdisciplinary interest in Ulster's material culture and social and cultural history. Through the 1970s and 1980s this institute built an enviable reputation for the quality of its humanistic researches, though literary culture has never been a primary focus of its attention.[6]

Literature certainly played a part in the quickening cultural self-consciousness of the North's intellectual life during the 1980s. The establishment of The Field Day Theatre Company in Derry in 1980 was probably a decisive event. This cultural and theatrical group, which brought together as directors the various talents of poets Seamus Heaney and Tom Paulin, playwright Brian Friel, singer David Hammond, and actor Stephen Rea, at its inception (when Friel and Rea were the founding presences) intended only to emulate the achievements of earlier Irish theatrical innovators—the Ulster Literary Theatre, for example, of pre-Partition days. However, it swiftly became a focus for a cultural debate stimulated in part by the series of pamphlets on political and cultural themes it issued and in part by its capacity to command public attention with such remarkable plays as its inaugural in 1980, Brian Friel's *Translations*. In these pamphlets and in their public statements the Field Day team certainly made culture and its relation to the political order a central question. Prominent among them was Seamus Deane, who in his *Heroic Styles: The Tradition of an Idea* (1984) insisted that "everything including our politics and our literature, has to be re-written—i.e. re-read."[7] Friel also saw the cultural issue as the heart of the enterprise, remarking in a 1982 interview published in Dublin that their endeavors "should lead to a cultural state, not a political state. And I think out of that cultural state, a possibility of a political state follows."[8]

Field Day unquestionably provoked responses in the North and elsewhere, some vigorously critical. The kernel of the criticism was that Field Day was simply using culture to repackage the political aims of a poorly disguised, all-too-familiar Irish nationalism. But whatever the force of such strictures (and to this writer it seemed unreasonable, given the national outlook of a majority of Ireland's inhabitants, that the possession of nationalist feelings and convictions should somehow condemn one

[6]In recent years the Institute of Irish Studies has in fact appointed several research fellows who have engaged in literary study.
[7]Seamus Deane, *Heroic Styles: The Tradition of an Idea* (Derry, Northern Ireland, 1984), p. 18.
[8]Brian Friel, quoted in John Gray, "Field Day: Five Years On," *The Linenhall Review* 2, 2 (Summer 1985): 5.

out of court), Field Day undoubtedly managed to set some of the terms of a cultural debate that enlivened conference halls and the pages of journals in the North and the rest of the country throughout the decade. Such periodicals as *Fortnight, The Linenhall Review,* and *The Honest Ulsterman,* which ran a "Critical Forum" for several issues under the editorship of Professor John Wilson Foster (one of Field Day's most astute critics), have all dealt with cultural topics. And the matter of culture began to engage the official mind too, with such bodies as Anglo-Irish Encounter and Co-operation North enjoying government support, so that by 1985 *The Linenhall Review* could editorialize:

What then of this new flurry of activity? The concept of "cultural co-operation" is a dangerously vague one which in the wrong circumstances sparks off a windy piety for which even good dinners do not compensate. Here the good faith of both the British and Irish governments must be called into question. They have played a not insignificant part in sparking off the new debate. Anglo-Irish Encounter is directly funded by both governments. Co-operation North, while independent, is grant aided by both governments, and no doubt its proceedings... will be welcomed in both Dublin and London. Can it be that both governments find the roar of cultural debate a useful distraction from the difficulties of political agreement?[9]

One antidote in recent years in the North of Ireland to the kind of windy piety which *The Linenhall Review* felt it necessary to warn against has been the writings of Edna Longley, the most formidable of the cultural critics to have emerged in the 1980s in the North. This Southern-born, Trinity College-educated professor of English at Queen's University began her career as a skilled practitioner of the close reading of poetry. But under the pressure, one presumes, of a grimly challenging local demand that the intellectual attend to the disorder in the streets, she has produced a body of polemical, probing, and thoroughly engaged cultural criticism. A controlling concern in her writings has been that the simplifications of monolithic conceptions of Irish identity should be subjected to rigorous deconstruction, and the cultural diversity of the Irish experience recognized. Constantly alert to those tendencies in Irish life that seek to impose totalizing concepts on political debate, she has proposed in a telling metaphor how the literature of the North could serve as a guide to future political structures in the country as a whole. It has been perhaps her most enabling insight:

[9]"View from The Linenhall," *The Linenhall Review*, 2, 2 (Summer 1985): 3.

The literature produced by the Ulster people suggests that, instead of brooding on Celtic and Orange dawns, its inhabitants might accept this province-in-two-contexts as a cultural corridor. Unionists want to block the corridor at one end, republicans at the other. Culture, like common sense, insists it can't be done. Ulster Irishness and Ulster Britishness are bound to each other and to Britain and Ireland. And the republic will have to come cleaner about its own *de facto* connections with Britain. Only by promoting circulation within and through Ulster will the place ever be part of a healthy system.[10]

Given such views and commitment to cultural analysis, it is not surprising that Longley has been to the fore in two of the most significant ventures in the cultural sphere of recent years in Northern Ireland: the founding of the John Hewitt International Summer School and the establishment of the Cultural Traditions Group. The annual Hewitt Summer School (inaugurated in summer 1988, the first such school in the province to emulate the many that have been a part of the Republic's intellectual and social life since the 1960s) has been notably well-attended and has been marked by the sense that Hewitt's regionalist ideals, developed in the 1940s, may have come into their own in a new "Europe of the regions." A prime mover in the school, Longley has been at pains in her writings and public statements to advert frequently to Hewitt's crucial role for contemporary ideology in the North:

John Hewitt, aside from his own poetry, is important in Northern Irish Literary history for three reasons.

Firstly, he tried to change the milieu where "the Ulster ideology... offered [the writer] no inspiration. The Ulster public offered him no livelihood." Secondly, he saw literature and the arts as indeed inseparable from their total environment. Thirdly he pioneered an indigenous cultural framework for Ulster Protestants: a framework which did not exclusively depend on imports or the Orange Lodge.[11]

The occasion of this statement was the second Cultural Traditions conference, held in March 1990 on the theme "Varieties of Britishness." The Cultural Traditions Group is an ad hoc committee of interested individuals "drawn together by the Central Community Relations Unit to explore ways of promoting a better understanding of, and a more constructive debate about, our different cultural traditions in Northern

---

[10]Edna Longley, quoted in Liam de Paor, *Unfinished Business: Ireland Today and Tomorrow* (London, 1990), pp. 148–9.

[11]Edna Longley, "Literature," in Maurna Crozier (ed.), *Cultural Traditions in Northern Ireland: Varieties of Britishness* (Belfast, 1990), p. 25.

Ireland."[12] Since its formation in autumn 1988 the group has organized two well-attended conferences, the first under the general rubric of "Varieties of Irishness," the second on the British identity, at which Longley commended Hewitt's regionalist thought. Purpose has been added to the deliberations of this group, which meets under the aegis of the Institute of Irish Studies at Queen's University, by the government support which in recent years has been dedicated to the development of cultural awareness in the province. One million pounds has been made available for various projects and undoubtedly the Cultural Traditions Group has had a useful role in identifying priorities for expenditure. But its more catalytic significance is to intensify the cultural debate in Northern Ireland in the conviction, in the words of the group's chair, James Hawthorne, that "cultural diversity and community relations cannot be separated."[13] That the deliberations of the group have not been informed by that blandness which can so readily accompany the ideal of community relations in contexts of communal conflict is evidenced by the rigorous contents of the two volumes of conference proceedings. These are essential reading for anyone involved in the contemporary cultural debate in the North and in Ireland as a whole. Indeed, Edna Longley, at the "Varieties of Britishness" conference, identified the importance of that debate in the context of the more immediate demands on political and social energy that the Northern Irish crisis imposes. Her words supply a program for all those who feel that inadequate attention has been given to the cultural basis of the Northern Irish conflict in the past, and offer hope that the 1990s will consolidate the gains made in cultural self-awareness in the previous decade:

I think many people in Northern Ireland lead a very unconscious, unreflective existence in which they are accepting a whole load of conditioning which they have never actually examined, and obviously a conference encouraging debate, if it affects anything, is going to be initially a very slow process. I think that the fact that the issue exists shows the lack of working and thinking in the past: the contentment of both communities to stew in their own juices and not, in fact through the study of literature or history or locality or whatever, to ask themselves any very serious or searching questions. I think we are unscrambling those two

---

[12]James Hawthorne, "Preface," in Crozier (ed.), *Cultural Traditions in Northern Ireland: Varieties of Britishness*, p. vi.
[13]James Hawthorne, "Preface," in Maurna Crozier (ed.), *Cultural Traditions in Northern Ireland: Varieties of Irishness* (Belfast, 1989), p. vii.

very powerful political ideologies that clashed earlier this century, and were ideologies of identity.

Until we have established a more complicated picture of these matters the political problems will not be properly solved, they will only be suppressed to rise again.[14]

[14]Longley, "Literature," p. 54.

Part III

In search of the politics of reconciliation

11

Conflict and the incentives to
political accommodation

DONALD L. HOROWITZ

Northern Ireland's conflict is intractable by Western standards. In some
key ways, Northern Ireland resembles the severely divided societies of
Asia and Africa more than it does the less severely divided multiethnic
societies of the West, such as Belgium, Canada, Switzerland, and the
Netherlands.

Later on, when I discuss some techniques that seem to reduce ethnic
conflict (and here I include religious and linguistic conflict), I shall refer
to what seems to work in those severely divided societies of Asia and
Africa. I shall do so because if a technique has an effect there it might
have an effect in Northern Ireland. In the European cases, by contrast,
there is an element of circularity: We cannot quite be sure whether the
Western cases are conflicts that are moderate because they have effectively
been controlled or whether they are effectively controlled because they
are moderate conflicts to begin with.

I said there were some resemblances between Northern Ireland and

DONALD L. HOROWITZ is Charles S. Murphy Professor of Law and Professor of Political
Science at Duke University. His publications include *Ethnic Groups in Conflict* and *A
Democratic South Africa?: Constitutional Engineering in a Divided Society*. He is a former
Fellow of the Woodrow Wilson Center.

An earlier version of this chapter appeared as "Community Conflict: Policy and Possibilities," Occasional Paper No. 1 in the series published by the Centre for the Study of
Conflict, University of Ulster (1990). The comparison of Sri Lanka and Malaysia draws
heavily on the author's "Incentives and Behaviour in the Ethnic Politics of Sri Lanka and
Malaysia," *Third World Quarterly* 11 (October 1989): 18–35. The concept of vote pooling
and the methods to induce it are discussed more fully in "Electoral Systems for Divided
Societies," which forms chapter 5 of the author's *A Democratic South Africa?: Constitutional Engineering in a Divided Society* (Berkeley: University of California Press, 1991).

severely divided societies of Asia and Africa. To put it another way, Northern Ireland is something of a deviant case in Western terms. How?

In ethnically divided societies of the West, there is, first, an important overarching level of national identity. A survey of Switzerland found that, despite ethnic differences, about half of all respondents identified themselves as "Swiss." In France, only 25 percent of French Basques called themselves "Basques," 20 percent called themselves "French," and the remaining 55 percent responded with "Basque-French" or "French-Basque." These are not findings that could be obtained in Nigeria, Malaysia, or Sri Lanka. And of course the very terms *unionist* and *nationalist* reveal that the nature of a supraethnic national identity is what is at issue in Northern Ireland as well.

Second, not only is there an overarching level of national identity but there are also alternative identities at the same substate level as ethnic identity. Belgium, for all its Fleming-Walloon differences, also has religious and class differences that compete for attention with ethnic differences. Switzerland has linguistic, class, religious, and cantonal differences. Canada has class, regional, and religious conflicts in addition to Anglophone-Francophone conflict. These differences show up in party organization, voting behavior, and the structure of divisive issues. In the multiethnic societies of Asia and Africa, wherever free elections prevail, parties tend to be organized closely along ethnic lines. In Western Europe and North America, they do not. In Belgium, the three main parties long bridged the Fleming-Walloon cleavage, and one of them, with its distinctly non-ethnic perspective—the Liberal Party—actually *increased* its support as ethnic issues gained in prominence. Ethnic issues never wholly preempted others in Belgium. Rather, a "triple issue spectrum"—language, class, and religion—characterizes political debate, with each issue changing the alignment of forces and to some extent neutralizing the others. In Switzerland, language is no stronger a predictor of party preference than is class, although it is somewhat stronger than religion. Ethnicity in the West typically does not displace all other forms of group difference. But one can hardly say that about Northern Ireland, where religion and ethnicity are not sources of alternating affiliations but are coterminous, where regional loyalties do not significantly crosscut ethnoreligious differences, and where class has been alleged to reinforce those ascriptive differences. So here, too, Northern Ireland resembles Malaysia, Sri Lanka, and Nigeria more than Belgium, Canada, and Switzerland, and this is reflected in the ethno-religious basis of party politics.

Third, there is inferential evidence that the intensity of ethnic conflict is lower in the West than it is in Asia and Africa. Surveys show French and Italian minorities in Switzerland are actually *more* satisfied with government and politics than is the German-speaking majority. Such phenomena are incompatible with strong ascriptive loyalties. There is also much less interethnic violence in Western countries. Once again, Northern Ireland is an exception—although it is not quite on a par with Asia and Africa. Intense mass hostility usually produces face-to-face ethnic riots and mass killings, as it did in Sri Lanka in 1983, not just terrorism. And in the most severely divided societies ascriptively based parties usually drive out completely the multiethnic parties of the center. Interestingly, in Northern Ireland in the 1970s, the Alliance Party generally held its own, with about 10 percent of the vote.

Fourth, there is the external factor. Some of the most severely divided societies are located on fault lines between two worlds: the Arab and the African, as in Mauritania, Chad, and Sudan; the Christian and the Muslim, as in Cyprus and Lebanon; the Dravidian and the so-called "Aryan," as in Sri Lanka; the Malay world and the Chinese world, as in Malaysia. In all these cases, there are external pulls, external influences, and especially external fears, such as the fear of the Sinhalese that the Sri Lankan Tamils are really the cutting edge of the invasion by the 50 million Tamils in India—and there is therefore a fear of being swamped by the people across the border. Northern Ireland, too, may lie between the Celtic world and the Anglo-Saxon world; and the fear of being swamped is not far from the surface. But, more to the point, the double minority issue is as familiar in Sri Lanka or Mauritania as it is in Northern Ireland.

Now that I have made Northern Ireland part of the Third World, at least in terms of *some* characteristics, I shall enumerate a few of the obstacles to accommodation in such deeply divided societies, some of the things it is futile to hope for, and some of the things it is by no means idle to hope for.

First of all, in such societies, many of the claims are zero-sum. That is because relative group advantage is the thing in issue. I refer here not just to advantage in the material sense but in the symbolic sense, because symbols tell us whose country this is, who is at home, who belongs, and who is worthy. Symbolic demands, if they reflect claims to the distribution of group worth and group legitimacy in the territory, are difficult to compromise.

Moreover, in such societies, we should not project our own good intentions onto policy-makers—often they, too, are participants in the conflict and have hostile feelings toward members of other groups. Even where they do not, they know that their followers do, and they know that to retain their ethnic following, they must pursue the conflict. For most politicians, most of the time, it is more rewarding to pursue the conflict than to pursue accommodation. Again, under conditions of free elections politicians who pursue a strategy of interethnic accommodation will usually lose more followers of their own group than they could conceivably hope to attract from across the ethnic divide.

But buried here is a prescription. It has two sides to it—negative and positive.

First, do not aim too high. Do not try to make people love each other, or at least do not put all your eggs in that basket. Do not try for national unity or national integration or nation-building. It took hundreds of years to produce integrated national entities where they exist, and severely divided societies like Northern Ireland cannot wait for that. For them, the short run is crucial.

Second, if much of the conflict revolves around politics, politicians, and their pursuit of group advantage, but politicians have no incentive to be accommodative, then they need to be provided with such incentives. The situation they face must be structured so that it is politically rewarding for them to act in an accommodative fashion.

In other words, the object of policy is not to surmount or obliterate or ignore ethnic differences, and not necessarily, in the short run at least, to reduce feelings of hostility, but to reduce the level of overt ethnic conflict behavior.

The aim, in other words, is to make moderation pay. There is a market, and there are market incentives in party politics and in leadership. Parties and leaders who do not supply the requisite hostility or promote ethnically exclusive policies demanded by the electoral market will find themselves without buyers for the product they do supply. Party A, representing Group A, can quickly be displaced by Party A_1, representing the same group, as soon as Party A is perceived as being too soft or as selling out group interests. Strategies of accommodation involve intervening in this market to change the incentive structure. The currency in this market consists of votes and support.

There are two main underlying mechanisms for doing this. The first involves instituting devices that have the effect of heightening incentives for interethnic cooperation on the part of politicians. The second involves devices that heighten intraethnic differences and therefore lessen inter-ethnic conflict, in two ways: (1) by making interethnic conflict relatively less important or (2) by increasing incentives for fractions of ethnic groups to reach out across ethnic boundaries and cooperate with fractions of other ethnic groups. These latter two tendencies are related, because a fraction of a group may have more need to reach out across ethnic lines.

Take the following situation, which is familiar in an array of ethnically divided societies, including Northern Ireland. Suppose there are two groups, A and B. A is 60 percent of the population, and B is 40 percent. Each group is represented by one party. Party A has a majority in 60 percent of the single-member constituencies in first-past-the-post elections. Elections are held: Party A wins 60 percent of the seats and forms the government in perpetuity. Party B and Group B are excluded from power permanently. This is a situation fraught with conflict: riots, secessionist violence (if groups are territorially concentrated), and coup attempts (if Group B predominates in the officer corps).

What to do? Be careful, because if you split Group A into two equal parts, Party A with 30 percent and Party A_1 with 30 percent, then Party B, with 40 percent, may win a majority of seats on a mere plurality of votes by repeated victories in three-way contests. The result will be an illegitimate government, because a minority has, only because of plurality electoral rules, captured the state machinery.

That is not to say that fragmenting the support of the Party A's of this world is always a bad idea—only that it is not always a good idea. For a case in which it was a good idea, consider Nigeria's second republic.

During its first republic, 1960–66, Nigeria consisted of three main regions, with a dominant group and a dominant party in each, all of them fighting to control the entire state. When one group—the Yoruba—split into two, one Yoruba fraction aligning with the Hausa-Fulani of the North and the other aligning with the Ibo of the East, there was bifurcation and a 60–40–type election, followed by a coup, riots, another coup, more riots, and a war of secession.

In 1978, when Nigeria went back to civilian rule, there was a keen desire to avoid a recurrence of this syndrome. The Nigerians particularly wanted to avoid having whoever controlled parliament control the whole state. So they opted for a presidential system and a separation of powers. But they went further. By then there were not three main regions but nineteen states. The old North was segmented into ten states, with Hausa-Fulani dominant in only five or six. How, then, to elect the president?

If the president were to be elected by a plurality, the Hausa-Fulani, the largest group, could win the presidency. If it were to be elected by a majority, no one would win the presidency. The Nigerians wanted the president to be a pan-ethnic figure. So they hit on the idea of plurality plus distribution. The winning candidate had to have the largest number of votes and no less than 25 percent of the vote in no fewer than two-thirds of the then-nineteen states. That meant that no two or three major groups could capture the presidency alone. To be successful, a presidential candidate would have to reach out broadly across ethnic lines for votes. Shehu Shagari, who won the 1979 election, did exactly that—he gained one-third of the popular vote and narrowly won 25 percent in two-thirds of the states. And he behaved as a pan-ethnic figure in office. Quite simply, he wanted to be reelected, and he understood how the electoral incentives were structured.

There are several points here. The first involves the division of territory. Changing the state boundaries in a federal system prevented the Hausa-Fulani from controlling the whole North by having a majority in a single Northern parliament. This partition of the North led to a flourishing of previously dormant regional opposition parties there. This in turn heightened the electoral incentives for presidential candidates from the North to reach out across ethnic lines for votes, because such candidates started out with a smaller Northern electoral base. The effects of slicing up the territory interacted with the effects of the electoral innovations previously described.

Second, the president was ethnically conciliatory because he depended on the votes of members of ethnic groups other than his own. The only way to get such votes and keep them is to accommodate the wishes, the claims, the sentiments of those other ethnic groups.

Third, this mechanism is not dependent on the existence of a presidential system. We can just as easily make legislators in a parliamentary system dependent on votes of members of ethnic groups other than their own. I discuss some ways to do this later in this chapter.

Fourth, the pooling of *popular votes* of members of otherwise antagonistic ethnic groups is far more likely to produce accommodative political behavior than is the mere pooling of *seats* of parties representing more than one ethnic group to form a government. Where Party A and Party B pool just their parliamentary seats, representing 50 percent plus one of all seats in the house, in order to form a government, where each party is dependent only on the votes of members of its own group, the result is only a coalition of convenience. Indeed, the partners in the coalition will often be those with literally no electoral overlap, for if they were rivals for some marginal voters, party officials of each would resist the formation of the coalition. So, such arrangements often are coalitions of opposites, and they quickly turn inconvenient. The stronger partner tries to induce aisle crossings, secure a majority, and push the other party out of the government. In any case, such coalitions (and there are many instances—Punjab before 1966, Benin, Uganda, Nigeria from 1960 to 1964) tend to dissolve acrimoniously over divisive ethnic policy issues.

Such results are much less likely where parties of different ethnic groups have pooled *seats and popular votes*—where, for example, in constituencies each cannot win, it has told its voters to vote for a party of the other ethnic group. In a divided society, it cannot do that unless it can assure its voters that, compared to the alternatives, this party is moderate and accommodating on ethnic issues of concern to its voters. Therefore, an arrangement based on vote pooling is a coalition of the moderate middle and not of the extremes, as coalitions of convenience tend to be.

Fifth, vote pooling will not be necessary unless there are more than two parties. For vote pooling to work, there needs to be some intraethnic division, or else there needs to be a plurality of ethnic groups that has not reduced itself to bifurcation.

When people who study Northern Ireland talk of electoral innovation in the service of accommodation, they often say that Northern Ireland has had an appropriate electoral reform, because it had proportional representation in the 1970s. They are therefore discouraged about the prospects for intergroup accommodation through the electoral process. Their discouragement, however, is unwarranted, for proportional representation (PR) does not necessarily produce vote pooling or coalitions committed to accommodation.

It is true that PR creates incentives for the proliferation of parties, because any party—or, in some systems, any party satisfying a minimum vote threshold—can secure representation in parliament. All else equal, the larger the number of parties, the less the chance that any one party can form a government alone. Consequently, the majority governments that are fostered by the first-past-the-post electoral system used in Great Britain and the United States are less likely under proportional representation. If, under PR, no party has a majority of seats, there will be a need to form a coalition.

Nevertheless, such a coalition generally will result from a mere pooling of seats, and not votes. Under the more extreme list systems of proportional representation, there is no occasion even to contemplate vote pooling. Each party will receive the same fraction of seats as it received of votes. Parties will seek to maximize the support of their own groups and will not jeopardize this by making appeals across group lines. The same is not necessarily true under the different form of proportional representation—the single transferable vote (STV)—used in the Irish Republic. STV is a preferential system. The voter may cast a ballot for more than one candidate for the same seat, in order of the voter's preference. Vote pooling across ethnic lines is therefore possible. The single transferable vote was utilized in the Northern Ireland elections of 1973, the elections that determined the future of the power-sharing executive. Unfortunately, that future turned out to be bleak. One crucial reason that the power-sharing executive did not succeed is that STV induced no substantial vote pooling.

The incentives to vote pooling are much too weak under STV to induce vote pooling across ethnic lines. The reason is that, under STV, it is easy to win a seat. If there are four seats in a constituency, just over one-fifth of the vote will suffice to secure election for a candidate. Under these rules, candidates (and parties) simply will appeal to members of their own group for votes, rather than undertake the riskier course of making reciprocal agreements to pool votes across group lines. This is exactly what happened in Northern Ireland in 1973. There are other systems of preferential voting—particularly, those with a majority threshold for election—that provide much stronger incentives to intergroup vote pooling, because the second and third preferences of voters will be crucial to victory. Without those strong incentives, which are not present in most PR systems, coalitions tend to be coalitions of convenience, assembled merely to gain a majority of seats, rather than coalitions committed to compromise. To put the point sharply, Northern Ireland has certainly not had an accommodative electoral reform.

The most reliable way to make interethnic moderation pay is to make some politicians reciprocally dependent on the marginal votes of members of groups other than their own. The electoral system can do this despite the wishes of the politicians, by making vote pooling profitable.

There are several ways of doing this. I shall illustrate one way rather quickly and two at greater length, because I can then also demonstrate the impact of such techniques by a paired comparison.

Lebanon is a severely divided society which had more than thirty years of peace because of intricate accommodative arrangements. Peace did not break down in Lebanon because of any fault in the electoral arrangements; it broke down *despite* these arrangements, because powerful forces overtook them.

All elected positions in Lebanon were assigned by sectarian group. The president was required to be a Maronite, the prime minister a Sunni, the speaker of the house a Shiite. Likewise, virtually all parliamentary seats were reserved. So it was Maronite versus Maronite, Sunni versus Sunni, etc. Immediately, there was intraethnic competition among politicians and a concomitant reduction of interethnic competition. But every voter voted for all the candidates running in the constituency. The typical parliamentary constituency was multimember, and each of the seats was reserved to a different group—for example, one Druze, one Sunni, one Shiite, one Maronite. This led to the creation of competing interethnic tickets, because a Sunni candidate, relying only on himself, could easily be defeated by a Sunni rival who added Druze, Shiite, and Maronite votes to his Sunni votes. So there was intraethnic competition *and* interethnic cooperation and moderation, because a Maronite candidate could not persuade his supporters to vote for a Sunni with whom he was aligned unless he could assure them that *this* Sunni was one who understood Maronite concerns. This, then, was a system with powerful tendencies toward conciliation. I cite it not because it is apt for Northern Ireland, but only to show how a clever system can be designed for this purpose in a severely divided society.

Now to a more detailed comparison, which shows that divided societies that do not design such systems can end up in a worse condition than even more severely divided societies that do. The comparison is Sri Lanka versus Malaysia.

Sri Lanka had the easier problem but political institutions that exacerbated it; Malaysia had the harder problem but institutions that ameliorated it—and the difference is cast in terms of incentives for politicians to behave moderately.

At independence, anyone forecasting the ethnic future of the two countries would have predicted far more difficulty for Malaysia than for Sri Lanka. Relative group proportions, conceptions of group legitimacy, recent political events, the relations of elites of the various groups, and the political culture of the two countries all suggested a Sri Lankan advantage.

1. *Numbers.* The Sri Lankan Tamils were a mere 11 percent of the

population at independence. The Malaysian Chinese were more than one-third and the Indians about 10 percent of the Malaysian population, so the non-Malay total was about half the Malaysian population.

2. *Indigenousness.* The Sri Lankan Tamils arrived, on average, one thousand years ago. The Chinese and Indians, on the other hand, were relatively recent migrants to Malaysia. The Sri Lankan Tamils were citizens. The Chinese and Indians, by and large, were not. The Tamils were legitimate participants in the political system and were early participants in the national movement. The Chinese were not accepted as legitimate participants in Malaysian politics. Segments of the Malay press were advocating the return of the Chinese to China. The Malays were regarded as "sons of the soil," having priority in the country. The Sinhalese did not use that term or make such distinctions.

3. *Events around independence.* Recent events were unconducive to peaceful ethnic relations in Malaya. During World War II, Chinese guerrillas, in conflict with the Japanese, had fought Malay villagers who resisted their exactions of food. After the war, the guerrillas emerged from the jungle, proclaimed the abolition of Malay sultanates, and purported to annex Malaya to China. Until the British completed the reoccupation of Malaya, there were bloodbaths up and down the peninsula. Thereafter, Chinese guerrillas returned to the jungle to fight the British and the largely Malay armed forces in the emergency of 1948–60. These battles had the character of ethnic hostilities, undermining the Chinese position in the country. In Ceylon, the Tamils were well represented in the Ceylon Defence Force during the war and in the Ceylon army after independence. Tamil leaders had asked for ethnically balanced representation in Parliament, but the British had rejected that. Independence nevertheless found the Tamils with ministerial portfolios.

4. *Elites.* Malay and Chinese elites were divided by the structure of educational institutions in colonial and post-colonial Malaya. By contrast, Sinhalese and Tamil elites were brought together by the educational system in Ceylon. The Malay top elite was segregated in the Malay College at Kuala Kangsar, which was modeled on the British public school. No comparable monoethnic institution existed in Ceylon. The result was that Malay and Chinese leaders were not, at first, on intimate terms, whereas Sinhalese and Tamil leaders frequently knew each other well. There was, in Ceylon, a genuinely intercommunal elite, sharing many common values. The same description would certainly not hold for the Malayan elite at independence.

5. *Interethnic diplomacy and political culture.* Malay politicians were quite discriminating and cautious about whom they would deal with. Some Malay newspapers were urging "no diplomacy with the Chinese." The Ceylonese, by contrast, had a bargaining political culture. No agreement was automatically foreclosed. Tamil parties dealt with several Sinhalese parties, and vice versa. "What are your terms?" was a phrase frequently heard. Party discussions often revolved around whether a better deal could be obtained from some party other than the one with which negotiations were being conducted. For interethnic negotiations, it is reasonable to assume that such a bargaining political culture is more advantageous than one that puts a premium on personal relations, is hesitant to deal at arm's length, and has a set of unwritten rules governing interethnic negotiations.

On all of these grounds, Sri Lanka started out with considerable advantages. But, despite those favorable conditions, Sri Lanka is in the midst of a violent ethnic conflict. Despite Malaysia's unfavorable conditions, Malaysia is at peace. The last serious episode of ethnic violence was in May 1969. This contrast is not fortuitous. Malaysia has had the more difficult problem, but it has also had better conflict management.

The most important contrast between Malaysian and Sri Lankan ethnic policies has been the role of interethnic political coalitions, based on vote pooling, in the two countries. The dominant parties in Sri Lanka have all been ethnically based, whereas the dominant force in Malaysia has been a permanent interethnic coalition of ethnically based parties—namely, the Alliance and its successor, the National Front.

By the mid-1950s, practically all Sri Lankan Tamils had abandoned Sinhalese parties and moved either to the Tamil Congress or the Federal Party. Thereafter, Sri Lanka's party system revolved around the competition of the two main Sinhalese parties for Sinhalese votes and the two main Tamil parties for Tamil votes until the two Tamil parties merged in 1972. The dynamics of intraethnic competition, especially for the Sinhalese vote, pushed the parties toward meeting ethnic demands and limited their leeway to make concessions across ethnic lines.

The rise of the Sri Lanka Freedom Party (SLFP) as the main competitor to the United National Party (UNP) in the 1950s went hand in hand with appeals to Sinhalese ethnic sentiment. After the landslide victory of the SLFP-led coalition in 1956, a "Sinhalese Only" language act was passed, and Tamil civil servants were discriminated against on linguistic grounds. Rebuffed at the polls, the UNP responded by becoming as anti-Tamil as the SLFP. When Mr. S. W. R. D. Bandaranaike attempted to cool down Sinhalese-Tamil tension by a compromise agreement with the Federal Party in 1957, the UNP campaigned against it, and the compromise was abandoned. From 1960 to 1965, when Mrs. Sirimavo Bandaranaike was in power, there was a further acceleration of favoritism toward Sinhalese Buddhists. The UNP-led coalition of 1965 to 1968 made some concessions to redress Tamil grievances, but these came to an abrupt halt when the SLFP opposed them and UNP backbenchers feared losing their seats to SLFP candidates if they went along. Interethnic compromise was strictly limited by intraethnic electoral competition between the two main Sinhalese parties. This is a phenomenon not entirely unknown in Northern Ireland.

Mrs. Bandaranaike's second regime, from 1970 to 1977, was characterized by a virulent anti-Tamil strain. In 1972, a new constitution was promulgated. By its terms, Buddhism was accorded a "foremost place" in the country. The constitution utterly ignored the Tamil presence in the country. Around the same time, a scheme to "standardize marks" was implemented. Its effect was to reduce the grades received by Tamil students on university entrance examinations, thereby depriving large numbers of Tamil students of the higher education for which they were plainly more qualified than many of the Sinhalese students who were admitted in their place. An entire half generation of recruits for Tamil separatist organizations was thereby created, and the seeds were planted for guerrilla warfare.

Underlying this process of bidding and outbidding for the Sinhalese vote was an electoral system that translated small swings in popular votes into large swings in seats. The system was first-past-the-post in mainly single-member, largely homogeneous constituencies. With multiparty competition in the Sinhalese South, it was often possible to win a parliamentary majority on a plurality of 30 to 40 percent of the popular vote. In every parliamentary election from 1952 to 1970—six times, in fact—there was alternation in office between the SLFP and the UNP. In the South, the vast majority of constituencies was overwhelmingly Sinhalese in composition. As a result, parties derived rich rewards from appealing to Sinhalese ethnic sentiment and opposing proposals to conciliate the Tamils.

The combination of (1) largely homogeneous constituencies, (2) plurality elections in mainly single-member constituencies, and (3) a competitive party configuration on the Sinhalese side that produced two main contenders for power and two plausible contenders for nearly every seat created a system exceedingly sensitive to Sinhalese opinion and inhospitable to interethnic accommodation.

Several of these conditions were later altered. In 1978, the UNP government promulgated a new constitution. A separately elected presidency was instituted. The president is now elected by a system of preferential voting that accords weight to voters' second choices in a way that these choices had not been weighted in plurality elections for Parliament. To be elected president, a candidate needs a majority. Under preferential voting, if no candidate receives a majority of first-preference ballots, second preferences of voters whose first choices are not among the top two candidates are then counted. Under this system, Tamil second preferences for president will be reallocated as if they were first preferences whenever the Tamil candidate is not among the top two, as, of course, he or she never will be. So Tamil second preferences could provide the margin of victory, and prudent presidential candidates could hardly ignore Tamil interests under such conditions. Since presidential candidates will make deals with Tamil parties to pool votes, and Tamil parties will only make such deals with Sinhalese candidates who are moderate on Tamil issues, candidates will sort themselves out with respect to their position on Tamil issues.

By the time the preferential voting system was put into effect, however, separatist violence had begun in earnest, and Sinhalese and Tamil opinion had so polarized that, in the short term at least, no electoral system could foster moderation. In the two presidential elections held under this system, the withdrawal of the Tamils from legitimate politics and civil war conditions have prevented the conciliatory features of this ingenious system from having an effect thus far.

Few conditions were different in Malaysia, and yet the results have been dramatically different. Malaysia also had first-past-the-post elections in single-member constituencies, as well as party competition revolving around attention to mutually exclusive ethnic claims. In contrast to Sri Lanka, however, interethnic compromise has also had a claim on party attention; and moderation, as well as extremism, has brought political rewards.

Three differences changed the balance of incentives. These related to timing, the composition of constituencies, and the role of political self-interest.

The first difference was fortuitous. Malaysians began working on interethnic accommodation early. They had had a bitter taste of violence during and after World War II and did not wait until accumulated grievances were about to break into widespread violence. But electoral incentives also played a big part, as I shall suggest.

The second difference is the existence of many more ethnically heterogeneous parliamentary constituencies in Malaysia than in Sri Lanka. In Malaysia, the electorate in the 1964 elections was 38 percent Chinese and 8 percent Indian. Forty percent of the parliamentary constituencies had Chinese pluralities and non-Malay majorities. Another 20 percent had an electorate that was at least 30 percent Chinese. In Sri Lanka, only 11 percent of parliamentary constituencies had a Sri Lankan Tamil plurality, and in all but one of these Tamils comprised the vast majority of the constituency. In 81 percent of all constituencies, Tamils constituted less than 10 percent of the electorate. In Malaysia, by contrast, Chinese comprised less than 10 percent of the electorate in only 18 percent of all constituencies—a graphic illustration of how much more heterogeneous Malaysian constituencies were. These contrasts occurred not just because the Chinese were more numerous than the Sri Lankan Tamils, but because the Tamils and the Sinhalese are much more regionally concentrated. So in overwhelmingly Sinhalese constituencies, there simply was no electoral constraint on taking anti-Tamil positions. The 1 or 2 percent of voters who were Tamil could hardly offer anything in return for the moderation of a Sinhalese candidate. Overall there were many more Sinhalese votes to be had by being extreme than there were Tamil votes to be had by being moderate. And likewise in the country as a whole: no Tamil party could help a Sinhalese party win a hotly contested Sinhalese-majority constituency by contributing marginal Tamil votes (and vice versa for Sinhalese help for Tamil candidates). Consequently, interethnic coalitions based on vote pooling were unlikely, since vote pooling could not really occur, given the nature of the territorial constituencies.

Malaysia's heterogeneous constituencies made ethnic calculations more complex. In many constituencies, Chinese voters could punish Malay extremists and reward moderates. There were not always more Malay votes to be gained than Chinese votes to be lost by taking extreme positions. By the same token, Chinese and Malay parties could pool votes profitably at the constituency level and come out ahead. Where there were more Malays than Chinese in a constituency, a Chinese party could urge its supporters to vote for a friendly Malay candidate, and vice versa where there were more Chinese than Malays in a constituency. Parties might still evolve along wholly ethnic lines, but, especially if there were more than one party per ethnic group, there would be countervailing incentives fostering interethnic coalition.

It is important to note that the structure of constituencies is not a given: it is not a function of mere demography and geography. If ethnic groups are geographically concentrated and heterogeneous constituencies are regarded as desirable, it is possible to do what the Nigerians did and what the Sri Lankans later did—namely, make the whole country one large heterogeneous constituency for the purpose of electing a president. And, to turn the conventional wisdom around, perhaps the greatest utility of a presidential system in a divided society has nothing to do with the separation of powers. Rather, it is that it permits the institution of electoral devices that can guarantee vote pooling across ethnic lines.

The third difference between Malaysia and Sri Lanka follows from the first two. An interethnic coalition was formed before independence, and it occupied the center of the ethnic spectrum. It was formed, not out of "statesmanship," not out of goodwill or tolerant attitudes—these were not always present—but out of selfish electoral calculations. The two parties that came together were in danger of losing crucial elections before independence that would undermine all their subsequent claims in negotiations for independence. These were town council elections, in which non-Malay votes were especially important. Once the coalition was formed for these elections and made permanent, other parties—all of them ethnically based—took extreme positions on the flanks, locking the coalition into the center. With Malay and Chinese votes split, the center coalition could not compete with the extreme parties in taking extreme positions, and there were often more votes to be had across ethnic lines by being conciliatory on ethnic issues than there were within one's own group by being extreme. Had the interethnic coalition not been formed, the configuration of Malaysian politics would resemble that of Sri Lankan politics, and Malaysian ethnic relations would be in the same parlous— or, very likely, even worse—condition.

If there are any morals in all of this for Northern Ireland, they would seem to be the following:

First, in a severely divided society, it is futile to devote too much attention to trying to make people love and respect each other. It is more fruitful to try to encourage decent behavior by politicians, whatever they may feel in their hearts.

Second, the most enduring basis for interethnic conciliation in a severely divided society, where communal allegiances are politicized, lies in an electoral system that creates some incentives that reward moderation, even though other incentives continue to reward extremism.

Third, an electoral reform without regard to all the functions of elections in severely divided societies—apart from the function of merely providing representation in accordance with numbers—will not help, may make things worse, and may convince people, incorrectly, that nothing works.

Fourth, a plan for "power-sharing" from the top down, without the appropriate, underlying electoral incentives for power-sharing, will fail and, furthermore, will reinforce the false notion that a substantial reform has been implemented without success. This is the sort of "power-sharing" Northern Ireland has attempted.

12

The origins and rationale of
the Anglo-Irish Agreement of 1985

GARRET FITZGERALD

On one issue in particular my views have remained constant throughout my life, that is, the futility of attempting to achieve Irish political unity by force or by constraint, or otherwise than with the free consent of a majority of the people of Northern Ireland.

A logical corollary of this stance has been a concern to develop a constructive dialogue between the Irish state and the unionist community in Northern Ireland, which must be linked to a move to create conditions within the Irish state that economically, socially, and culturally would be attractive rather than repellent to Northern unionists.

Such a policy, however, should not be pursued at the expense of the nationalist minority in Northern Ireland; on the contrary, I believe that the removal of discrimination could logically be facilitated by an improvement in North-South relations, which would eliminate a primary cause of the pursuit by unionists of discriminatory policies against the Northern nationalist minority, namely, fear of being overwhelmed by Irish nationalism.

Nevertheless, there can be no disguising the fact that in the pursuit of such a policy, tensions could arise from time to time between a proper concern for the right of the nationalist population in Northern Ireland to be free from discrimination and the longer-term objective of improving relations with the unionist community.

In 1968–69 the inability of unionism to react constructively to the

GARRET FITZGERALD was leader of Fine Gael, 1977–87; Irish Minister for Foreign Affairs, 1973–77; and Taoiseach (prime minister), 1981–82 and 1982–87. He is the author of *Planning in Ireland, Towards a New Ireland, Unequal Partners,* and *All in a Life.*

civil rights movement—which in practical terms involved the nationalist minority's seeking belatedly to opt into the Northern Ireland system on a basis of equal treatment—created tensions, which led to the suspension of devolved government in Northern Ireland in 1972. The aftermath of these events provided an opportunity for the Irish government that took office in 1973 to seek to pursue a constructive relationship with the unionist leadership under Brian Faulkner. This effort, which contributed to the signing of the Sunningdale Agreement, failed because of the resistance of important elements of unionism to the provisions of that agreement for power-sharing in Northern Ireland and a new North-South relationship through a Council of Ireland. The experiment collapsed after the Ulster Workers' Council strike of May 1974.

In the aftermath of these events the future of Northern Ireland was clouded in uncertainty. The British government was less than candid with the Irish government about the subsequent review of its policy on Northern Ireland and in particular about its discussions with Sinn Féin in early 1975, which seemed at the time open to the interpretation of being in some sense a preparation for a possible British withdrawal from Northern Ireland. During that year of uncertainty the Irish government pursued a dual policy of seeking to reassure the nationalist minority while avoiding any specific commitment as to the course of action it would pursue in the event of a British withdrawal, and at the same time establishing a constructive, unofficial relationship with the leaders of the Official Unionist Party who had been involved in the process of undermining the Sunningdale Agreement. During 1976 and the first half of 1977, these contacts with Official Unionists proved particularly friendly and fruitful. However, they do not appear to have been maintained following the change of government in the South in June 1977.

In opposition, Fine Gael produced a policy document on Northern Ireland in 1979. This included a suggestion for a possible loose confederation of two Irish states that would devolve upwards—to a confederal government in which both parts of Ireland would be *equally* represented—powers in relation to external affairs, security, and monetary matters, as well as some financial matters. The two states could have different heads of state to whom and by whom ambassadors could be accredited. Northern Ireland, sharing equally in this confederal structure, would have a right to alternate with the Southern state in key positions in the confederal government, and also in respect of Irish representation in the European Community.

This proposal was relatively well received by unionists in Northern Ireland; Harry West, who was then leader of the Official Unionist Party, while describing it as "of no interest," nevertheless said that his party would be willing to have talks on it. The leader of another small unionist party of that period, Ernest Baird, said that it would be wrong to dismiss it. Ian Paisley somewhat pointedly avoided committing himself either way on the proposals in the document.

The Fine Gael/Labour government elected in June 1981 was deeply preoccupied during its early weeks in office with the hunger strike, but in August a Northern Ireland review conference of ministers and officials decided to give priority to developing our contacts with leading unionists including, if at all possible, Ian Paisley, with a view to seeing how they could become involved in structures that might flow from the joint-studies process that had been initiated following the summit meetings between Charles Haughey and Margaret Thatcher the previous year. It was also agreed at this conference that it would be desirable to modify the provisions of Articles 2 and 3 of our constitution with regard to Northern Ireland, with a view to creating more favorable conditions where possible for discussions with unionists. It was as a result of this that I launched the idea of a constitutional review in a radio broadcast in September 1981.

Meanwhile I had taken steps to secure a presentation of the unionist case to public opinion in the Republic by encouraging a visit of a unionist group led by Bob McCartney. The aim was to alert public opinion in our state to the issues that would have to be confronted in any negotiations with the unionists.

At that stage the full impact of the hunger strike on nationalist opinion in Northern Ireland had not become clear. It became evident during 1982 that the handling of the hunger strike by the British government had radicalized a significant proportion of nationalist opinion in Northern Ireland, leading to considerable additional support for Sinn Féin and the Irish Republican Army (IRA). I came to the conclusion then that, whatever my own personal commitment to seeking progress by dialogue with the unionists rather than by talking over their heads to the British, I could not in conscience persist with such a policy if, as then seemed likely, such persistence in an approach that showed no signs of yielding any results in the foreseeable future were merely to play into the hands of the IRA, even further increasing, perhaps to a dangerous degree, support for the IRA in Northern Ireland. Nor in prevailing circumstances could I reasonably reject the need to combine some kind of "Irish dimension" with our devolution policy, for to do so merely would have contributed further to a possibly disastrous radicalization of Northern nationalist opinion and an erosion of the position of the Social Democratic and Labour Party (SDLP) in favor of Sinn Féin.

These issues were now emerging as potential threats to the security of the island, including the Republic. If the IRA became able to claim credibly to enjoy majority support within the nationalist community in Northern Ireland, it could not be excluded that it might be emboldened to raise the threshold of violence to the point of risking outright civil war in the North, something from which it had always hitherto drawn back when its activities had seemed in danger of producing such a result. Nevertheless, in the Dimbleby Lecture, "Irish Identities," which I delivered on BBC Television in May 1982, I still placed the main emphasis on a need to seek common ground between the two traditions in Northern Ireland with a view to providing structures that would respect their diversity. Moreover, I went on to say, we should seek to create in our own state the kind of pluralist society that might have evolved if Ireland had not been divided sixty years earlier.

I also suggested in this lecture the introduction of an all-Ireland policing and judicial system that would help the British and ourselves ensure that members of the IRA could not evade arrest and conviction by passing rapidly from one jurisdiction to another. And with regard to an eventual political solution I suggested that we should look for a structure, however novel, that would enable the people of Ireland to tackle together things that could not be done as well separately, such as security and the pursuit of the interests of all the Irish people in the European Community where these interests differed from those of Britain. I also proposed that Ireland and Britain should move toward a form of common citizenship.

This lecture thus foreshadowed some of the themes that were to be taken up in the New Ireland Forum in 1983–84 and in the Anglo-Irish negotiations of 1984–85—although at the time of the lecture I had not come to a firm conclusion as to the details of the approach I would adopt in relation to these issues when in government again.

Later, in October 1982, SDLP leader John Hume told me of his intention to propose the establishment of a nationalist Council for a New Ireland. I saw merit in seeking to establish common ground among nationalists North and South as a preliminary to negotiations with the British government directed toward reducing the alienation of the minority in Northern Ireland. However, it seemed to me desirable to provide an opportunity for a wider discussion that would involve unionists as well as nationalists, although I recognized that it was most improbable that the unionist parties as such would join in such an enterprise. In a speech in October 1982 in Pittsburgh, Pennsylvania, I therefore proposed consultations involving all the parties in the Dáil together with "all in Northern Ireland who might be willing to talk to us, however informally, whether they be organized in political parties or not, and whether they sought, opposed, or (less probably!) were indifferent to, the development of a new political relationship between North and South." The discussion should be "with all in Northern Ireland who may see merit in reducing tension within our island, and should be designed to seek the help of those concerned in identifying those aspects of the Constitution, laws, and social arrangements of our State which pose obstacles to understanding amongst the people of this island."

On my reelection to government in December 1982, these ideas began to take more concrete shape in my mind. The fact that Sinn Féin had secured 10 percent of the vote in Northern Ireland—over a quarter of the total nationalist vote—in the Assembly election in October, and the likelihood that it would build on this to increase its share of the vote still further, imbued me with a sense of urgency about securing arrangements that would reduce the alienation of a large part of the nationalist minority from the institutions of Northern Ireland. I believed that this might be achieved by seeking some form of joint authority in Northern Ireland that would involve the Irish government in a manner that might end the alienation of the minority and make it possible to secure nationalist support for the institutions of government and policing in Northern Ireland.

I recognized, however, that such a move would be seen or represented by Fianna Fáil as an unacceptable compromise that fell short of the aspiration to Irish unity. I also realized that opposition from this source could make it impossible for me to secure the necessary public support for my objective of creating the conditions in which peace and stability could be restored to Northern Ireland and the IRA marginalized.

It was in this context that I presented to the government my idea of a New Ireland Forum that would both provide a platform for the presentation of the unionist case to public opinion in the Republic, with a view to generating a more informed public approach to the Northern Ireland problem, and at the same time hopefully secure a sufficient measure of support or acceptance on the part of Fianna Fáil for my proposed approach to the problem of the alienation of the minority in the North.

The initial reaction of the government to my proposal was strongly negative; only two ministers supported me. However I secured immediately a reversal of this initial negative reaction. I then presented my proposal to John Hume, making it clear to him that I was not prepared to accept his narrower concept of a nationalist Council for a New Ireland, and seeking his support for a New Ireland Forum open to all parties. Once he accepted my proposal I asked him to assist me in securing acceptance by Fianna Fáil of the establishment of this forum, acceptance that I felt might not be withheld once the SDLP had agreed to participate. This tactic was successful: the New Ireland Forum was established, and started working in May 1983.

What I hoped to secure from the forum in practical terms was a two-fold result:

First, I hoped that there would emerge from it a set of principles for the achievement of peace and stability in Northern Ireland—which was the stated aim of the forum, the terms of reference of which deliberately contained *no* reference to Irish unity—and that these principles would provide a common basis upon which the Irish and British governments could proceed in relation to negotiations.

The second result I hoped to achieve was the emergence of a number of "models" for a possible eventual resolution of the Northern Ireland problem. These would include, as well as a unitary state and a federation or confederation, the idea of joint sovereignty or joint authority—leaving open, however, other possible models that could emerge from negotiations. By securing acceptance in the report of the forum of a joint-sovereignty or joint-authority model I would, I believed, have eliminated, or at any rate greatly weakened, a possible Fianna Fáil objection to whatever might eventually emerge from a negotiation, which would inevitably be something other than a united Ireland.

These twin objectives were in fact secured in the report of the forum even though this outcome was somewhat obscured by the attempt of the Fianna Fáil leader, Charles Haughey, when presenting his views on the report, to suggest that the parties to the forum had agreed that a unitary state was "the only solution"—a view the other parties had specifically and unwaveringly refused to accept.

Meanwhile, in summer 1983 I authorized a "deniable" approach to the British government designed to attract the attention and interest of

Prime Minister Margaret Thatcher as she prepared to establish the priorities for her second term of office. This approach involved a suggestion of a willingness on our part to assist in defusing nationalist alienation through our direct involvement in the security process in Northern Ireland, should this commend itself to the British government.

In November, at a summit meeting with the British prime minister, I explained the rationale for the New Ireland Forum and what I hoped would emerge from it. I confirmed our willingness to consider joint action in Northern Ireland, should this commend itself to the British government. But the issue of joint action was not pursued between us at this meeting because of Margaret Thatcher's sensitivity to the possibility of questions in Parliament on this issue as a result of a recent airing of it in the media. I also reluctantly agreed that no negotiations would take place between the two governments until the forum report had been completed and publicized. My approach secured the prime minister's interest and was in fact followed in March 1984 by a British initiative along lines that, however, did not commend themselves to us.

After presentation of the forum report in May 1984 we initiated formal discussions with the British government at official level, presenting the three models set out in the report and filling out the joint-authority proposal. This latter proposal of ours provided for the exclusion of defense, foreign policy, and finance from the scope of joint authority, although there might be consultations on these issues, and certain functions such as representation of some or all of Northern Ireland's interest in the European Community could, by agreement between the two governments and after consultation with the Northern Ireland Assembly, pass from British to Irish responsibility. Joint authority, the establishment of which we saw as an exercise of sovereignty by the United Kingdom, was proposed, involving a full-time cabinet minister from each government; it would directly control certain reserved areas until such time as responsibility for these was transferred to a Northern Ireland executive. In the security area, a system of joint command was proposed with alternating command at the highest level, and an all-Ireland court was also envisaged. As a basis for negotiations along these lines we proposed early agreement on a public statement that the two governments based themselves on the principles set out in the "Present Realities and Future Requirements" section of the forum report. These proposals had been formally authorized by our government, after a full discussion in cabinet.

However, in the light of a reported negative initial reaction from the

British prime minister to our suggestions, I came to the conclusion shortly afterward that if the initiative were not to founder very quickly we should indicate at least a possibility of movement on Articles 2 and 3 of our constitution in return for a major package involving some form of joint authority.

In July 1984 we received the formal British response to our proposals, which involved rejection of the unitary state and the federal and confederal models. However, we were told that the British government had been much more cautious about rejecting the joint-authority proposal, although what it had really concentrated on had been our openness to other views, which had been expressed in the final paragraph of the forum report. There was acceptance of the need for some sort of joint action in security operations. However, the British saw insuparable difficulties with anything that looked like joint sovereignty and felt that the distinction we had made between joint authority as an exercise of sovereignty and actual sharing of sovereignty would seem very fine to unionists in Northern Ireland. They had, however, been trying to find a way around this and they wondered if a system of government in Northern Ireland in which the Irish government would have a part, but which would not seem to involve a derogation of British sovereignty and yet would be seen by the nationalist minority as an effective protection of its interests, would be possible. An Irish resident presence in Belfast could be an element in such a package.

It was on this basis that negotiations proceeded in the months that followed. But with the involvement of the Northern Ireland Office in the British negotiating team from September onward and the appointment of Douglas Hurd as Northern Ireland secretary there was a noticeable retreat on the part of the British negotiators. At the summit meeting in November 1984 the British government not only pulled back from positions that had hitherto been under discussion but played down the value of amending Articles 2 and 3—the importance of which I had stressed in a private discussion with Margaret Thatcher at the outset of this meeting—and pressed the view that the more limited proposals it was now putting forward could be implemented without our having to change our constitution.

Although the discussion at this meeting had thus taken a highly negative turn, the agreed communiqué had a positive tone, and at a subsequent press conference the British prime minister went to considerable trouble to present our discussions in a most positive light. Unhappily, the tone of voice in which she responded to a particular question about the three forum models had a totally negative impact on the minds of the media, who came to the conclusion that the negotiations were effectively at an end.

However, the extremely negative reaction that this comment induced not merely in Ireland but also in British political circles and among the public in Britain and elsewhere, together with concern expressed about the situation to the British prime minister by President Ronald Reagan at a meeting between the two shortly afterward in Washington, led to a radical reconsideration of the British stance. In January 1985 the British put forth proposals of a much more substantial character than those adumbrated at the November summit, making it clear at the same time that they were not seeking or expecting an amendment to Articles 2 and 3 as a *quid pro quo* for what they were now suggesting.

The new British proposals involved the establishment, within the Anglo-Irish intergovernmental framework set up in 1981, of a joint body to consider—in relation to Northern Ireland—legal matters, relations between the police and the community, prisons policy, security coordination, and political human rights questions, as well as other topics that might be agreed. Within this joint body every effort would be made to resolve differences rather than simply report them to the two governments. There would be a joint secretariat in Belfast with ministers from the two governments as joint chairs of the joint body. The question of joint or mixed courts for terrorist crimes would be considered by a subcommittee. In relation to policing, the body would put in hand a program of action that would include, among other things, the establishment of local consultative machinery, improvements in the handling of complaints, and action to increase the proportion of Catholics in the Royal Ulster Constabulary (RUC), the main object of all this being to make the police more readily acceptable among the nationalist community. There was to be a new structure to protect human rights and to prevent discrimination, and our views would be taken into account in appointments to a number of bodies. Finally the proposal for a British-Irish parliamentary tier was described as "still open."

It was on this basis that the negotiations proceeded during early 1985. By the end of April, however, it was becoming clear that our proposals for "confidence-building measures," as they were then described, which would involve the RUC and the Ulster Defence Regiment (UDR) and would include a possible review of prison sentences related to a reduction of violence, were not being given adequate attention on the British side. When I met Margaret Thatcher in Milan in June our discussions centered on these issues. In response to her reaction to the effect that, on their side, they were already afraid they had gone too far, I made it clear that our government had come to the conclusion that unless these "associated measures," as they were by now being described, were implemented simultaneously with the signing of the agreement, the government could not back the agreement. After a somewhat heated discussion the prime minister conceded that steps could be taken in respect of these matters, but suggested that these steps should be described as "implementing part of the agreement" rather than as involving "associated measures."

In the months that followed, agreement was reached in relation to issues such as the accompaniment of the British Army and the UDR by the police and the appointment of additional Catholic judges to the higher courts in Northern Ireland with a view to modifying a religious imbalance in these courts.

The primary concern of the Irish government throughout the negotiations had been to secure an outcome likely to have a significant impact on the alienation of much of the nationalist population from the political and security systems in Northern Ireland. While the outcome of the negotiations, in relation to security matters in particular, fell short of our objectives, with the result that it seemed unlikely that the particular aim of achieving a full identification by the minority with the policing system in Northern Ireland would be achieved, we judged that the proposed new structure would significantly enhance support among the nationalist community for constitutional politics, and would have a significant adverse effect on support for and tolerance of the IRA within this community.

From early in 1985 onward there was concern among members of the Irish government as to the possible reaction of unionists to an agreement along the lines that seemed to be emerging. In contacts with unionist politicians around that time we formed the impression that, especially in the case of the Official Unionist Party, some of those concerned had a very good idea of what was in preparation as a result of informal briefings by British officials without, however, having seen the actual language proposed, and that they did not seem to find these ideas as alarming as expected. When we had passed on this impression to the British in February they had responded by saying there was not a monolithic unionist view; they wondered if the Official Unionists would "come up to scratch," and if they could deliver the voters if Paisley sought a massive disapproval vote. Several months later we were given further information by a senior unionist politician concerning the briefing on the negotiations which he had received from a Northern Ireland Office official.

The question of unionist attitudes to the impending agreement was raised again by members of the government at a meeting in mid-September at which further information was sought on the contacts we had been having with representatives of the different parties and other interests in Northern Ireland. A report on this was furnished to a government meeting at the beginning of October. In this report the government was told that an important factor in assessing the current mood in Northern Ireland was that there had been widespread leaking by the British side of the progress achieved and about the discussions taking place between the two governments. These leaks had included information on the possibility of some form of Irish presence in Belfast, of significant changes in the security area involving the RUC and UDR, and of a proposal by us for a mixed court for the trial of terrorist offenses. Our officials also understood that as James Molyneaux, leader of the Official Unionist Party, was a privy councillor, the British government probably had kept him well informed on a Privy Council basis as the talks had progressed. Reference was also made to numerous contacts that our officials had had with members of the Official Unionist Party and the Democratic Unionist Party (DUP), which had indicated that briefings of varying content had been given to a number of members of these two parties.

The report went on to say that there were indications that there would be significant opposition to the agreement from the unionists; a leading DUP member had told us that the argument the British government would use in trying to sell an agreement to the unionists, to the effect that it would help to defeat the IRA, would not be enough to compensate for what the unionists would see as an infringement of sovereignty. Moreover, leading members of the Official Unionist Party had told us that their party would oppose any role for Dublin other than a minimal consultative one. If a ministerial or official presence in Belfast were involved, it would be "very difficult" for unionists to see that as other than an infringement of sovereignty.

Nevertheless, this report to the government continued, it was widely believed by serious observers and among middle-class moderate unionists with whom we had been in touch, that the vast majority of the unionist population wanted peace and stability and would be prepared to accept a role for the Irish government and some form of power-sharing for Northern nationalists if the result were to be peace in Northern Ireland. Some unionist politicians had been more forthcoming and less belligerent in private than in public.

In a verbal briefing accompanying the memorandum, I told my colleagues that we had indicated to the British government that we had felt there could be a case for a more formal briefing of the unionists on the agreement, but that the British had made the point that there was a great difference between the unionists and the SDLP. The latter wanted the negotiations to succeed if the outcome were right in their view, but there was no similar guarantee as regards the unionists. Our response to this had been that any such briefing would require the use of judgment and discretion, but that if possible a situation should be devised such that the unionists could not say afterward, "Of course, if you had told us what was going on . . . " We had made clear to the British that, while it was the view of our ministers that the British should consider briefing the unionists, we recognized that of course they might judge that it was better not to do so. In response to this, the British had said that they had in fact thought about it, and that "something had been given to Molyneaux in his role as a Privy Councillor" but not to the DUP on the same scale, because, of course, its leader Ian Paisley was not a privy councillor.

On the basis of this information, and in the light of hints to us from some unionist sources that public indignation against an agreement would be accompanied by a measure of private acquiescence, I offered some reassurance to the members of the government who were concerned about the possibility of unionist political reaction. At the same time, however, I told them that the best information we had would suggest that there could be a significant violent backlash from paramilitaries on both sides.

It later became clear that we had overestimated the extent of briefing that had been provided by the British to Molyneaux personally and had underestimated Molyneaux's unwillingness to face realities—encouraged, we heard later, by Enoch Powell. It was only after the agreement had been signed that we were told that it had come as a great shock to Molyneaux; that he had refused a Privy Council briefing, contrary to what we had earlier understood; and that his contacts with Enoch Powell, and perhaps with a member of the British cabinet, had led him to believe there would be no agreement, or at any rate that there would be no agreement that did not include an amendment of Articles 2 and 3. Accordingly he had discounted all the media leaks that had been intended to alert him and his colleagues to what was likely to emerge.[1] Despite efforts on my own part, there had been no contact between our government and Molyneaux during this period.

From all this it will be clear that the agreement was never envisaged by the Irish government as an attempt to "downface" the unionists, as they subsequently alleged. From the inception of the whole process that led to the agreement the objective had been to weaken support for the IRA by reducing the alienation of the nationalist minority in Northern Ireland and to stabilize the position in that area by creating conditions in which this minority could identify with the system of authority there as it had not previously been able to do.

It should, of course, be added that until the eve of the signing of the agreement we were uncertain also about the nature of the reaction to it that we could expect from Northern nationalists. From an early stage the SDLP leader, John Hume, had been kept in touch with developments, and during the first half of 1985 the deputy leader, Seamus Mallon, and two other leading members were brought into our confidence. However, they quite properly retained their independence of action, pending consultation with their colleagues when the agreement finally was settled.

The form the agreement eventually took was less helpful than we had originally hoped in terms of ending nationalist alienation and securing nationalist acceptance of the institutions and security structure in Northern Ireland, and until a couple of days before the agreement was signed we were not certain that it would secure the support of all the leading members of the SDLP. In the final discussion that took place with the SDLP leaders, I told them that what had emerged fell short of our aspirations and that in signing it the Irish government realized it was taking a considerable risk—as of course the SDLP would be doing in supporting it. But within the agreement there was, I believed, a potential for much more progress—and even if we failed I had no doubt that it had been worth trying. The SDLP leaders then gave the agreement their unanimous support.

It should be said that both governments anticipated a significant increase in violence from both the IRA and loyalist paramilitaries in the

---

[1]Subsequent to the publication of my autobiography (*All in a Life*) in 1991 a statement was issued by the Official Unionist Party to the effect that from January 1985 onward it had in fact been kept informed of the developing negotiations by a civil servant and that the agreement did not therefore come as a surprise. The above account of the position as seen by the Irish and British governments must be read in this context.

aftermath of the agreement and made preparations to deal with such a contingency. In the event, however, there was no significant upsurge in violence in the period immediately following the agreement, and the level of violence in 1986 was no greater than in the immediately preceding year—contrary to the impression subsequently fostered by some interested parties.

One further point should, perhaps, be added by way of footnote. In the early months of 1985 there were indications that support for the IRA had already started to wane and that the danger that had led us to initiate these negotiations—that the IRA might be encouraged by increased support among the nationalist minority in Northern Ireland to raise the level of violence to a civil-war level—was diminishing. Nevertheless, although the urgency of securing an agreement was somewhat reduced as a result of this apparent reduction in support for the IRA, we remained convinced that the alienation problem among the nationalist community continued to be a major one and that an agreement along the lines that eventually emerged remained desirable with a view to overcoming this problem.

13

Ethnicity, the English, and Northern Ireland: comments and reflections

LORD ARMSTRONG

In a number of the contributions to this volume there have been references to the "ethnicity" of the Irish, and one contributor refers to the "ethnicity" of the English, which he says is about to be "interrogated." I am not quite sure what that means, but it sounds like something that happens—or used to happen—in the Ljubjanka. I realize that I feel very uncomfortable with this concept of the "ethnicity" of the English. That is perhaps a very English thing to feel, but I am not at all sure that there is any. I can recognize an English national identity and character, but I cannot recognize an English "ethnicity." If there is any, it is certainly less than that of the Scots or the Welsh or the Irish.

The English are an ethnic cocktail, with more ingredients than most cocktails: Celtic, Latin, Anglo-Saxon, Viking, Norman, Gallic—without taking account of recent immigrations. They have had a monarchy for more than a thousand years, but since 1066 the royal family has been by turns Norman, French, Welsh, Scottish, and German. Even now it carries more Scottish than native English genes. And then the English have accepted being governed by Scottish, Welsh, and Irish prime ministers, as well as by English men and women—and indeed, memorably, by someone who was by origin a Portuguese Jew.

Perhaps this comparative lack of English ethnicity is one of the abiding

Lord Armstrong of Ilminster was Secretary of the Cabinet and Head of the Home Civil Service in Britain in the 1980s. His public career also included positions as Private Secretary to the Chancellor of the Exchequer and Principal Private Secretary to the Prime Minister.

problems in Anglo-Irish relations: The English are not really able to understand in others what they lack in themselves.

I am inclined to agree with those who say that in Anglo-Irish relations we should not let ourselves be dominated by history. We should use it to understand where we are and why we are there. But when we come to think about and work for the future, having climbed the ladder of history, we should do well to throw it away. I do not believe that, at any rate in this sphere of human affairs, history is a good guide to the future.

The Anglo-Irish Agreement of November 1985 was, as has already been said, part of a process. Some would trace it back to the meeting between Margaret Thatcher and Charles Haughey in 1980, and to the communiqué which included that famous phrase, "the totality of relationships"—a phrase which I learned later not to use too often. I think that a case could be made for going back further than that, to the Sunningdale Agreement and the idea of a Council of Ireland. However that may be, the process of discussion of which the agreement was the outcome had its beginning in the second half of 1983.

The agreement can be attributed to the initiative and farsightedness of Margaret Thatcher and Garret FitzGerald. In the second half of 1983 both had recently won general elections, the results of which allowed each of them to look forward to a period of four years before another election had to be held. Thatcher, a unionist by instinct and conviction, was none the less an intensely pragmatic politician. She could see that the "rolling devolution" initiative taken in Northern Ireland in 1982 was not getting anywhere, and that there was no prospect of movement on that front. In the face of the continuing costs of the situation in Northern Ireland, and above all the cost in terms of human lives, she felt the need to do something—if not necessarily to solve the problem of Northern Ireland, at least to see if it might be possible to move it out of the impasse in which it seemed frozen.

Thatcher also had what was perhaps the advantage that, although she had read extensively on the historical background of the problem, it was for her just history and not—as it sometimes seems to be for the Irish—a backward extension of the present: it was not part of her personal experience. She was relatively free of historical baggage or hang-ups, and she liked and respected her Irish counterpart, whom she had gotten to know in the course of meetings of the European Council.

For Garret FitzGerald the work of the New Ireland Forum was clearly an important, even necessary, preliminary to the decision to try to seek an Anglo-Irish agreement. With its reexamination, and to some extent redefinition, of the aspirations of Irish nationalism, the New Ireland Forum report gave him an opportunity to go into the negotiations with somewhat more room for maneuver than he might otherwise have had.

The negotiations between the two teams of officials had a number of favorable characteristics. First, those of us responsible for the detailed discussion and negotiation had a clear political direction from both sides to work for an agreement. Aware as we all obviously were of the history of Anglo-Irish relations, we did not allow ourselves to be overshadowed or cowed by it. Indeed, I think we all saw it as a challenge to achieve something that would constitute an improvement, and perhaps if we were lucky and successful, a turning point, in Anglo-Irish relations after long years of distance and suspicion. Second, like our respective prime ministers, we had no problem meeting and doing business together as equal representatives of independent sovereign states. This was helped by the fact that Dermot Nally and I had worked together as fellow members of the international group of permanent representatives for the purpose of preparing economic summits—as sherpas, in short—when Ireland had the presidency of the Council of Ministers of the European Community in 1979. Third, while both teams were working under clear political directions as to the national objectives to be achieved and the national interests to be safeguarded, and faithfully carried out the instructions and upheld the interests of their respective governments, we all shared a degree of personal commitment to succeed, and developed a relationship of trust which ripened over the months into abiding friendship.

If I may once again make a personal point, you cannot sit at the cabinet table in 10 Downing Street discussing matters relating to Ireland, as I did so often, and not be conscious of all that has happened there before in discussion about affairs in Ireland and relations between Britain and Ireland, without feeling conscious of the opportunity that you may have, no doubt to get it wrong again, but also perhaps, for once, to get it even slightly right. The negotiations had limited ambitions:

1. To bring (as I have already said) some movement into the situation
2. To respect and preserve unimpaired the sovereignty of each government with respect to the territory in which it exercised the responsibilities of government

3. To confirm between the two governments, in an agreement that would have the force and quality of an international treaty, the status of Northern Ireland, in a form which the Irish government judged would not be in violation of the Irish constitution

4. To create an agreement that would be perceived to be as unthreatening as possible to the position of the unionists (We of course recognized that they were bound to view as profoundly objectionable any negotiations, and especially an agreement, between the two governments that in giving the Irish government a framework in the form of a conference in which it could put forward views and proposals relating to the interests of the minority community, provided that government with an institutionalized say in the management of affairs in Northern Ireland.)

5. To create a structure that, while it admitted a participation by the parties in Northern Ireland, did not depend on it

6. To give the nationalists in Northern Ireland the sense of being at least indirectly represented in the counsels of government in Northern Ireland

7. Not to preclude the possibility of agreement among the parties in Northern Ireland on the establishment of a devolved administration there (In fact it is provided in the agreement that substantial parts of it would be superseded and would have to be reviewed if a devolved administration were brought into being.)

8. To provide an institutional framework for improving cooperation between London (and Belfast) and Dublin on cross-border affairs (including security) and other matters of common interest, and for dealing with the sorts of disagreements bound to occur from time to time

9. To create an agreement and a relationship with some prospect of surviving changes of government in London and in Dublin

It may not be very heroic to create something that is intended to last only until there is something better to put in its place; but in the circumstances I do not think that it was a negligible achievement.

What of the future? I am only a bureaucrat, and a retired one at that. I do not ask to see the distant scene; one step is enough for me. I should find it difficult to construct a rational basis for optimism in relation to Northern Ireland, but then a few years ago who could have foreseen the astonishing developments in Eastern Europe? But if there is to be a prospect for hope in Northern Ireland, and in Anglo-Irish relations in which the problems of Northern Ireland make up so large an element, I think that it has to be on the three following bases:

1. Having used the map of history to discover where we are and how we got there, we should not rely on that map when we come to chart the course on which we should be going.
2. We should base relations and decisions on respect for independence and on what Garret FitzGerald has called "equality of esteem," whether between the British and the Irish or between the unionists and the nationalists.
3. We should remember the European dimension. Both the United Kingdom and the Republic of Ireland are members of the European Community. We cannot and should not aspire to buck the facts of geography. We inhabit neighboring offshore islands in a wider and probably growing community of European nations. Our own traditions and identities are not threatened by that. The challenge to us both is to harness those traditions and identities in a framework that respects our independence and equality as sovereign states and our shared interests as members of, and neighbors in, the European Community. The Anglo-Irish Agreement is the beginning of a response to that challenge.

This is the opportunity that beckons. It is an opportunity which we have never had before, and that is one of the reasons why we must not be trammeled by history. It is part of a wider European challenge, a challenge to transcend the enmities, rivalries, and resentments of the past. And it calls for wisdom, understanding, statesmanship, and vision of the highest order.

14

The Anglo-Irish Agreement:
a device for territorial management?

PAUL ARTHUR

Until Western social scientists can encompass such hard cases as Northern Ireland in their theories of politics, only modest claims should be made on behalf of putative general theories.[1]

The political cohesion of the United Kingdom—its "identity" if you like—cannot lie in loyalty to the nation. There is no British nation: there are only British citizens. Loyalty, if it means anything, must mean loyalty to the idea of the Union: the willing community of peoples united not by creed, colour or ethnicity but by recognition of the authority of that Union.[2]

In an impressive historical overview, Jim Bulpitt offers a simple definition of the structure of power in the United Kingdom. He calls it the "Dual Polity": "a structure of territorial politics in which Centre and periphery had relatively little to do with each other" and in which "until recently the Centre sought not to govern the United Kingdom, but to manage it."[3] He suggests that "in terms of a Centre's management of its domestic environment it will attempt to construct what can be labelled an external support system, that is to say it will attempt to minimise the impact of external forces on domestic politics, or ensure that these forces are favourable to the maintenance of domestic tranquillity."[4]

PAUL ARTHUR is Professor of Politics, University of Ulster, Jordanstown, Northern Ireland. Among his publications are *The People's Democracy 1968–72, Government and Politics of Northern Ireland,* and *Northern Ireland Since 1968.*

[1] R. Rose, *Governing without Consensus: An Irish Perspective* (London, 1971), p. 19.
[2] A. Aughey, *Under Siege: Ulster Unionism and the Anglo-Irish Agreement* (Belfast, 1989), p. 24.
[3] J. Bulpitt, *Territory and Power in the United Kingdom: An Interpretation* (Manchester, 1983), p. 238.
[4] Ibid., p. 59.

This chapter examines the Bulpitt thesis in the light of developments over the past decade and, in particular, the impact of the 1985 Anglo-Irish Agreement. The continuing crisis in Northern Ireland suggests that territorial management is in some disarray. Peripheral dissidents have been setting the agenda and the search for a new governing class within Northern Ireland has been futile to date. The analysis in this chapter concentrates on Northern Ireland, but we shall pay some obeisance to the larger picture and the "variety of contradictory tendencies" to be found in the international scene:

The first is the universal recognition of territorial sovereignty as the differentiating principle in the international arena. But there is also a second conflicting trend: the erosion of boundaries through the increasing interdependencies of modern economic life. Thus, while political systems are boundary-maintaining systems, markets—although dependent for their creation upon political power and economic networks—are not.... A third identifiable trait is the result of the power differentials among nations and the tensions between bounded political systems and unbounded exchanges such as economic, ideological or informational transactions.[5]

These remarks are particularly relevant to British political discourse in the late twentieth century. To William Wallace, Britain's predicament is its preoccupation with sovereignty reinforced by a sense of separateness from the European continent in contrast to the shared values of the English-speaking community.[6] Wallace bemoans the fact that this "preoccupation with sovereignty—in particular, with the nature of the formal European commitment—has distracted attention from the progressive informal encroachment of international linkages on British autonomy."[7] The result is that certain historical myths shape practical policy and cloud the assessment of contemporary options.

Bulpitt is aware of this propensity for mythmaking. His study is an exercise in demythology, an acknowledgment of the significance of world systems and a plea for a "return to history." We may draw different conclusions from his analysis, but we recognize his exposure of the "highly ambiguous" political settlement worked out in the years follow-

[5]F. Kratochwil, "Of Systems, Boundaries and Territoriality: An Enquiry into the Formation of the State System," *World Politics* 39, 1 (1986): 42–3.
[6]W. Wallace, "What Price Independence? Sovereignty and Interdependence in British Politics," *International Affairs* 62, 3 (1986): 367–89.
[7]Ibid., p. 368.

ing 1688, and the center's failure to develop "any positive Unionist culture [—the] idea that the United Kingdom was 'one and indivisible.' "[8]

I

If there was ever an example of political ambiguity, Northern Ireland
stands as the supreme visual aid. Since its creation in 1920–21 there has
been no shortage of definitions of its constitutional status. The most
acceptable (because the most broad-brush) appears to be that of Budge
and O'Leary: "a self-governing province with some of the trappings of
sovereignty."[9] Precisely how much "sovereignty" was always a matter
of dispute. Shortly after Partition, for example, the British government
had proposed that parliamentary responsibility for both parts of Ireland
be assumed by the secretary of state for the colonies even though Northern
Ireland was neither a dominion nor a colony. The proposal was not
accepted by Sir James Craig's government because he feared that Northern Ireland's interests would suffer if they were represented by a minister
who had to balance Northern Ireland's representations with those of the
Irish Free State.

In the ensuing years a one-sided contest was waged to push the limits
of Northern Ireland's autonomy. Perhaps the classic debate took place
when Labour was returned to power after 1945. Unionists feared that
the Clement Attlee government was antipartitionist and for a period an
intense debate was conducted inside the Northern Ireland cabinet on the
merits of dominion status. The idea was dropped once it became clear
that Labour would continue the policy of noninterference in Northern
Ireland's internal affairs.

In the aftermath of the signing of the Anglo-Irish Agreement in 1985
we have been witnessing the same fundamental debate over the province's
place in United Kingdom politics, in particular a debate between those
who favor devolution and those who believe that the only safeguard lies
in Northern Ireland's thorough integration into the British political system. The most articulate exposition of this debate comes from Arthur
Aughey who (borrowing a phrase from Robert Berki) sees the present
distinction between devolution and integration in unionist politics as that
"between the idealism of nostalgia and the idealism of imagination."[10]

8Bulpitt, *Territory and Power*, pp. 54, 81–2, 96–7.
9I. Budge and C. O'Leary, *Belfast: Approach to Crisis: A Study of Belfast Politics 1613–
1970* (New York, 1973), p. 143.
10Aughey, *Under Siege*, p. 124.

Aughey places himself firmly on the side of the imagination. Indeed it might be said that he has adopted the heroic mode: "The task of unionism is to bring the parliament of the United Kingdom back to its true principles. The argument of unionism is that a great wrong has been done, not just to the citizens of Ulster, but to the whole British way of political life."[11]

In this respect Northern Ireland may be at the center of the debate on territoriality and identity. Given that it is a community noted for its insularity, there is a certain irony in viewing it as being in the vanguard of the drive toward a positive unionist culture. That irony is compounded by the fact that the most unionist of prime ministers, Margaret Thatcher, is derided as the person who has done most to undermine the "idea" of the Union. Nonetheless, it is conceivable that by inadvertently concentrating minds on this very question she went some little way in raising a fundamental debate about the nature of the Union at a time of closer European political cooperation. Individuals can shape history, but in turn they are molded by history. Nowhere is this more apparent than in Thatcher's contribution to the politics of territoriality within the United Kingdom. She inherited certain givens from her predecessors. Her contribution was to accelerate the process whereby (to paraphrase Bulpitt) the most extreme example of duality was/is Northern Ireland. Some consider it so extreme an example that it must challenge Bulpitt's assertion that "the situation in Britain differed only in degree, not in kind."

The first given inherited by the Conservatives in 1979 was "British history." In a speculative essay, J. G. A. Pocock comments on the elasticity of the concept of British history. It is relevant here to quote from it:

But the term "British history" has been used here to express the need for something that shall include both the attempt to incorporate Ireland within English or British political structures, and the reactions against that attempt and its consequences. The history of Irish nationality is as much a part of "British history" in this sense as is the history of Union and Empire, and "British history" thus denotes the historiography of no single nation but of a problematic and uncompleted experiment in the creation and interaction of several nations. At this point "British history" becomes independent of Anglo-Irish union and will continue as long as there are a number of nations inhabiting the "Atlantic archipelago." But "British history" does not stop there; it extends itself into oceanic, American and global dimensions. . . . Our "British history" . . . includes the history of English-speaking America down to the point—however we determine it—when the United States is seen to have created a distinctive political culture and

[11]Ibid., p. 86.

embarked upon a constitutional and global history that demands to be treated in its own terms. The pattern resembles that of Irish history in the sense that Anglicization and the revolt against Anglicization unite in determining it; "Ireland," however, is not able to depart from that archipelagic history of which "America" ceased to be an extension.[12]

We shall see that some of those elements of "British history"—particularly "America" and "Ireland"—impinged on the United Kingdom's domestic political process to add another dimension to the "Northern Ireland problem." In the meantime we should acknowledge that Pocock's analysis has the merit of imposing a proper perspective on the problem: a sense of scale, of time, of geopolitics, and of the dynamism of state and ethnic relationships.

"Ireland" may have departed the United Kingdom in 1922 but its presence—whether at archipelagic or Commonwealth level—continued to be palpable in British constitutional evolution. The "Irish dimension" is the second given that Thatcher inherited. Her contribution was to put it on a sounder institutional footing. The third given was what Bulpitt refers to as the "contractual nature of the union."[13] Events since 1969 have challenged that allegedly cozy relationship. If we wish to understand the present tense of territorial politics inside the United Kingdom, we need to examine all three givens in reverse order.

II

The Conservative Party manifesto of 1979 paid scant attention to Northern Ireland, save to stress the traditional policy of defeating terrorism and of maintaining the Union "in accordance with the wish of the majority in the Province." A cryptic reference to future government stated that in the "absence of devolved government, we will seek to establish one or more elected regional councils with a wide range of powers over local services." This policy bore the imprimatur of Airey Neave, opposition spokesperson on Northern Ireland and Thatcher confidant. His assassination by the Irish National Liberation Army (INLA) on 30 March 1979 robbed the prime minister of a secretary of state for Northern Ireland, but not necessarily of a policy. The Tories had a comfortable House of Commons majority and the enthusiastic support of the Ulster

[12]J. G. A. Pocock, "The Limits and Divisions of British History: In Search of the Unknown Subject," *American Historical Review* 87, 2 (1982): 318.
[13]Bulpitt, *Territory and Power*, p. 98.

Unionist Party (UUP), led by James Molyneaux. His mentor, Enoch Powell, made no secret of his integrationist stance: in March 1979 Powell announced that "local democracy" rather than devolved government was the cause to be pursued because devolution would endanger the unity of the United Kingdom.

There was no reason to anticipate major opposition from Labour. Under Roy Mason (secretary of state, September 1976 to May 1979), Labour had made no serious effort at constitutional innovation but followed what an official of the Northern Ireland Office had called a "cotton wool" policy. Basically both parties were engaged in a retreat from the Sunningdale Agreement: Ulster was not yet ripe for bold constitutional experiments like power-sharing. The appointment of Humphrey Atkins, a man without previous cabinet experience or any knowledge of Northern Ireland, as the new secretary of state seemed to confirm that a period of consolidation was under way.

Within a matter of months Thatcher did a U-turn. The government produced a consultative document in November, "The Government of Northern Ireland: A Working Paper for a Conference."[14] It sought no more than "the highest level of agreement... which will best meet the immediate needs of Northern Ireland." It narrowly circumscribed the areas for discussion—debate on Irish unity, confederation, Ulster independence, and the constitutional status of the province were ruled out of order—and an appendix containing six illustrative models of systems of government was added to open up discussions. In addition, the prime minister appointed a high-powered cabinet committee to oversee the exercise: it included Humphrey Atkins, Francis Pym, William Whitelaw, Lord Hailsham, and Sir Ian Gilmour. She had invested considerable prestige in the exercise, with some commentators alluding to the Rhodesian negotiations.

The putative conference was endorsed, initially, only by the biconfessional Alliance Party. The two voices of unionism—Ian Paisley's Democratic Unionist Party (DUP) and Molyneaux's UUP—were engaged in a battle for dominance of the unionist electorate, a contest occurring along the devolution-integration axis. Notwithstanding a highly personal alliance forged by Paisley and Molyneaux in the aftermath of the Anglo-Irish Agreement, unionist politics throughout the 1980s were absorbed

---

[14]Great Britain, *Parliamentary Papers*, "The Government of Northern Ireland: A Working Paper for a Conference" (1979), Cmnd. 7763.

by this debate. That may not be altogether surprising because it is a fundamental debate over the nature of the Union, about the Dual Polity, and about whether a positive unionist culture could be constructed. The historian of unionism has commented that unionists did not develop a coherent political philosophy: "No constructive philosophy had been developed over the years of struggle to equip Ulster Unionists to govern a state they had neither expected nor wanted."[15] The issue for the 1980s was not simply whether or not they were equipped to run the province, but what was to be their relationship with the center. Since the committee led by Atkins could not resolve this issue—because the UUP refused to participate—then the next attempt might provide some answers.

That was to be the experiment in "rolling devolution" sponsored by Atkins's successor, Jim Prior. The Prior initiative to establish a Northern Ireland Assembly owed something to the new secretary of state's political ambitions, but also to the devolution-integration debate. The very fact that devolution was being sought suggested that integrationism was on the wane. As much had been recognized by Molyneaux, who led a revolt against the Prior bill in Parliament. He knew he did not stand alone. Prior has recorded that the prime minister opposed it in cabinet, describing it as "a rotten Bill."[16] Suffering an unusual fate for a constitutional bill, the Prior bill was subjected to a guillotine motion. When it came to debate on the second reading no major party leader spoke—nor did any of the five former secretaries of state for Northern Ireland. The authors of the standard work on the Northern Ireland Assembly find this lack of interest difficult to explain, although they do acknowledge that the bill's passage through the Commons coincided with the Falklands War.[17]

The prime minister's hostility would be understandable if it had been based on an antipathy toward the Dual Polity, but later events suggest that that was not her motivation. However, it does explain Molyneaux's attitude. Despite opposition the bill became law and the Northern Ireland Assembly was established. From the outset the UUP leader engaged in diversionary tactics. As leader of the largest party—twenty-six members to the DUP's twenty-one, the Social Democratic and Labour Party's fourteen, Alliance's ten, Sinn Féin's five, and two independent unionists—he sent a letter to all elected members inviting them to a meeting on 1

[15]P. Buckland, *The Factory of Grievances* (Dublin, 1979), p. 5.
[16]J. Prior, *A Balance of Power* (London, 1986), p. 199.
[17]C. O'Leary et al., *The Northern Ireland Assembly 1982–1986: A Constitutional Experiment* (London, 1988), pp. 70–9.

November 1982 to discuss the deteriorating security situation. During the four-year lifetime of the Assembly—it was dissolved by the government on 23 June 1986—the UUP boycotted proceedings twice, in all for a period of about eight months. In the vital role of scrutinizing the record of direct rule, UUP members attended just over half of the committee sessions. By contrast, the DUP had a 72 percent attendance record and the Alliance 68 percent.[18] In these circumstances the DUP introduced a motion on 10 May 1983 designed to "flush out" those members against devolution. It was aimed at the UUP leadership and led to the longest debate in the brief history of the Assembly. All of this fitted into a pattern detected by Molyneaux some years earlier. In a House of Commons debate on the Atkins initiative Molyneaux made a thinly disguised attack on Ian Paisley when he referred to the whole exercise as "a continuation of the cynical game of what may be called leadership destruction which has been going on in one form or another for the past ten years."[19] Among other matters, Molyneaux may have been alluding to the British imposition on Northern Ireland of the single-transferable-vote system of proportional representation, which had enabled the DUP to challenge the UUP for unionist supremacy; the Sunningdale experiment of power-sharing with its detested Irish dimension; and an insistence by successive governments that they would not tolerate unionist intransigence and misbehavior. Indeed, in his memoirs a former home secretary had gone so far as to hint at the conditions of membership in the United Kingdom:

So long as the majority of people in Northern Ireland wished to remain part of the United Kingdom there could be no possible question of their right to do so, but this must be on two conditions. First, that United Kingdom standards of political behaviour were accepted, and secondly, that the overall authority of the Westminster parliament was recognised as in the rest of the United Kingdom.[20]

The implication appeared to be that Northern Ireland was stretching the patience of British politicians and that not only was the Dual Polity in doubt but the Union itself. How better to demonstrate one's unionism than to wish away the Dual Polity and embrace full integration? That seemed to be Molyneaux's tactic, but he knew he led a party that had enjoyed the fruits of a devolved system for more than fifty years and that he had to persuade the center of the merits of such a policy. In both cases

[18]Ibid., p. 164.
[19]*Parliamentary Debates,* Commons, 5th ser., 988, 209, 579.
[20]R. Maudling, *Memoirs* (London, 1978), p. 187.

it meant breaking the habits of generations. And that entailed high-risk strategy, because as Bulpitt points out,

the Unionist elite could not afford to lose disputes with the United Kingdom Centre. As a result, it was very reluctant to initiate conflict situations, and above all to publicise them. ... The Ulster Unionists were ideal collaborators: stable, quiescent, efficient and yet fundamentally weak in their relationship with the Centre.[21]

Events since 1972 challenged that assertion. And events after 1985 illustrated the prescience in Bulpitt's next sentence: "The Northern Ireland model was sustained by the Centre's indifference, not by peripheral strength."

III

The "Irish dimension" was acknowledged as early as October 1972 in a British discussion paper, "The Future of Northern Ireland" (paras. 76–8), and alluded to by Humphrey Atkins in the parliamentary debate on his initiative:

The geographical and historical facts of life oblige us to recognise the special relationship that exists between the component parts of the British Isles. ... We do improve our chances of success by recognising that the Republic is deeply interested in what happens in Northern Ireland. ... There will continue to be a practical "Irish dimension."[22]

In fact, the Irish dimension predated direct rule. It had not really disappeared with Partition—for example, Irish influence in shaping the contours of the new Commonwealth through the Statute of Westminster (1931) was considerable. Even after Ireland left the Commonwealth and became a republic in 1948, its influence was such that its citizens were not treated as aliens in Britain; its appearance in *The Diplomatic Service List: An Official Year Book* under the "List of British Representatives in the Commonwealth and the Republic of Ireland" suggests that, in British eyes, Ireland was not even properly foreign.

That is not to say that relations between Britain and Ireland since 1969 have not been frosty, but at least there has been mutual recognition of a need to work together. A dispassionate examination of the contemporary dimension would reveal three elements. First, it is based on the

[21]Bulpitt, *Territory and Power*, p. 146.
[22]*Parliamentary Debates*, Commons, 5th ser., 998, 209, 557.

constitutional guarantee—Northern Ireland's present status is secure and subsequent change can be effected only through consent—although skeptics have challenged the security of the present status and the ambivalence of the concept of consent. Second, in keeping with the two states' accession to the European Community, the dimension stresses functional cooperation. Third, its antiterrorism aspirations should never be underestimated.

From a Dublin perspective different nuances might be emphasized. The British government had declared in 1969 that Northern Ireland was purely a matter of domestic British concern, an assertion that was accepted at the United Nations. Much that has passed since has tested the rigidity of that position. As early as 1973 the Irish government believed that it had had some success in shaping the white paper, "Northern Ireland Constitutional Proposals,"[23] in which power-sharing and the Irish dimension became practical politics. After all, London had sought and received Dublin's views before the final drafting. The foreign minister, Garret FitzGerald, told the Dáil, "The document...I understand, from my subsequent contacts, [is] to be taken fully into consideration and to influence the shaping of the White Paper."[24]

This cursory discussion of the Irish dimension serves as a rehearsal for the debate over the Anglo-Irish Agreement. It is an illustration of the tentative shift toward joint action on the Northern Ireland problem. And the demise of joint action as a result of the Ulster Workers' Council strike in 1974 was a valuable lesson for the two governments when they came together to devise the 1985 agreement. It also suggests that the Dual Polity on the British mainland might be of a different order than that of the Northern Ireland model. Scotland, for example, does not present the same security threat, and it lacks that extra leverage provided by an external guarantor.

IV

Bulpitt has suggested that one of the challenges to the old regime of the Dual Polity has been the collapse of the external support system.[25] His analysis recognizes the significance of the international system in contrast

---

[23]Great Britain, *Parliamentary Papers,* "Northern Ireland Constitutional Proposals" (1973), Cmnd. 5259.
[24]*Dáil Éireann Debates,* 265, 832, 9 May 1973.
[25]Bulpitt, *Territory and Power,* p. 167.

to much of the insularity of Ulster unionism. Interdependence has become
the name of the game and myths about "special relationships" are being
laid to rest. This section is concerned with the conflicting conceptions
about the role the United States has played (and continues to play) in
the Anglo-Irish relationship. It will be suggested that until recent years
the potential for U.S. intervention has been exaggerated, but that from
the mid-1970s onward the role of the U.S. has shifted from one of benign
concern to incremental involvement; and that the Irish question has begun
to have an effect on the U.S. domestic political process.

The nature of the Anglo-American relationship has been well
documented. David Vital has depicted three characteristics: its longev-
ity—some date it back to December 1895; its prime (but not exclusive)
military value to the British; and its asymmetry, signifying different things
to either side: "Indeed, as a political concept, the 'special relationship'
is largely a British creation which few influential Americans have accepted
without serious reservations."[26] In recent years a greater sense of realism
and perspective has crept into British analyses. David Reynolds, surveying
the postwar literature on the topic, finds that it ranges from the senti-
mental—"Little seemed impossible.... Certainly in the year 1952 it was
by no means beyond the range of possibility that the deed of 1776 might
in some sense be undone" (H. C. Allen)—to the realistic: "Undoubtedly
the relationship remains special in quality in some of its aspects—such
as intelligence and nuclear matters. Yet it is no longer special in importance, either to America or to the world at large. That is the difference
between the 1980s and the 1940s."[27] A glance at a range of issues in
which the United Kingdom was bypassed is indicative of its diminishing
influence: the abrupt end of Lend-Lease; the insistence on sterling con-
vertibility; the refusal to share nuclear technology; the exclusion of the
United Kingdom from the ANZUS Pact; the failure to join the Baghdad
Pact; Suez and much of the Middle East policy generally; cancellation
of the Skybolt weapons system in 1962; the decision to deploy neutron
bombs in Western Europe in 1978; the hostage rescue mission to Iran
in April 1980; the pressure to cancel the Soviet gas pipeline from Siberia
to Western Europe in 1982; the launching of the Strategic Defense Initiative in 1983; Afghanistan, Central America, and Angola; intimations
in 1985 that the limits of the SALT II Treaty would be exceeded; the air

[26]D. Vital, *The Making of British Foreign Policy* (Boston, 1968), pp. 36–7.
[27]D. Reynolds, "Rethinking Anglo-American Relations," *International Affairs* 65, 1 (1988–
89): 89–111.

raids on Libya in 1986 (the decision to attack, that is, rather than the use of British air bases); and the Reykjavik summit in 1986.

That ledger illustrates the changing nature of geopolitical relationships and *may* be one (very small) indication of why the Irish question has been permitted a higher visibility in the American political process. Certainly it was the Irish government's view that its influence was growing, a fact confirmed in a statement made by the Taoiseach at a St. Patrick's Day luncheon in 1988 in Washington hosted by Speaker of the House Jim Wright. In what may have been unconscious irony Charles Haughey said that there "are no two countries anywhere in the world which have such a special relationship as ours."

Haughey may have had some reason for his optimism. In the 1980 census 43.7 million Americans (19 percent of the population) identified themselves as of Irish ethnic origin or heritage group. The Irish diplomatic mission in the United States was once described by one of Speaker of the House Thomas "Tip" O'Neill's aides as "second only to that of the Israelis";[28] and the *U.S. News and World Report* (17 June 1984) listed the Irish Republic as the fifth largest group lobbying the U.S. government, based on its reputed $5.5-million expenditure in 1984. These figures are provided simply to suggest that the United States is being used as a second front in the conflict over Northern Ireland.

There is nothing new in this, of course. As early as 1855 a British home secretary warned of the danger to British interests of what he called the "Irish nation" in the United States. Despite Irish-American illusions, the Irish question was not an issue in Washington until the 1970s, except during World War I, when the

Irish question was transformed from an essentially domestic problem into one occupying the stage of international politics. This arose from two main issues: Ireland's possible effect on the European balance of power up to August 1914 and, subsequently, her growing role in Anglo-American relations.[29]

A study of Washington's Irish policy between 1916 and 1986 found nothing positive in the U.S.-Irish "special relationship" during the 1940s, 1950s, and 1960s.[30] Ireland was considered in the British sphere of responsibility, and American foreign policy was pro-British.

Spheres of responsibility constitute one of three new devices for man-

[28]J. Holland, *The American Connection* (New York, 1987), p. 129.
[29]S. Hartley, *The Irish Question as a Problem in British Foreign Policy 1914–18* (New York, 1987), p. 5.
[30]S. Cronin, *Washington's Irish Policy 1916–86* (Dublin, 1987).

aging the international system, the other two being *spheres of abstention* and *functional regimes*. It is conceivable that the management of the Northern Ireland problem has moved from a sphere of responsibility to a functional regime:

Basically, functional regimes "unbundle" the package of rights inherent in territorial sovereignty. Functionalism has therefore sometimes been advocated as an alternative organisational principle for international life. Functional regimes, it was hoped, would not only downgrade the importance of national boundaries, but could, through the expansion of transboundary cooperative networks, lead to "peace in parts."[31]

We can begin to detect a shift in that direction in the mid-1970s. In 1973 it was noted in a Federal Bureau of Investigation memorandum that "the Irish Problem has become a serious problem and a source of embarrassment to the United States," the embarrassment arising from the fact that Americans were the Irish Republican Army's main source of money and weapons.[32] The U.S. government's difficulty was that it was dealing with a conflict between two of its oldest allies, and one of them (in the Downing Street declaration of August 1969) made it patently clear that the problem was one internal to the United Kingdom. Until both the United Kingdom and Ireland acted in tandem there was little that the United States could do by way of positive action.

The beginnings of a joint approach were evident in 1977. Following discussions with both governments, President Jimmy Carter issued a statement in which he condemned violence, expressed support for a peaceful solution in which the Irish government would be involved, and promised United States investment assistance in the event of such a settlement:

The United States wholeheartedly supports peaceful means for finding a just solution that involves both parts of the community of Northern Ireland and protects human rights and guarantees freedom from discrimination—a solution that the people in Northern Ireland as well as the Governments of Great Britain and Ireland can support.... United States Government policy on the Northern Ireland issue has long been one of impartiality, and that is how it will remain.

There are several points to be made about Carter's statement. The first is that it treated the Northern Ireland conflict as a legitimate concern of U.S. foreign policy—the phrase used by the American ambassador in

[31]Kratochwil, "Of Systems," pp. 48–9.
[32]Jack Holland, *The American Connection: US Guns, Money and Influence in Northern Ireland*, (New York, 1987), p. 39.

Dublin (9 September 1977) was that the United States was "neutral but not indifferent." The second is that the sentiments expressed were not far removed from those written into the preamble of the Anglo-Irish Agreement in November 1985. The third is that it skated over the "internal jurisdiction" issue by referring to three entities: Northern Ireland, Great Britain, and Ireland. The fourth is that President Carter specifically raised human rights and discrimination issues, both of which were to be exploited by Irish-American lobbyists in the coming years.

In fact, insofar as we can speak of American intervention, it occurred at three levels:

1. Intervention as mediation
2. Intervention in the furtherance of the protection of human rights
3. Geopolitical aspects of intervention, especially at the functional level of controlling the "network of international terrorism"

In an address to a joint session of the U.S. Congress on 20 February 1985, Prime Minister Thatcher recognized the depth of American interest when she devoted a section of her address to the question of Ireland: "Garret FitzGerald and I will continue to consult together in the quest for stability and peace in Northern Ireland. We hope we will have your continued support for our joint efforts to find a way forward."

That support was forthcoming for the signing of the Anglo-Irish Agreement and was tangible in United States support for the International Fund for Ireland established under Article 10(a) of the agreement. By 1990 the United States had made a grant of $150 million, by far the largest sum from any individual donor. American government support has also enabled the United States to keep a watching brief on political activity within Ireland, a fact acknowledged by Assistant Secretary Rozanne Ridgway in evidence she gave to the Senate Foreign Relations Committee on 10 April 1986: "We are confident that the independent nature of the Fund and its management operation will ensure adherence to the objectives spelled out in the Agreement and specifically with respect of human rights, equal employment opportunity and reconciliation." And in the opinion of Hadden and Boyle, "it would appear that the chief donor to the Fund has had considerable influence over the Board in the framing of its main policy."[33]

[33]T. Hadden and K. Boyle, *The Anglo-Irish Agreement: Commentary, Text and Official Review* (London, 1989), p. 58.

V

In a work on the Northern Ireland problem in a comparative context, Frank Wright asserts that the "relationship between Britain, Ireland and Northern Ireland is more like that of a disputed nationality zone with dependency upon two powers."[34] That much appears to have been recognized by the two signatories to the Anglo-Irish Agreement as they searched for novel approaches to an intractable problem. The Irish authorities recognized their contradictions from an early stage. Articles 2 and 3 of their 1937 constitution claim jurisdiction over the territory of Northern Ireland. This was fine so long as Dublin governments had no dealings with Belfast. However, difficulties arose after October 1968 when Dublin attempted "to persuade the British to carry out jurisdictional acts *within* Ireland, to bring about reforms or changes in Northern Ireland."[35]

These difficulties were compounded by the failure of the reform program and the imposition of direct rule. Now there could be no pretense: The Irish government was caught in a contradiction. On the one hand the 1937 constitution accepts some obligation to speak on behalf of the people of Northern Ireland; on the other Dublin has "in effect also recognised British rights in Ireland and this entangles them in the implications of the constitutional claim."[36] Taoiseach Liam Cosgrave recognized this theoretical difficulty when he attempted a practical reply to a Dáil question on 28 March 1973: "Northern Ireland affairs are primarily the responsibility of the Taoiseach. In so far as those affairs affect relations with Britain they are also, of course, the concern of the Minister for Foreign Affairs." That was a neat if evasive reply because no Taoiseach can admit publicly that Northern Ireland is a foreign affairs issue.

One route out of the contradiction was to recognize "the totality of relationships within these islands," a phrase which appeared in the communiqué following the second Anglo-Irish summit in December 1980. Another was the establishment of a Joint Steering Group of British and Irish officials (30 January 1981) given the task of analyzing "the reasons for misconceptions in each country over attitudes and government policies in the other" and considering "measures which the two Governments

---

[34]F. Wright, *Northern Ireland: A Comparative Analysis* (Dublin, 1987), p. 218.
[35]L. de Paor, "The Case for the Retention of Articles 2 and 3," *The Irish Times*, 4 September 1981.
[36]Ibid.

might take jointly or separately to remove such misconceptions and improve mutual understanding."

A third route was to sign the Anglo-Irish Agreement. Its potential was recognized by William Shannon, a former American ambassador to Ireland:

Never before has Britain formally acknowledged that Ireland has a legal role to play in governing the north. Although it is far short of an acceptance of the principle of a united Ireland the agreement contradicts cherished beliefs of the unionist majority in Northern Ireland: the belief that the north is exclusively British territory, that its affairs are purely an internal British concern, and that the Republic of Ireland, although a neighbour, is to be regarded as in all respects a foreign country.[37]

It is precisely this potential and the implications of outside "interference" which so upset the unionist majority. The machinery of the agreement, for example, is similar in many respects to that of the European Community's Council of Ministers, and there is little doubt that the European context has reinforced Anglo-Irish contacts through frequent meetings of foreign ministers and of prime ministers. One Irish official on the Commission of the European Communities has commented:

The effects of common United Kingdom and Irish membership of the Community and particularly their attitudes to the emerging Community are so great that Anglo-Irish relations can hardly usefully be discussed except in that context. This, in my view, is healthy for both partners as it substitutes an agreeably wider embrace for what has been an excessive intimacy.[38]

Garret FitzGerald has described Dublin's new relationship with Britain through the agreement as being "beyond a consultative role, necessarily because of the sovereignty issue, falling short of an executive role." Whatever the precise position, it is another novel step in constitutional evolution in that "problematic and uncompleted experiment in the creation and interaction of several nations."[39] It suggests that Britain and Ireland have recognized the advantages of interdependence and that they are following a reasonably familiar track. Hadfield notes, "It is not unprecedented for the United Kingdom Government through the treaty-ratification power to give other States an influence in the internal affairs

[37]W. Shannon, "The Anglo-Irish Agreement," *Foreign Affairs* 64, 4 (Spring 1986): 850.
[38]E. Gallagher, "Anglo-Irish Relations in the European Community," *Irish Studies in International Affairs* 2, 1 (1985): 35.
[39]J. G. A. Pocock, "The Limits and Divisions of British History: In Search of the Unknown Subject", *American Historical Review* 82, no. 2 (1982): 318.

of the United Kingdom—the machinery for enforcing the European Convention on Human Rights has just that effect." But he goes on to make the telling point that where "the Agreement may differ from the European Convention is possibly in its lack of reciprocity: the United Kingdom Government does not seem to have the same degree of influence over affairs in the Irish Republic as the latter has over the affairs of the former."[40]

Given that state of affairs, where stands the Dual Polity? It is worth noting that its construction was quintessentially the work of the center—"a political-administrative community composed of senior ministers and top civil servants."[41] The key player in selling the Anglo-Irish Agreement to the British prime minister was Sir Robert (now Lord) Armstrong, the cabinet secretary. He worked in great secrecy with a tiny group of senior officials, none of whom had served in the Northern Ireland civil service.

At the very least the continued working of the agreement suggests that not only does the center believe that it cannot govern this part of the kingdom, but that the best it can do is manage the problem with the assistance of the Republic of Ireland. No one doubts that Northern Ireland remains within the United Kingdom if only in a semidetached condition. Unemployment at 14.1 percent is double the United Kingdom average, yet the province remains highly dependent on Britain: The public sector accounts for 40 percent of total employment and government spending in Northern Ireland is 40 percent above the U.K. average.[42]

But it is its ambiguous constitutional position that worries the majority population. On the day after the signing of the agreement the deputy leader of the Democratic Unionist Party, Peter Robinson, spoke of being "on the window ledge of the Union." None sees the government attempting to develop a positive unionist culture. Indeed Margaret Thatcher may have challenged the (Ulster) unionist concept of "community." In a stimulating discussion of community, Geraint Parry asserts that one "can only speak of self-determination or of liberty within tradition if the boundaries of the community correspond to the boundaries of those sharing the particular tradition."[43] Northern Ireland's boundaries were

---

[40]B. Hadfield, "The Anglo-Irish Agreement—Blue Print or Green Print?" *Northern Ireland Legal Quarterly* 37, 1 (Spring 1986): 10.

[41]Bulpitt, *Territory and Power*, p. 237.

[42]*The Irish Times*, 28 March 1990.

[43]G. Parry, "Tradition, Community and Self-Determination," *British Journal of Political Science* 12, 4 (October 1982): 413–14.

drawn in a restrictive way. The agreement may be a fundamental challenge to that exclusivism.

After the events in Eastern Europe in 1989, the secretary general of the North Atlantic Treaty Organization, Manfred Woerner, could assert in July 1990 that "the Cold War belongs to history." Events in Ireland—indeed the lack of any apparent political movement—have to be examined against this backdrop. The vocabulary of political science needs to be scrutinized to consider if it meets the demands of the late twentieth century. The Anglo-Irish Agreement may have played some modest role in that respect. At the very least it has induced attitudinal change inside Northern Ireland. It has been innovative in its joint approach to the Northern Ireland problem by moving it from (following Kratochwil) a sphere of responsibility to that of a functional regime. In Irish terms that may be cataclysmic.

15

A new Ireland in a new Europe

JOHN HUME

The major developments that have been taking place in Europe, the creation of the Single Market and now the drive toward European political union, have profound implications for relations within Ireland, relations between Ireland and Britain, and, therefore, what has become known as the Irish problem, which today disfigures the North of Ireland.

A half century ago, World War II was in progress. Not for the first time in this century, millions of people were being slaughtered and cities across Europe were being devastated. Difference for the nth time in centuries was pushed to the point of division, and the terrible price in human terms was again being paid. Once again nationality was more important than humanity.

If someone had stepped forth then and declared that in fifty years' time all that would have changed and that we would be moving toward a united Europe, in which difference and identity would be respected, in which the French would still be French and the Germans would still be German, that person would have been described as a fool or a dreamer. But it has happened, and it has profound lessons for areas of conflict everywhere, and especially Ireland, both parts of which are now part of the emerging unity of Europe. If the deep bitterness that separated peoples like the French and the Germans, a bitterness far deeper than the one

JOHN HUME, MP, MEP, is Leader of the Social Democratic and Labour Party. A founding member of the party in 1970, he was Deputy Leader until 1979 and has served as Leader ever since. He was a member of the Northern Ireland Parliament, the power-sharing executive of 1974, and the Northern Ireland Assembly. He has been a member of the European Parliament since 1979, and a Westminster MP since 1983. He is the author of *Northern Ireland: A British Problem* and *Europe of the Regions*.

that divides the people of Ireland, could be laid aside, why cannot the Irish do likewise?

Change in the European order is continuing apace at two levels. One is the growing integration of the European Community based on the realization that the democratic nation-state is no longer a sufficient political entity to allow people to have adequate control over the economic and technological forces that affect people's opportunities and circumstances. The task is to ensure that those arrangements and institutions which develop shared policies and programs are democratically based. The issue is the need to optimize the real sovereignty of the peoples of Europe rather than ossify our democratic development around limited notions of national sovereignty that only give space to multinational vested interest.

However, there is a second level on which the European order is changing. The transforming scene in Eastern and Central Europe has opened the prospect of the Common European Home. That has been powerfully symbolized by the Paris Charter signed at a meeting of the Conference on Security and Cooperation in Europe (CSCE) in late 1990. The process represented by the Paris Charter marks a fundamental change in the nature of the defense and security debate in Europe. That has significance in British and Irish relationships because it underscores the fact that whatever strategic considerations inspired British attitudes toward Ireland in the past are obsolescent if not already obsolete.

This is in turn reinforced by the ongoing development of the European Community. The EC dimension has significance beyond the strategic consideration. It represents a changing economic interface between countries. In the Single Market the border will be no more in real terms than a county boundary as goods, people, and services move freely across it. This is already evident in areas such as agriculture, tourism, energy, and transport, all central to our economic future and all of which will be intensified when we become the offshore island of a united Europe, the only part that has no land link with the rest. The process of the Single Market underlines the fact that whatever economic considerations historically informed British policy on Ireland can no longer be held to apply. It is notable that Margaret Thatcher, that most dominant premier, in the end fell essentially on the issue of Europe. This indicates just how far-reaching, even in crusty Tory quarters, is the reappraisal of Britain's place in the world in the context of new European configurations. Against that background, a reappraisal of Britain's role in Ireland is hardly refutable.

In a speech in late 1990, the then British secretary of state for Northern Ireland, Peter Brooke, stated in bald terms that Britain has no selfish strategic or economic interest in Ireland. He asserted that Britain is not out to manipulate or maintain its presence or Partition in Ireland as a means of fulfilling British interests. He stressed that Britain is not opposed to political unity in Ireland and went further in saying that if a majority of people in Northern Ireland expressed a wish for a united Ireland, then Britain would make the necessary political provision to facilitate that. Although such expression of Britain's position is novelly lucid, the essence of this position was contained in the Anglo-Irish Agreement of 1985. That implicitly declared Britain to be neutral or agnostic on the question of a united Ireland.

As such the agreement removed any possible justification for violence by the Irish Republican Army (IRA) or any other group claiming to fight for Irish unity or freedom. We in the Social Democratic and Labour Party (SDLP) see it as part of our task in searching for peace to spell that message out to the political leadership of the republican movement, which espouses and uses violence. Accordingly in talks with Sinn Féin we challenged their justification for violence. As far as Sinn Féin was concerned, IRA violence was basically legitimate and effective because it was aimed at removing a British presence in Ireland based on strategic and economic self-interest. We offered an alternative analysis of the motives behind Britain's current function in relation to Ireland based on our understanding of the Anglo-Irish Agreement (and the process involved in that agreement) and on our reading of the changes taking place at the European level. In failing to persuade Sinn Féin of this analysis it was my understanding that its members deemed the evidence to support the SDLP contentions insufficient.

I contend that the evidence which has mounted since then makes irrefutable our challenge to Sinn Féin's justification for violence. If that party held our interpretation of the Anglo-Irish Agreement to be speculative and implicit, Brooke's statement corroborates our case in a way that is both authoritative and explicit. Consistent with our case, the ongoing effects of economic integration in the EC increasingly diminish the relevance of notions that Britain does or can defend a singular economic self-interest by its presence and financial outlay in Northern Ireland. Furthermore, both the nature of the EC's development and the factors represented by the new relationships and role of the CSCE deny realism to the suggestion that Britain's position in Ireland is today guided by strategic interests.

It is of course true that historically British involvement in Ireland was motivated by both strategic sensitivities and economic selfishness. It should not be overlooked that Ireland has had links with continental Europe for centuries, evidence of which can still be found in many parts of the Continent today. It was precisely those links that brought England into Ireland in the first place because the English regarded Ireland as the backdoor for their European enemies. The 1690 Battle of the Boyne was a major battle in a European war in which Dutch, Danes, Germans, French, and English all fought. The Plantation of Ulster was England's response to O'Neill's and O'Donnell's links with Spain. The Act of Union of 1800 was England's response to the French revolutionaries' invasion of Ireland in 1798.

Now that has all changed. Britain is pooling sovereignty not just with France and Spain but with Ireland and eight other European countries as well. Sovereignty and independence, the issues at the heart of wars in Europe and the issues at the heart of the British-Irish quarrel, have changed their meaning. The basic needs of all countries have led to shared sovereignty and interdependence as we move inevitably toward the United States of Europe and as we in Ireland rid ourselves of the obsession with Britain and rebuild our links with the rest of Europe. This is fundamentally changing British-Irish relations. The two governments together participate in the ongoing process to achieve progress across the ever expanding range of EC issues. Common membership in a new Europe moving toward unity has provided a new and positive context for the discussion and exercise of sovereignty in these islands.

This is a context in which there is a prevailing acknowledgment that the nation-state is not the last word in polity creation. There is increasing acceptance that policies and agencies operating only on a nation-state basis cannot properly cope with wider economic and technological forces and trends which bear on our social circumstances and impact on our environment. If democracy is to keep pace with reality, we have to implement new frameworks and programs better-suited to the scale and scope of those factors that require democratic control if the needs and will of the people are to prevail. Shared sovereignty and interdependence are therefore the issue because they are the method by which we can optimize democratic policy-making in so many matters. The traditional notions of absolute and indivisible national sovereignty and territorial jealousy are now so inadequate that their promotion is destructive.

All this clearly has significance for Ireland given that the historic difficulties in relationships within the island and between Britain and itself have hinged on attitudes and aspirations concerning sovereignty, territory, and the achievement or maintenance of separateness. The new European scene offers a psychological framework in which such issues can no longer be pursued in absolutist terms. There is and will be growing appreciation that the value of interdependence can be achieved without sacrificing the validity of independence. The importance of this for a situation that has been described as one of conflicting nationalisms should not be overlooked.

The attitude of "Ourselves Alone" ("Sinn Féin") is certainly not a viable political approach, whether it be of the Ulster unionist or Irish nationalist variety. Some Irish nationalists and some unionists have indicated that they regard European integration as the enemy's "latest trick." For one, the EC is suspect because it undermines national sovereignty and the British have particular influence. For the other, it undermines U.K. sovereignty and is a device that will remove the border in Ireland by stealth. In treating the EC as an alien arrangement contriving threats to their purpose and identity, these groups are confirming an inherent lack of self-confidence in the very identity and values which, they claim, distinguish their people. It is hardly surprising that they should believe that European unity, cooperation, and pooling elements of sovereignty threaten their position. They have believed that respectful accommodation with others *on the same island* would betray or undermine their tradition.

It can be argued that experience of the European process is having an educative effect on such attitudes. Issues can be seen in a wider context than the narrow ground of our traditionally disputed local political arena. People can see others with deep and marked historical and cultural differences working together, compromising and cooperating without any sacrifice of principle. They see this being done through agreed-upon institutions and frameworks.

The EC's structures were designed to allow diverse peoples to grow together at their own speed, as well as to enable EC institutions themselves to change and develop in order to keep pace with that growth and social, economic, and environmental realities. There are lessons in that for our quest for political arrangements that can accommodate different interests and identities, promote cooperation, provide for common needs, and allow for agreed development and adjustment in the future.

I believe that we are benefiting from exposure to a political ethos and modalities which are not as psychologically constraining as the ethos of "winner takes all" and the constitutional stagnancy of the British system. Both unionist and nationalist have sought to express their rights in terms of their territorial majority and other norms of the British system and nineteenth-century nationalism, but are now realizing that there are other valid norms to assimilate.

The changes that have taken place in Europe offer, then, the prospect that bitter conflict and tension can be replaced by cooperation and partnership without anyone being cast as victor or vanquished and without anyone losing distinctiveness or identity.

In this regard, it is surely significant that Franco-German reconciliation needed to find a wider forum to bring about the most lasting changes in France's and Germany's respective approaches. The sheer intensity and massiveness of the historical pressures toward division were transformed in the broader context of the original Community. It is also significant that the Community came into being in limited areas that went to the heart of the relationships between the founding countries. They began with their common ground. They began with coal and steel, the critical products for waging war in Europe, and sovereignty was pooled in these areas.

If countries and peoples that slaughtered one another by the millions, twice in this century alone, can lay aside their past, can build institutions that respect their differences, that allow them to work their common ground together, to spill their sweat and not their blood and to grow together at their own speed toward a unity that respects their diversity and evolves through patient agreements, cannot we on a small island do likewise? Indeed, given that both parts of Ireland have already voted for that European process, have agreed to the pooling of sovereignty and new relations with Greeks, French, Germans, Spanish, Dutch, Danes, and so forth, is it not long past time when we should build new relationships with one another?

We should also bear in mind that the Single Market will have an important impact on the border as we know it in Ireland. It will allow the border to ebb substantially from economic life on the island. It also provides a context that will require and should inspire policy programs and administrative instruments that will be cross-border and all-Ireland in scope. This in itself cannot remove the political division. But it will allow the real essence of that division to be addressed rather than be distorted and deepened by economic, social, and administrative divergences and rivalries.

It is not Panglossian to suggest that people from both traditions in Ireland can absorb the lessons of European harmonization and achieve convergence in the expression and pursuit of their identities and interests. A European dimension is hardly a new factor in Ireland's long-running problems. Remember that events celebrated by unionists such as the Siege of Derry and the Battle of the Boyne were not just local religious battles. They were part of a much wider European power play. On the republican and nationalist side Wolfe Tone is generally regarded as the father of Irish republicanism. His inspiration came from the French Revolution and its intellectual protagonists, and French military assistance was central to his strategy for rebellion.

Therefore both traditions—as instanced by unionist invocations of "civil and religious liberty" and nationalist espousals of republican ideals—have derived much of their strength or rationale from events or ideals originating elsewhere in the Europe of the past. Is it too much to suggest that we can share together in the spirit of the changing and future Europe?

Having presented the potential for new relationships within Ireland and between Ireland and Britain against the background of a changed and changing Europe, I should perhaps indicate something of the role Ireland might play in that context.

Whatever its ideological affinities, Ireland has remained aloof from military alliances. Current developments serve more to vindicate that position than to invalidate it. They do, however, call for a realignment of that neutrality to present realities and potential achievements.

In this I suggest not that Ireland join the North Atlantic Treaty Organization (NATO), whose relevance is more questionable now than previously. Instead, I suggest that Ireland can play a particular role in promoting and enhancing the possibilities offered by the CSCE scenario. I believe that it can identify a common cause not just with other neutral Western states but also with countries of Central and Eastern Europe that wish to escape responsibly from the notion of two military conglomerates. In doing so, Ireland can play a role that would complement the efforts of those in NATO member states who want to work to achieve real and complete pan-European security, offering true peace.

In the EC context, I think that Ireland has a particularly strong interest in ensuring that EC policy processes and programs carry a strong regional orientation. This is part of ensuring the democratic effectiveness and legitimacy of the EC and the equity of its policies. I suspect that in this we would have common cause with people in the regions of Britain and other countries.

I also believe that an Ireland at peace with itself and with its neighbor can properly address itself to what is almost a political calling—to carry a particular regard for the rights and needs of the developing world into its EC activities. As almost the only state in the EC to have been colonized rather than to have colonized, it should be able to promote an intelligent empathy with the less fortunate countries and peoples whom EC policies can affect so strongly. As a people who suffered famine and underdevelopment, the Irish know that these hardships and obscenities are not simply the product of natural disasters but, rather, result from exploitation, unequal power relationships, unjust economic relationships, and indifference to a common humanity. That should inspire them to persuade and support others in the pursuit of a new international economic order.

These considerations combine to suggest that in finding its place in a new Europe the new Ireland would be not at a point of arrival but, rather, at a point of departure on a challenging journey on which it can maturely discharge a responsibility to, and with, the peoples with whom it shares the European continent and the larger world.

Bibliography

Compiled by JOHN WHYTE

Adams, Gerry. *Falls Memories.* Dingle, Ireland, 1982.

——. *The Politics of Irish Freedom.* Dingle, Ireland, 1986.

——. *A Pathway to Peace.* Cork, Ireland, 1988.

Adamson, Ian. *Cruthin: The Ancient Kindred.* Newtownards, Northern Ireland, 1974.

——. *The Identity of Ulster.* Belfast, 1981.

Akenson, Donald Harmon. *Education and Enmity: The Control of Schooling in Northern Ireland 1920–50.* Newton Abbot, England, 1973.

——. *A Mirror to Kathleen's Face: Education in Independent Ireland, 1922–1960.* Montreal, 1975.

——. *Between Two Revolutions: Islandmagee, County Antrim 1798–1920.* Dublin, 1979.

Alliance. *What Future for Northern Ireland? Report of the Alliance Commission on Northern Ireland.* London, 1985.

Anglo-Irish Agreement. Dublin, 1985.

Antipode. 1980, 12, no. 1. Special issue on Ireland.

Arthur, Andrew. "Attitude Change and 'Neuroticism' among Northern Irish Children Participating in Joint-Faith Holidays." M.Sc. thesis, Queen's University of Belfast, 1974.

Arthur, Paul. *Government and Politics of Northern Ireland.* 2nd ed. London, 1987.

Aughey, Arthur. *Under Siege: Ulster Unionism and the Anglo-Irish Agreement.* Belfast, 1989.

Aunger, Edmund A. "Religion and Occupational Class in Northern Ireland," *Economic and Social Review* 7, no. 1 (October 1975): 1–18.

——. *In Search of Political Stability: A Comparative Study of New Brunswick and Northern Ireland.* Montreal, 1981.

Austin, Roger. "The Dividing Line," *Junior Education* (November 1986): 12–13.

Bailey, Sydney D. *Human Rights and Responsibilities in Britain and Ireland: A Christian Perspective.* Basingstoke, England, 1988.

Baker, John. Sermon preached in Westminster Abbey, Matins, Advent Sunday, 30 November 1980.

The editors are grateful to Jean for permission to use an abridged version of the bibliography that appeared in John Whyte, *Interpreting Northern Ireland* (Clarendon Press, Oxford, England, 1990).

————. "Ireland and Northern Ireland," *The Furrow* 33, no. 1 (January 1982): 13–21.

Bambery, Chris. *Ireland's Permanent Revolution.* London, 1986.

Barrington, Donal. *Uniting Ireland.* Dublin, 1959.

Barrington, Ruth. *Health, Medicine and Politics in Ireland 1900–1970.* Dublin, 1987.

Barritt, Denis P. *Northern Ireland: A Problem to Every Solution.* London, 1982.

Barritt, Denis P., and Charles F. Carter. *The Northern Ireland Problem.* 2nd ed. London, 1972.

Barton, Brian. *Brookeborough: The Making of a Prime Minister.* Belfast, 1988.

Beattie, Geoffrey W. "The 'Troubles' in Northern Ireland," *Bulletin of the British Psychological Society* 32 (June 1979): 249–52.

Beckett, Ian F. W. *The Army and the Curragh Incident 1914.* London, 1986.

Beckett, Ian F. W., and Keith Jeffery. "The Royal Navy and the Curragh Incident," *Historical Research* 62, no. 4 (February 1989): 54–69.

Belfrage, Sally. *The Crack: A Belfast Year.* London, 1987.

Bell, Desmond. "Acts of Union: Youth Sub-Culture and Ethnic Identity amongst Protestants in Northern Ireland," *British Journal of Sociology* 38, no. 2 (1987): 158–83.

Bell, Geoffrey. *The Protestants of Ulster.* London, 1976.

————. *Troublesome Business: The Labour Party and the Irish Question.* London, 1982.

————. *The British in Ireland: A Suitable Case for Withdrawal.* London, 1984.

[Bennett]. *Report of the Committee of Inquiry into Police Interrogation Procedures in Northern Ireland* (the Bennett Report). London, 1979.

Bew, Paul, Peter Gibbon, and Henry Patterson. *The State in Northern Ireland, 1921–72: Political Forces and Social Classes.* Manchester, 1979.

Bew, Paul, and Henry Patterson. *The British State and the Ulster Crisis: From Wilson to Thatcher.* London, 1985.

[BICO]. *On the Democratic Validity of the Northern Ireland State,* British and Irish Communist Organisation, Policy Statement no. 2. Belfast, 1971.

————. *The Two Irish Nations: A Reply to Michael Farrell.* Belfast, 1971.

————. *The Home Rule Crisis, 1912–1914.* 2nd ed. Belfast, 1972.

————. *The Economics of Partition.* 4th ed. Belfast, 1972.

————. *"Ulster as It Is": A Review of the Development of the Catholic Protestant Political Conflict in Belfast between Catholic Emancipation and the Home Rule Bill.* Belfast, 1975.

————. *Imperialism,* British and Irish Communist Organisation, Policy Statement no. 8. Belfast, 1975.

————. *Against Ulster Nationalism.* 2nd ed. Belfast, 1977.

Biggs-Davison, John. *Ulster: Six British Counties,* Salisbury Papers no. 10. London, n.d., 1982?

Birrell, Derek. "Relative Deprivation as a Factor in Conflict in Northern Ireland," *Sociological Review,* ns, 20, no. 3 (1972): 317–43.

Birrell, Derek, and Alan Murie. *Policy and Government in Northern Ireland: Lessons of Devolution.* Dublin, 1980.

Blacking, John, Kieran Byrne, and Kate Ingram. "Looking for Work in Larne: A Social Anthropological Study." In Donnan and McFarlane, eds. (1989), pp. 67–89.

Blackman, Tim, Eileen Evason, Martin Melaugh, and Roberta Woods. "Housing and Health: A Case Study of Two Areas in West Belfast," *Journal of Social Policy* 18, no. 1 (January 1989): 1–26.

Blanshard, Paul. *The Irish and Catholic Power.* London, 1954.

Blythe, Ernest (1955). *See* de Blaghd (1955).

Boal, F. W. "Territoriality on the Shankill-Falls Divide, Belfast," *Irish Geography* 6, no. 1 (1969): 30–50.

——. "Territoriality and Class: A Study of Two Residential Areas in Belfast," *Irish Geography* 6, no. 3 (1969): 229–48.

Boal, F. W., P. Doherty, and D. G. Pringle. *The Spatial Distribution of Some Social Problems in the Belfast Urban Area,* Northern Ireland Community Relations Commission Research Paper. Belfast, 1974.

Boal, F. W., and J. Neville H. Douglas. *Integration and Division: Geographical Perspectives on the Northern Ireland Problem.* London, 1982.

Boal, F. W., and David Livingstone. "Protestants in Belfast: A View from the Inside," *Contemporary Review* 248, no. 1433 (April 1986): 169–75.

Boal, F. W., Russell C. Murray, and Michael A. Poole. "Belfast: The Urban Encapsulation of a National Conflict." In Susan C. Clarke and Jeffrey L. Obler, eds., *Urban Ethnic Conflict: A Comparative Perspective,* Comparative Urban Studies Monograph no. 3, pp. 77–131. Chapel Hill, N.C., 1976.

Boserup, Anders. "Contradictions and Struggles in Northern Ireland," *Socialist Register* (1972): 157–92.

Bowen, Kurt. *Protestants in a Catholic State: Ireland's Privileged Minority.* Montreal, 1983.

Bowman, John. *De Valera and the Ulster Question 1917–1973.* Oxford, England, 1982.

Boyce, D. G. *Englishmen and Irish Troubles: British Public Opinion and the Making of Irish Policy 1918–22.* London, 1972.

——. *Nationalism in Ireland.* London, 1982.

Boyd, Andrew. *Holy War in Belfast.* Tralee, Ireland, 1969.

——. *Have the Trade Unions Failed the North?* Cork, Ireland, 1984.

Boyle, J., J. Jackson, B. Miller, and S. Roche. "Attitudes in Ireland," Report no. 1, *Summary Tables of Attitudes in N. Ireland.* Belfast, 1976.

Boyle, Kevin, and Tom Hadden. *Ireland: A Positive Proposal.* Harmondsworth, England, 1985.

Brett, C. E. B. *Housing a Divided Community.* Dublin and Belfast, 1986.

Brewer, John D., Adrian Guelke, Ian Hume, Edward Moxon-Browne, and Rick Wilford. *The Police, Public Order and the State: Policing in Great Britain, Northern Ireland, the Irish Republic, the USA, Israel, South Africa and China.* Basingstoke, England, 1988.

Brooke, Peter. *Ulster Presbyterianism.* Dublin, 1987.

Bruce, Steve. *God Save Ulster! The Religion and Politics of Paisleyism.* Oxford, England, 1986.

Buchanan, R. H., and B. M. Walker, eds. *Province, City and People: Belfast and Its Region.* Antrim, Northern Ireland, 1987.

Buckland, Patrick. *Irish Unionism, I: The Anglo-Irish and the New Ireland.* Dublin, 1972.

——. *Irish Unionism, II: Ulster Unionism and the Origins of Northern Ireland, 1886–1922.* Dublin, 1973.

——. *The Factory of Grievances: Devolved Government in Northern Ireland 1921–1939.* Dublin, 1979.

———. *A History of Northern Ireland*. Dublin, 1981.

Buckley, Anthony D. *A Gentle People: A Study of a Peaceful Community in Ulster*. Cultra, Northern Ireland, 1982.

———. "Playful Rebellion: Social Control and the Framing of Experience in an Ulster Community," *Man* ns 18, no. 2 (1983): 383–95.

———. "Walls within Walls: Religion and Rough Behaviour in an Ulster Community," *Sociology* 18, no. 1 (1984): 19–32.

———. "Collecting Ulster's Culture: Are There Really Two Traditions?" In Alan Gailey, ed., *The Use of Tradition: Essays Presented to G. B. Thompson*, pp. 49–60. Cultra, Northern Ireland, 1988.

Budge, Ian, and Cornelius O'Leary. *Belfast: Approach to Crisis: A Study of Belfast Politics, 1613–1970*. London, 1973.

Bufwack, Mary F. *Village without Violence: An Examination of a Northern Irish Community*. Cambridge, England, 1982.

Bulmer, Martin, with Keith G. Banting, Stuart S. Blume, Michael Carley, and Carol H. Weiss. *Social Science and Social Policy*. London, 1986.

Burton, Frank. *The Politics of Legitimacy: Struggles in a Belfast Community*. London, 1978.

Cairns, Ed. "The Development of Ethnic Discrimination in Children in Northern Ireland." In Harbison, ed. (1983), pp. 115–27.

———. "Intergroup Conflict in Northern Ireland." In Henri Tajfel, ed., *Social Identity and Intergroup Relations* (Cambridge, England, 1982), pp. 277–97.

———. *Caught in Crossfire: Children and the Northern Ireland Conflict*. Belfast, 1987.

———. "Social Identity and Inter-group Conflict in Northern Ireland: A Developmental Perspective." In Harbison, ed. (1989), pp. 115–30.

Callaghan, James. *A House Divided: The Dilemma of Northern Ireland*. London, 1973.

———. *Time and Chance*. London, 1987.

Calvert, Harry. *The Northern Ireland Problem*. London, 1972.

[Cameron]. *Disturbances in Northern Ireland: Report of the Commission Appointed by the Governor of Northern Ireland* (the Cameron Report). Belfast, 1969.

Campaign for Social Justice. *Northern Ireland: The Plain Truth*. 1st ed. Dungannon, Northern Ireland, 1964.

———. *Northern Ireland: The Plain Truth*. 2nd ed. Dungannon, Northern Ireland, 1969.

Campbell, Colin. "Social Relations in Glenarm, a Northern Ireland Village." M.A. thesis, Queen's University, Belfast, 1978.

Campbell, Gregory. *Discrimination: The Truth*. Derry, Northern Ireland, n.d.

Canning, David, Barry Moore, and John Rhodes. "Economic Growth in Northern Ireland: Problems and Prospects." In Teague, ed. (1987), pp. 211–35.

Carr, Alan. *The Belfast Labour Movement 1885–1893*. Belfast, 1974.

Carson, William S. *Ulster and the Irish Republic*. Belfast, 1957.

Cathcart, Rex. *The Most Contrary Region: The BBC in Northern Ireland 1924–1984*. Belfast, 1984.

Cavanagh, Colm. "How We All Became Sectarian." In *Community Work in a Divided Society*, comp. Hugh Frazerê, pp. 33–6, Belfast, 1981.

Cecil, Rosanne, John Offer, and Fred St. Leger. *Informal Welfare: A Sociological Study of Care in Northern Ireland*. Aldershot, England, 1987.

Chambers, Gerald. *Equality and Inequality in Northern Ireland*, Part 2: "The Workplace," Policy Studies Institute Occasional Paper no. 39. London, 1987.

Clancy, Patrick, Sheelagh Drudy, Kathleen Lynch, and Liam O'Dowd, eds. *Ireland: A Sociological Profile*. Dublin, 1986.

Clarke, Desmond. *Church and State: Essays in Political Philosophy*. Cork, Ireland, 1985.

Cohen, Anthony P. *Belonging: Identity and Social Organization in British Rural Cultures*. Manchester, 1982.

Collins, Martin, ed. *Ireland after Britain*. London, 1985.

Collins, Tom. *The Centre Cannot Hold: Britain's Failure in Northern Ireland*. Dublin, 1983.

Committee for Social Science Research in Ireland. *Report on Research Awards in the Disciplines of Economics, Politics and Social Science and under the Conflict Programme for the Period 1974–1987*. Dublin, 1988.

Compton, Paul. "Religious Affiliation and Demographic Variability in Northern Ireland," *Institute of British Geographers: Transactions*, ns 1, no. 4 (1976): 433–52.

———. *Northern Ireland: A Census Atlas*. Dublin, 1978.

———. "The Other Crucial Factors Why Catholics Don't Get More Jobs," *Belfast Telegraph*, 28 October 1980, p. 8.

———, ed. *The Contemporary Population of Northern Ireland and Population-Related Issues*. Belfast, 1981.

———. "An Evaluation of the Changing Religious Composition of the Population in Northern Ireland," *Economic and Social Review* 16, no. 3 (April 1985): 201–24.

———. "Population." In Buchanan and Walker, eds. (1987), pp. 237–61.

———. Letter in *Fortnight* 259 (February 1988): 19.

Compton, Paul, R. J. Cormack, and R. D. Osborne. "Discrimination Research 'Flawed.' " *Fortnight* 258 (January 1988): 11–12.

Compton, Paul, and John Coward. *Fertility and Family Planning in Northern Ireland*. Aldershot, England, 1989.

Compton, Paul, and John F. Power. "Estimates of the Religious Composition of Northern Ireland Local Government Districts in 1981 and Change in the Geographical Pattern of Religious Composition between 1971 and 1981," *Economic and Social Review* 17, no. 2 (Spring 1986): 87–105.

Conroy, John. *War as a Way of Life: A Belfast Diary*. London, 1988.

Cooney, John. *The Crozier and the Dáil: Church and State in Ireland 1922–1986*. Cork, Ireland, 1986.

Corken, James Peter. "The Development of the Teaching of Irish History in Northern Ireland in Its Institutional and Political Context." M.A. thesis, Queen's University of Belfast, 1989.

Cormack, R. J., and R. D. Osborne, eds. *Religion, Education and Employment: Aspects of Equal Opportunity in Northern Ireland*. Belfast, 1983.

———. "Fair Shares, Fair Employment: Northern Ireland Today," *Studies* 76, no. 303 (Spring 1989): 49–54.

Cormack, R. J., R. D. Osborne, and E. P. Rooney. *Religion and Employment in Northern Ireland: 1911–1971*. Belfast, 1984.

Cormack, R. J., R. D. Osborne, and W. T. Thompson. *Into Work? Young School*

Leavers and the Structure of Opportunity in Belfast, Fair Employment Agency, Research Paper no. 5. Belfast, 1980.

Covello, Vincent T., and Jacqueline A. Ashby. "Inequality in a Divided Society: An Analysis of Data from Northern Ireland," *Sociological Focus* 13, no. 2 (April 1980): 87–98.

Coward, John. "Demographic Structure and Change." In Clancy et al., eds. (1986), pp. 176–97.

Cox, W. Harvey. "Who Wants a United Ireland?" *Government and Opposition* 20, no. 1 (Winter 1985): 29–47.

———. "Public Opinion and the Anglo-Irish Agreement," *Government and Opposition* 22, no. 3 (Summer 1987): 336–51.

Critchley, Julian. *Ireland: A New Partition,* Bow Group Occasional Paper. London, 1972.

Cronin, Seán. *Irish Nationalism: A History of Its Roots and Ideology.* Dublin, 1980.

Crotty, Raymond. *Ireland in Crisis: A Study in Capitalist Colonial Underdevelopment.* Dingle, Ireland, 1986.

Crozier, Maurna. " 'Powerful Wakes': Perfect Hospitality." In Curtin and Wilson, eds. (1989), pp. 70–91.

Curran, Frank. *Derry: Countdown to Disaster.* Dublin, 1986.

Curtin, Chris, and Thomas M. Wilson, eds. *Ireland from Below: Social Change and Local Communities.* Galway, Ireland, 1989.

Daly, Mary. *An Economic and Social History of Ireland since 1800.* Dublin, 1981.

Dangerfield, George. *The Damnable Question: A Study in Anglo-Irish Relations.* London, 1977.

Darby, John. *Conflict in Northern Ireland: The Development of a Polarised Community.* Dublin, 1976.

———, ed. *Northern Ireland: The Background to the Conflict.* Belfast, 1983.

———. *Intimidation and the Control of Conflict in Northern Ireland.* Dublin, 1986.

Darby, John, and Seamus Dunn. "Segregated Schools: The Research Evidence." In Osborne, Cormack, and Miller, eds. (1987), pp. 85–97.

Darby, John, and Geoffrey Morris. *Intimidation in Housing,* Northern Ireland Community Relations Commission, Research Paper. Belfast, 1974.

Darby, John, D. Murray, D. Batts, S. Dunn, S. Farren, and J. Harris. *Education and Community in Northern Ireland: Schools Apart?* Coleraine, Northern Ireland, 1977.

Davey, Ray. *Take Away This Hate: The Story of a Search for Community.* Corrymeela, Northern Ireland, n.d.

Davis, E. E., and R. Sinnott. *Attitudes in the Republic of Ireland Relevant to the Northern Ireland Problem, I, Descriptive Analysis and Some Comparisons with Attitudes in Northern Ireland and Great Britain* (no vol. II). Dublin, 1979.

———. "The Controversy Concerning Attitudes in the Republic to the Northern Ireland Problem," *Studies* 69 (Autumn-Winter 1980): 179–92.

Davis, E. E., et al. *Some Issues in the Methodology of Attitude Research,* Economic and Social Research Institute, Policy Research Series, no. 3. Dublin, 1980.

De Blaghd, Earnán. *Briseadh na Teorann.* Dublin, 1955.

Dent, Martin. "The Feasibility of Shared Sovereignty (and Shared Authority)." In Townshend, ed. (1988), pp. 128–56.

De Paor, Liam. *Divided Ulster*. Harmondsworth, England, 1970.

———. *The Peoples of Ireland: From Prehistory to Modern Times*. London, 1986.

Department of Economic Development. *Equality of Opportunity in Employment in Northern Ireland: Future Strategy Options, a Consultative Paper*. Belfast, 1986.

Devlin, Bernadette. *The Price of My Soul*. London, 1969.

Dewar, M. W., John Brown, and S. E. Long, eds. *Orangeism: A New Historical Appreciation*. Belfast, 1967.

Dilley, Roy. "Boat Owners, Patrons and State Policy in the Northern Ireland Fishing Industry." In Donnan and McFarlane, eds. (1989), pp. 122–47.

Donnan, Hastings, and Graham McFarlane, eds. *Social Anthropology and Public Policy in Northern Ireland*. Aldershot, England, 1989.

Doob, Leonard W., and William J. Foltz. "The Belfast Workshop: An Application of Group Techniques to a Destructive Conflict." *Journal of Conflict Resolution* 17, no. 3 (September 1973): 489–512.

———. "The Impact of a Workshop upon Grass-Roots Leaders in Belfast," *Journal of Conflict Resolution* 18, no. 2 (June 1974): 237–56.

Douglas, J. Neville H., and Frederick W. Boal. "The Northern Ireland Problem." In Boal and Douglas, eds. (1982), pp. 1–18.

Dunn, Seamus, John Darby, and Kenneth Mullan. *Schools Together?* Coleraine, Northern Ireland, 1984.

Dwyer, T. Ryle. *Eamon de Valera*. Dublin, 1980.

———. *De Valera's Darkest Hour: In Search of National Independence, 1919– 1932*. Cork, Ireland, 1982.

———. *De Valera's Finest Hour: In Search of National Independence, 1932– 1959*. Cork, Ireland, 1982.

Edwards, Owen Dudley. *The Sins of Our Fathers: Roots of Conflict in Northern Ireland*. Dublin, 1970.

Edwards, Ruth Dudley. *Patrick Pearse: The Triumph of Failure*. London, 1977.

Elliott, S., and F. J. Smith. *Northern Ireland: The District Council Elections of 1985*. Belfast, 1986.

Elliott, S., and Richard A. Wilford. *The 1983 Northern Ireland Assembly Election*, Studies in Public Policy, no. 119. Glasgow, 1983.

Ellis, Ian M. *Peace and Reconciliation Projects in Ireland*. 2nd ed. Belfast, 1984.

Eversley, David. *Religion and Employment in Northern Ireland*. London, 1989.

Eversley, David, and Valerie Herr. *The Roman Catholic Population of Northern Ireland in 1981: A Revised Estimate*. Belfast, 1985.

Fair Employment Agency. *Eleventh Report and Statement of Accounts of the Fair Employment Agency for Northern Ireland*. London, 1988.

Fairleigh, John. "Personality and Social Factors in Religious Prejudice." In Fairleigh et al. (1975), pp. 3–13.

Fairleigh, John, et al. *Sectarianism—Roads to Reconciliation: Papers Read at the 22nd Annual Summer School of the Social Study Conference*, St. Augustine's College, Dungarvan, Ireland, 3–10 August 1974. Dublin, 1975.

Fanning, Ronan. "Britain, Ireland and the End of the Union." In *Ireland After the Union: Proceedings of the Second Joint Meeting of the Royal Irish Academy and the British Academy, London, 1986*. Oxford, England, 1989.

Farrell, Michael. *Northern Ireland: The Orange State*. 1st ed. London, 1976.

————. *Northern Ireland: The Orange State.* 2nd ed. London, 1980.

————. *Arming the Protestants: The Formation of the Ulster Special Constabulary and the Royal Ulster Constabulary 1920–27.* London, 1983.

————, ed. *Twenty Years On.* Dingle, Ireland, 1988.

Faughnan, Seán. "The Jesuits and the Drafting of the Irish Constitution of 1937." *Irish Historical Studies* 26, no. 101 (May 1988): 79–102.

Faulkner, Brian. *Memoirs of a Statesman.* London, 1978.

Fee, Frank. "Responses to a Behavioural Questionnaire of a Group of Belfast Children." In Harbison, ed. (1983), pp. 31–42.

————. "Educational Change in Belfast Schoolchildren 1975–1981." In Harbison, ed. (1983), pp. 44–58.

Fennell, Desmond, ed. *The Changing Face of Catholic Ireland.* London, 1968.

————. *The State of the Nation: Ireland Since the Sixties.* Swords, Ireland, 1983.

————. *Beyond Nationalism: The Struggle against Provinciality in the Modern World.* Swords, Ireland, 1985.

————. *Nice People and Rednecks: Ireland in the 1980s.* Dublin, 1986.

————. *The Revision of Irish Nationalism.* Dublin, 1989.

Fields, Rona. *Society under Siege: A Psychology of Northern Ireland.* Philadelphia, 1977.

FitzGerald, Garret. *Towards a New Ireland.* London, 1972.

————. *Irish Identities,* The Richard Dimbleby Lecture. London, 1982.

————. *All in a Life.* Dublin, 1991.

Fogarty, Michael, Liam Ryan, and Joseph Lee. *Irish Values & Attitudes: The Irish Report of the European Value Systems Study.* Dublin, 1984.

Fraser, Morris. *Children in Conflict.* London, 1973.

Fraser, T. G. *Partition in Ireland, India and Palestine: Theory and Practice.* London, 1986.

Gafikin, Frank, and Mike Morrissey. "Poverty and Politics in Northern Ireland." In Teague, ed. (1987), pp. 136–59.

Gallagher, Anthony M. "Intergroup Relations and Political Attitudes in Northern Ireland." M.Sc. thesis, Queen's University of Belfast, 1982.

Gallagher, Eric, and Stanley Worrall. *Christians in Ulster, 1968–80.* Oxford, England, 1982.

Gallagher, Frank. *The Indivisible Island: The History of the Partition of Ireland.* London, 1957.

Gallagher, Michael. *The Irish Labour Party in Transition 1957–1982.* Dublin, 1982.

Gallagher, Tom. "Religion, Reaction and Revolt in Northern Ireland: The Impact of Paisleyism in Ulster," *Journal of Church and State* 23, no. 3 (Autumn 1981): 423–44.

Galliher, John F., and Jerry L. DeGregory. *Violence in Northern Ireland: Understanding Protestant Perspectives.* Dublin, 1985.

Galway, R. "The Perception and Manipulation of the Religious Identities in a Northern Irish Community." M.A. thesis, Queen's University of Belfast, 1978.

Garvin, Tom. "The North and the Rest: The Politics of the Republic of Ireland." In Townshend, ed. (1988), pp. 95–109.

Gibbon, Peter. *The Origins of Ulster Unionism: The Formation of Popular Protestant Politics and Ideology in Nineteenth-Century Ireland.* Manchester, 1975.

————. "Some Basic Problems of the Contemporary Situation," *Socialist Register* (1977), pp. 81–7.

Gibson, Norman. "The Northern Problem: Religious or Economic or What?" *Community Forum* 1, no. 1 (Spring 1971): 2–5.

Gilmour, David. *Lebanon: The Fractured Country.* London, 1983.

Girvin, Brian. "Social Change and Moral Politics: The Irish Constitutional Referendum 1983," *Political Studies* 34, no. 1 (March 1986): 61–81.

———. "National Identity and Conflict in Northern Ireland." In Brian Girvin and Roland Sturm, eds., *Politics and Society in Contemporary Ireland,* pp. 105–34. Aldershot, England, 1986.

———. "The Divorce Referendum in the Republic, June 1986," *Irish Political Studies* 2 (1987): 93–9.

Glassie, Henry. *Passing the Time: Folklore and History of an Ulster Community.* Dublin, 1982.

Goudsblom, Johan. *Dutch Society.* New York, 1967.

Graham, Donald. "Discrimination in Northern Ireland: The Failure of the Fair Employment Agency," *Critical Social Policy* (Summer 1984): 40–54.

Gray, Tony. *The Orange Order.* London, 1972.

Greaves, C. Desmond. *The Irish Crisis.* London, 1972.

Gree, John E. "Viewing 'the Other Side' in Northern Ireland: Openness and Attitudes to Religion among Catholic and Protestant Adolescents," *Journal for the Scientific Study of Religion* 24, no. 3 (1985): 275–92.

Gudgin, Graham. "Prospects for the Northern Ireland Economy: The Role of Economic Research." In Jenkins, ed. (1989), pp. 69–84.

Guelke, Adrian. *Northern Ireland: The International Perspective.* Dublin, 1988.

Gwynn, Denis. *The History of Partition (1912–1925).* Dublin, 1950.

Haagerup, N. J., rapporteur. *Report Drawn Up on behalf of the Political Affairs Committee on the Situation in Northern Ireland,* European Parliament Working Documents, 1983–1984, document 1-1526/83, 19 March 1984 (the Haagerup Report).

Hall, Michael. *Ulster: The Hidden History.* Belfast, 1986.

Harbinson, John F. *The Ulster Unionist Party, 1882–1973: Its Development and Organisation.* Belfast, 1973.

Harbison, Joan, ed. *Children of the Troubles: Children in Northern Ireland.* Belfast, 1983.

———, ed. *Growing Up in Northern Ireland.* Belfast, 1989.

Harris, Rosemary. *Prejudice and Tolerance in Ulster: A Study of Neighbours and "Strangers" in a Border Community.* Manchester, 1972.

Harrison, Henry. *Ulster and the British Empire, 1939: Help or Hindrance?* London, 1939.

Hartz, Louis. *The Founding of New Societies: Studies in the History of the United States, Latin America, South Africa, Canada, and Australia.* New York, 1964.

Hastings, Max. *Ulster 1969: The Fight for Civil Rights in Northern Ireland.* London, 1970.

Hechter, Michael. *Internal Colonialism: The Celtic Fringe in British National Development, 1536–1966.* London, 1975.

Heskin, Ken. *Northern Ireland: A Psychological Analysis.* Dublin, 1980.

———. "Social Disintegration in Northern Ireland: Fact or Fiction?" *Economic and Social Review* 12, no. 2 (January 1981): 97–113.

———. "Societal Disintegration in Northern Ireland: A Five-Year Update," *Economic and Social Review* 16, no. 3 (April 1985): 187–99.

Heslinga, M. W. *The Irish Border as a Cultural Divide.* Assen, Netherlands, 1962; repr. 1971.

Hewitt, Christopher. "Catholic Grievances, Catholic Nationalism and Violence in Northern Ireland during the Civil Rights Period: A Reconsideration," *British Journal of Sociology* 32, no. 3 (September 1981): 362–80.

———. "Discrimination in Northern Ireland: A Rejoinder," *British Journal of Sociology* 34, no. 3 (1983): 446–51.

———. "Catholic Grievances and Violence in Northern Ireland," *British Journal of Sociology* 36, no. 1 (1985): 102–5.

———. "Explaining Violence in Northern Ireland," *British Journal of Sociology* 38, no. 1 (1987): 88–93.

Hickey, John. *Religion and the Northern Ireland Problem.* Dublin, 1984.

Hogan, G. W. "Law and Religion: Church-State Relations in Ireland from Independence to the Present Day," *American Journal of Comparative Law* 35, no. 1 (Winter 1987): 47–96.

Howe, Leo. "Unemployment: Doing the Double and Labour Markets in Belfast." In Curtin and Wilson, eds. (1989), pp. 144–64.

———. " 'Doing the Double' or Doing Without: The Social and Economic Context of Working 'On the Side' in Northern Ireland." In Jenkins, ed. (1989), pp. 164–77.

Hunter, John. "An Analysis of the Conflict in Northern Ireland." In Rea, ed. (1982), pp. 9–59.

Hurley, Michael, ed. *Irish Anglicanism 1869–1969.* Dublin, 1970.

Inglis, Tom. *Moral Monopoly: The Catholic Church in Modern Irish Society.* Dublin, 1987.

Institute for Representative Government. *Fair Employment or Social Engineering? Submission to the Department of Economic Development on the White Paper, "Fair Employment in Northern Ireland."* Belfast, 1989.

Irish Episcopal Conference. *Submission to the New Ireland Forum.* Dublin, 1984.

Irish Information Partnership. "Information Service on Northern Ireland Conflict and Anglo-Irish Affairs. Extracts from Forthcoming Edition of Agenda: Summary Tables." 11 August. London, 1989.

Jackson, Harold. *The Two Irelands: A Dual Study of Inter-Group Tensions,* Minority Rights Group, Report no. 2. London, 1971.

Jackson, T. A. *Ireland Her Own: An Outline History of the Irish Struggle for National Freedom and Independence.* London, 1946.

Jahoda, Gustav, and Susan Harrison. "Belfast Children: Some Effects of a Conflict Environment," *Irish Journal of Psychology* 3, no. 1 (1975): 1–19.

Jalland, Patricia. *The Liberals and Ireland: The Ulster Question in British Politics to 1914.* Brighton, England, 1980.

Jenkins, Richard. *Hightown Rules: Growing Up in a Belfast Estate.* Leicester, England, 1982.

———. *Lads, Citizens and Ordinary Kids: Working-Class Youth Life-Styles in Belfast.* London, 1983.

———. "Bringing It All Back Home: An Anthropologist in Belfast." In Colin Bell and Helen Roberts, eds., *Social Researching: Politics, Problems, Practice,* pp. 147–64. London, 1984.

———. "Northern Ireland: In What Sense 'Religions' in Conflict?" In Richard Jenkins, Hastings Donnan, and Graham McFarlane, *The Sectarian Divide in Northern Ireland Today,* Royal Anthropological Institute of Great Britain and Ireland, Occasional Paper no. 41, pp. 1–21. London, 1986.

————, ed. *Northern Ireland: Studies in Social and Economic Life*. Aldershot, England, 1989.

Johnson, David. *The Interwar Economy in Ireland*, Studies in Irish Economic and Social History, no. 4. Dundalk, Ireland, 1985.

Jones, Emrys. "The Distribution and Segregation of Roman Catholics in Belfast," *Sociological Review* 4 (1956): 167–89.

————. *A Social Geography of Belfast*. London, 1960.

Jones, Thomas. *Whitehall Diary, III, Ireland 1918–1925*. Edited by Keith Middlemas. London, 1971.

Jowell, Roger, and Colin Airey, eds. *British Social Attitudes: The 1984 Report*. Aldershot, England, 1984.

Kee, Robert. *The Green Flag: A History of Irish Nationalism*. London, 1972.

Kelley, Jonathan, and Ian McAllister. "The Genesis of Conflict: Religion and Status Attainment in Ulster, 1968," *Sociology* 18, no. 2 (May 1984): 171–90.

Kennedy, Dennis. *The Widening Gulf: Northern Attitudes to the Independent Irish State 1919–49*. Belfast, 1988.

Kennedy, Kieran A., Thomas Giblin, and Deirdre McHugh. *The Economic Development of Ireland in the Twentieth Century*. London, 1988.

Kennedy, Liam. *Two Ulsters: A Case for Repartition*. Belfast, 1986.

Kennedy, Robert E., Jr. *The Irish: Emigration, Marriage, and Fertility*. Berkeley, Calif., 1973.

Kenny, Anthony. *The Road to Hillsborough: The Shaping of the Anglo-Irish Agreement*. Oxford, England, 1986.

Keogh, Dermot. *The Vatican, the Bishops and Irish Politics 1919–39*. Cambridge, England, 1986.

————. "The Constitutional Revolution: An Analysis of the Making of the Constitution," *Administration* (special number, "The Constitution of Ireland, 1937–1987") 35, no. 4 (1987): 4–84.

[Kilbrandon]. *Northern Ireland: Report of an Independent Inquiry, Chairman Lord Kilbrandon* (the Kilbrandon Report). London, 1984.

Kirk, Thomas. "The Religious Distribution of Lurgan with Special Reference to Segregational Ecology." M.A. thesis, Queen's University of Belfast, 1967.

Kovalcheck, Kassian A. "Catholic Grievances in Northern Ireland: Appraisal and Judgement," *British Journal of Sociology* 38, no. 1 (1987): 77–87.

Kremer, John, Robert Barry, and Andrew McNally. "The Misdirected Letter and the Quasi-Questionnaire: Unobtrusive Measures of Prejudice in Northern Ireland," *Journal of Applied Social Psychology* 16, no. 4 (1986): 303–9.

Kuhn, Thomas S. *The Structure of Scientific Revolutions*. 2nd ed. Chicago, 1970.

Kuper, Leo. *Genocide: Its Political Use in the Twentieth Century*. Harmondsworth, England, 1981.

Labour Party. *New Rights, New Prosperity and New Hope for Northern Ireland: A Policy Statement of the National Executive Committee of the Labour Party*. London, 1987.

————. *Towards a United Ireland: Reform and Harmonisation: A Dual Strategy for Irish Unification*. London, 1988.

Laffan, Michael. *The Partition of Ireland 1911–1925*. Dundalk, Ireland, 1983.

Larsen, Sidsel Saugestad. "The Two Sides of the House: Identity and Social Organisation in Kilbroney, Northern Ireland." In Cohen (1982), pp. 131–63.

————. "The Glorious Twelfth: A Ritual Expression of Collective Identity." In Cohen (1982), pp. 278–91.

Lawlor, Sheila. *Britain and Ireland 1914–23*. Dublin, 1983.

Lawrence, R. J. *The Government of Northern Ireland: Public Finance and Public Services 1921–1964.* Oxford, England, 1965.

Lee, Joseph. "Some Aspects of Modern Irish Historiography." In Ernst Schulin, ed., *Gedenkschrift Martin Gohring: Studien zur europaischen Geschichte.* Wiesbaden, Germany, 1968.

Lee, Joseph, and Gearóid O Tuathaigh. *The Age of de Valera.* Dublin, 1982.

Lee, Raymond M. "Interreligious Courtship in Northern Ireland." In Mark Cook and Glenn Wilson, eds., *Love and Attraction: An International Conference.* Oxford, England, 1979.

Lennon, Brian. "A Wider View from a Local Housing Estate," *Studies* 73, no. 292 (1984): 309–17.

Leyton, Elliott. "Opposition and Integration in Ulster," *Man* ns 9 (1974): 185–98.

———. *The One Blood: Kinship and Class in an Irish Village,* Newfoundland Social and Economic Studies no. 15. St. John's, Nfld., 1975.

Lijphart, Arend. *Class Voting and Religious Voting in the European Democracies,* Survey Centre, Occasional Paper no. 8. Glasgow, 1971.

———. *The Politics of Accommodation: Pluralism and Democracy in the Netherlands.* 2nd ed. Berkeley, Calif., 1975.

———. Review article, "The Northern Ireland Problem: Cases, Theories, and Solutions," *British Journal of Political Science* 5 (1975): 83–106.

———. *Democracy in Plural Societies: A Comparative Exploration.* New Haven, Conn., 1977.

Long, S. E. " 'The Union: Pledge and Progress' 1886–1967." In Dewar, Brown, and Long, eds. (1967), pp. 147–200.

Longford, Earl of, and Anne McHardy. *Ulster.* London, 1981.

Longford, Earl of, and Thomas P. O'Neill. *Eamon de Valera.* Dublin, 1970.

Loughlin, James. *Gladstone, Home Rule and the Ulster Question 1882–93.* Dublin, 1986.

Lustick, Ian. *State-Building Failure in British Ireland and French Algeria.* Berkeley, Calif., 1985.

LWT. *From the Shadow of the Gun: The Search for Peace in Northern Ireland.* London, 1984.

Lyons, F. S. L. *Charles Stewart Parnell.* London, 1977.

McAllister, Ian. *The 1975 Northern Ireland Convention Election,* University of Strathclyde, Survey Research Centre, Occasional Paper no. 14. Glasgow, 1975.

———. *The Northern Ireland Social Democratic and Labour Party: Political Opposition in a Divided Society.* London, 1977.

———. "The Devil, Miracles and the Afterlife: The Political Sociology of Religion in Northern Ireland," *British Journal of Sociology* 33, no. 3 (September 1982): 330–47.

———. "Religious Commitment and Social Attitudes in Ireland," *Review of Religious Research* 25, no. 1 (September 1983): 3–20.

McAllister, Ian, and Brian Wilson. "Bi-confessionalism in a Confessional Party System: The Northern Ireland Alliance Party," *Economic and Social Review* 9, no. 4 (April 1978): 207–25.

McAnallen, Martin. "Minority Interaction in a Small Northern-Irish Village." M.A. thesis, Queen's University of Belfast, 1977.

McAteer, Fergus. *Won't You Please Sit Down?* Derry, Northern Ireland, 1972.

McCann, Eamonn. *War and an Irish Town*. 1st ed. Harmondsworth, England, 1974.
———. *War and an Irish Town*. 2nd ed. London, 1980.
———. *Bloody Sunday in Derry—What Really Happened*. Dingle, Ireland, 1992.
McCartney, R. L., Sean Hall, Bryan Somers, Gordon Smyth, H. L. McCracken, and Peter Smith. "The Unionist Case." Typescript. Belfast, 1981.
McCashin, Anthony. "Social Policy, 1957–82," *Administration* (special number, "Unequal Achievement: The Irish Experience, 1957–1982") 30, no. 2–3 (1982): 203–23.
McClean, Raymond. *The Road to Bloody Sunday*. Swords, Ireland, 1983.
McCluskey, Conn. *Up off Their Knees: A Commentary on the Civil Rights Movement in Northern Ireland*. Galway, Ireland, 1989.
McCreary, Alf. *Corrymeela: The Search for Peace*. Belfast, 1975.
McCrudden, C. "The Experience of the Legal Enforcement of the Fair Employment (Northern Ireland) Act 1976." In Cormack and Osborne, eds. (1983), pp. 201–21.
MacDonald, Michael. *Children of Wrath: Political Violence in Northern Ireland*. Cambridge, England, 1986.
McFarlane, W. Graham. "Gossip and Social Relationships in a Northern Irish Village." Ph.D. thesis, Queen's University of Belfast, 1978.
———. "Mixed Marriages in Ballycuan, Northern Ireland," *Journal of Comparative Family Studies* 10, no. 2 (Summer 1979): 191–205.
———. "Dimensions of Protestantism: The Working of Protestant Identity in a Northern Irish Village." In Curtin and Wilson, eds. (1989), pp. 23–45.
MacIver, Martha Abele. "Ian Paisley and the Reformed Tradition," *Political Studies* 35, no. 3 (September 1987): 359–78.
McKee, Eamonn. "Church-State Relations and the Development of Irish Health Policy: The Mother-and-Child Scheme, 1944–53," *Irish Historical Studies* 25, no. 98 (November 1986): 159–94.
McKeown, Ciaran. *The Passion of Peace*. Belfast, 1984.
McKeown, Kieran. "A Critical Examination of Some Findings of the Davis and Sinnott Report," *Studies* 69, no. 274 (Summer 1980): 113–20.
McKeown, Michael. *The Greening of a Nationalist*. Lucan, Ireland, 1986.
———. *Two Seven Six Three: An Analysis of Fatalities Attributable to Civil Disturbances in Northern Ireland in the Twenty Years between July 13, 1969 and July 12, 1989*. Lucan, Ireland, 1989.
MacLaughlin, James G., and John A. Agnes. "Hegemony and the Regional Question: The Political Geography of Regional Industrial Policy in Northern Ireland, 1945–1972," *Annals of the Association of American Geographers* 76, no. 2 (1986): 247–61.
McLoone, James, ed. *Being Protestant in Ireland*. Belfast and Dublin, 1985.
McMahon, Deirdre. *Republicans and Imperialists: Anglo-Irish Relations in the 1930s*. New Haven, Conn., 1984.
McNabb, Patrick. "A People under Pressure." Paper presented to Lancaster University Conference on Northern Ireland. 1971.
McNeill, Ronald. *Ulster's Stand for Union*. London, 1922.
MacRae, John. "Polarisation in Northern Ireland: A Preliminary Report." Lancaster, England, 1966.
McWhirter, Liz. "Contact and Conflict: The Question of Integrated Education," *Irish Journal of Psychology* 6, no. 1 (1983): 13–27.

——. "Looking Back and Looking Forward: An Inside Perspective." In Harbison, ed. (1983), pp. 127–57.

Mair, Peter. "Breaking the Nationalist Mould: The Irish Republic and the Anglo-Irish Agreement." In Teague, ed. (1987), pp. 81–110.

Mansergh, N. "The Government of Ireland Act, 1920: Its Origins and Purposes. The Working of the 'Official' Mind." In J. G. Barry, ed., *Historical Studies, IX, Papers Read before the Irish Conference of Historians, Cork, 29–31 May 1971*, pp. 19–48. Belfast, 1974.

Marrinan, Patrick. *Paisley: Man of Wrath*. Tralee, Ireland, 1973.

Martin, John. "The Conflict in Northern Ireland: Marxist Interpretations," *Capital and Class* 18 (Winter 1982): 56–71.

Marx, Karl, and Frederick Engels. *On Ireland*. London, 1971.

Miller, David. *Queen's Rebels: Ulster Loyalism in Historical Perspective*. Dublin, 1978.

Miller, Robert. *Attitudes to Work in Northern Ireland*, Fair Employment Agency, Research Paper no. 2. Belfast, 1978.

——. "Religion and Occupational Mobility." In Clancy et al., eds. (1986), pp. 221–43.

——. "Evaluations Research 'Ulster Style': Investigating Equality of Opportunity in Northern Ireland," *Network: Newsletter of the British Sociological Association* 42 (October 1988): 4–7.

Miller, Robert, and Robert Osborne. "Why Catholics Don't Get More Jobs: A Reply," *Belfast Telegraph*, 4 November 1980, p. 12.

Mogey, John M. *Rural Life in Northern Ireland: Five Regional Studies Made for the Northern Ireland Council of Social Service (Inc.)*. London, 1947.

Moloney, Ed, and Andy Pollak. *Paisley*. Swords, Ireland, 1986.

Moody, T. W., and J. C. Beckett. *Ulster Since 1800*. 2 vols. London, 1954, 1957.

Moore, Jonathan. "Historical Revisionism and the Irish in Britain," *Linenhall Review* 5, no. 3 (Autumn 1988): 14–15.

Morgan, Austen. "Politics, the Labour Movement and the Working Class in Belfast 1905–1923." Ph.D. thesis, Queen's University of Belfast, 1978.

——. *James Connolly: A Political Biography*. Manchester, 1988.

Morgan, Austen, and Bob Purdie, eds. *Ireland: Divided Nation, Divided Class*. London, 1980.

Moxon-Browne, E. "The Water and the Fish: Public Opinion and the Provisional IRA in Northern Ireland." In Paul Wilkinson, ed., *British Perspectives on Terrorism*, pp. 41–72. London, 1981.

——. *Nation, Class and Creed in Northern Ireland*. Aldershot, England, 1983.

Moynihan, Maurice, ed. *Speeches and Statements by Eamon de Valera 1917–73*. Dublin, 1980.

Munck, Ronnie. *Ireland: Nation, State, and Class Conflict*. Boulder, Colo., 1985.

Murphy, Dervla. *A Place Apart*. London, 1978.

——. *Changing the Problem: Post-forum Reflections*, Lilliput Pamphlets no. 3. Gigginstown, Ireland, 1984.

Murray, Dominic. *Worlds Apart: Segregated Schools in Northern Ireland*. Belfast, 1985.

Murray, Dominic, and John Darby. *The Vocational Aspirations and Expectations of School Leavers in Londonderry and Strabane*, Fair Employment Agency, Research Paper no. 6. Belfast, 1980.

Nairn, Tom. *The Break-up of Britain*. London, 1977.

Nelson, Sarah. "Protestant 'Ideology' Considered: The Case of 'Discrimination.' " In Ivor Crewe, ed., *British Political Sociology Yearbook, II, The Politics of Race*. London, 1975, pp. 155–87.

————. *Ulster's Uncertain Defenders: Protestant Political, Paramilitary and Community Groups and the Northern Ireland Conflict*. Belfast, 1984.

New Ireland Forum. *Report of Proceedings* nos. 1–13. Dublin, 1983–84.

————. *Report*. Dublin, 1984.

————. *The Macroeconomic Consequences of Integrated Economic Policy, Planning and Co-ordination of Ireland*, study prepared for the New Ireland Forum by Davy Kelleher McCarthy Ltd., economic consultants, and commentary on the study by Professor Norman Gibson and Professor Dermot McAleese. Dublin, 1984.

New Ulster Movement. *The Reform of Stormont*. Belfast, 1971.

————. *A Commentary on the Programme of Reforms for Northern Ireland*. Belfast, 1971.

————. *The Way Forward*. Belfast, 1971.

————. *Two Irelands or One?* Belfast, 1972.

————. *Violence and Northern Ireland*. Belfast, 1972.

————. *A New Constitution for Northern Ireland*. Belfast, 1972.

————. *Tribalism or Christianity in Ireland?* Belfast, 1973.

New Ulster Political Research Group. *Beyond the Religious Divide*. Belfast, 1979.

North-Eastern Boundary Bureau. *Handbook of the Ulster Question*. Dublin, 1923.

Northern Friends Peace Board. *Orange and Green: A Quaker Study of Community Relations in Northern Ireland*. Sedbergh, England, 1969.

Northern Ireland Assembly. *Report: The Investigation by the Fair Employment Agency for Northern Ireland into the Non-industrial Northern Ireland Civil Service*. Belfast, 1984.

Northern Ireland Census 1981: Religion Report. Belfast, 1984.

Northern Ireland Office. *The Future of Northern Ireland: A Paper for Discussion*. London, 1972.

O'Brien, Conor Cruise. *States of Ireland*. London, 1972.

————. *Neighbours: The Ewart-Biggs Memorial Lectures 1978–1979*. London, 1980.

O'Carroll, John P., and John A. Murphy, eds. *De Valera and His Times*. Cork, Ireland, 1983.

O'Connell, James. "Conflict and Conciliation: A Comparative Approach Related to Three Case Studies—Belgium, Northern Ireland, and Nigeria." In Townshend, ed. (1988), pp. 157–91.

O'Donnell, E. E. *Northern Irish Stereotypes*. Dublin, 1977.

O'Dowd, Liam, Bill Rolston, and Mike Tomlinson. *Northern Ireland: Between Civil Rights and Civil War*. London, 1980.

O Gadhra, Nollaig. "Appreciation: Earnán de Blaghd, 1880–1975," *Éire-Ireland* 11, no. 3 (1976): 93–105.

O Glaisne, Risteard. *Ian Paisley agus Tuaisceart Éireann*. Dublin, 1971.

O'Halloran, Clare. *Partition and the Limits of Irish Nationalism: An Ideology Under Stress*. Dublin, 1987.

O'Hearn, Denis. "Catholic Grievances, Catholic Nationalism: A Comment." *British Journal of Sociology* 34, no. 3 (1983): 438–45.

250   JOHN WHYTE

——. "Again on Discrimination in the North of Ireland: A Reply to the Rejoinder," *British Journal of Sociology* 36, no. 1 (1985): 94–101.

——. "Catholic Grievances: Comments," *British Journal of Sociology* 38, no. 1 (1987): 94–100.

O'Hegarty, P. S. *A History of Ireland Under the Union, 1801 to 1922.* London, 1952.

O'Leary, Brendan. "Explaining Northern Ireland: A Brief Study Guide," *Politics* 5, no. 1 (1985): 35–41.

O'Leary, Cornelius. "The Irish Referendum on Divorce," *Electoral Studies* 6, no. 1 (1986): 69–74.

O'Leary, Cornelius, and Tom Hesketh. "The Irish Abortion and Divorce Referendum Campaigns," *Irish Political Studies* 3 (1988): 43–62.

Oliver, John. *Ulster Today and Tomorrow*, vol. 44, broadsheet no. 574. London, 1978.

——. *Working at Stormont.* Dublin, 1978.

O'Malley, Padraig. *The Uncivil Wars: Ireland Today.* Belfast, 1983.

O'Neill, Terence. *Ulster at the Crossroads.* London, 1969.

——. *The Autobiography of Terence O'Neill, Prime Minister of Northern Ireland 1963–1969.* London, 1972.

Osborne, Robert D. "Denomination and Unemployment in Northern Ireland," *Area* 10, no. 4 (1978): 280–3.

——. "Religious Discrimination and Disadvantage in the Northern Ireland Labour Market," *International Journal of Social Economics* 7, no. 4 (1980): 206–83.

——. "What About the Other Minority?" *Fortnight* 196 (August 1983): 14.

Osborne, Robert D., and R. J. Cormack. "Conclusions" and "The Last Word." In Cormack and Osborne (1983), pp. 222–33 and 238–42.

——. "Higher Education: North and South," *Administration* 33, no. 3 (1985): 326–54.

——. "Unemployment and Religion in Northern Ireland," *Economic and Social Review* 17, no. 3 (April 1986): 215–23.

——. *Religion, Occupations and Employment 1971–1981*, Fair Employment Agency, Research Paper no. 11. Belfast, 1987.

——. "Gender and Religion as Issues in Education, Training and Entry to Work." In Harbison, ed. (1989), pp. 42–65.

Osborne, Robert D., R. J. Cormack, and R. L. Miller, eds. *Education and Policy in Northern Ireland.* Belfast, 1987.

Osborne, Robert D., R. J. Cormack, N. G. Reid, and A. P. Williamson. "Class, Sex, Religion and Destination: Participation and Higher Education in Northern Ireland," *Studies in Higher Education* 9, no. 2 (1984): 123–37.

Paisley, Ian R. K., Peter Robinson, and John D. Taylor. *Ulster: The Facts.* Belfast, 1982.

Paisley, Rhonda. *Ian Paisley, My Father.* Basingstoke, England, 1988.

Palley, Claire. *The Evolution, Disintegration and Possible Reconstruction of the Northern Ireland Constitution*, repr. from the *Anglo-American Law Review.* London, 1972.

Patterson, Henry. *Class Conflict and Sectarianism: The Protestant Working Class and the Belfast Labour Movement 1868–1920.* Belfast, 1980.

Pickvance, T. J. *Peace Through Equity: Proposals for a Permanent Settlement of the Northern Ireland Conflict.* Birmingham, 1975.

Poole, Michael A. "Religious Residential Segregation in Northern Ireland." In Boal and Douglas (1982), pp. 281–308.

———. "The Demography of Violence." In Darby, ed. (1983), pp. 151–80.

Poole, Michael A., and F. W. Boal. "Religious Residential Segregation in Belfast in mid-1969: A Multi-level Analysis." In B. D. Clark and M. D. Gleave, eds., *Social Patterns in Cities*, Special Publication no. 5. London, 1973, pp. 1–40.

Pringle, D. G. *One Island, Two Nations?: A Political Geographical Analysis of the National Conflict in Ireland*. Letchworth, England, 1985.

Prior, James. *A Balance of Power*. London, 1986.

Probert, Belinda. *Beyond Orange and Green: The Political Economy of the Northern Ireland Crisis*. London, 1978.

Project Team. *Belfast: Areas of Special Social Need. Report by Project Team 1976*. Belfast, 1977.

Randall, Vicky. "The Politics of Abortion in Ireland." In Joni Lovenduski and Joyce Outshoorn, eds., *The New Politics of Abortion*, pp. 67–85. London, 1986.

Rea, Desmond, ed. *Political Co-operation in Divided Societies: A Series of Papers Relevant to the Conflict in Northern Ireland*. Dublin, 1982.

Reed, David. *Ireland: The Key to the British Revolution*. London, 1984.

Rees, Merlyn. *Northern Ireland: A Personal Perspective*. London, 1985.

Road to Partition: 1914–1919, The. Belfast, 1974.

Roberts, David A. "The Orange Order in Ireland: A Religious Institution?" *Government and Opposition* 2, no. 3 (Summer 1987): 315–35.

Robinson, Alan. "Education and Sectarian Conflict in Northern Ireland," *The New Era* 52, no. 1 (January 1971): 384–8.

———. "If You Lived in Northern Ireland—Would *Our* Child Be Fighting in the Streets?" *Where* 57 (May 1971): 133–6.

Rolston, Bill. "The Limits of Trade Unionism." In O'Dowd, Rolston, and Tomlinson (1980), pp. 68–94.

———. "Reformism and Sectarianism: The State of the Union after Civil Rights." In Darby, ed. (1983), pp. 197–224.

Rolston, Bill, and Mike Tomlinson. *Unemployment in West Belfast: The Obair Report*. Belfast, 1988.

Rolston, Bill, Mike Tomlinson, Liam O'Dowd, Bob Miller, and Jim Smyth. *A Social Science Bibliography of Northern Ireland 1945–1983*. Belfast, 1983.

Rose, Richard. *Governing without Consensus: An Irish Perspective*. London, 1971.

———. *Northern Ireland: A Time of Choice*. London, 1976.

Rose, Richard, Ian McAllister, and Peter Mair. *Is There a Concurring Majority About Northern Ireland?*, Studies in Public Policy no. 22. Glasgow, 1978.

Rowthorn, Bob. "Northern Ireland: An Economy in Crisis." In Teague, ed. (1987), pp. 111–35.

Rowthorn, Bob, and Naomi Wayne. *Northern Ireland: The Political Economy of Conflict*. Cambridge, England, 1988.

Russell, James. "Sources of Conflict," *Northern Teacher* 11, no. 3 (1974): 3–11.

Russell, James, and James A. Schellenberg. "Political Attitude Structure of Schoolboys in Northern Ireland," *Irish Journal of Psychology* 3, no. 2 (1976): 73–86.

Ryan, Desmond, ed. *Socialism and Nationalism: A Selection from the Writings of James Connolly.* Dublin, 1948.

Ryan, Liam. "The Church and Politics: The Last Twenty-Five Years," *The Furrow* 30, no. 1 (January 1979): 3–18.

SACHR (Standing Advisory Commission on Human Rights). *Religious and Political Discrimination and Equality of Opportunity in Northern Ireland: Report on Fair Employment.* London, 1987.

Salters, John. "Attitudes towards Society in Protestant and Roman Catholic School Children in Belfast." M.Ed. thesis, Queen's University of Belfast, 1970.

Schmitt, David. "Equal Employment Opportunity as a Technique toward the Control of Political Violence: The Case of Northern Ireland's Fair Employment Agency," *Current Research on Peace and Violence* 3, no. 1 (1980): 33–46.

Shanks, Amanda. *Rural Aristocracy in Northern Ireland.* Aldershot, England, 1988.

Shannon, Catherine B. *Arthur J. Balfour and Ireland, 1874–1922.* Washington, D.C., 1988.

Shea, Patrick. *Voices and the Sound of Drums: An Irish Autobiography.* Belfast, 1981.

Shearman, Hugh. *Not an Inch: A Study of Northern Ireland and Lord Craigavon.* London, 1942.

———. *Anglo-Irish Relations.* London, 1948.

———. "Conflict in Northern Ireland," *Year Book of World Affairs* 24 (1970): 40–53.

———. "Conflict in Northern Ireland," *Year Book of World Affairs* 36 (1982): 182–96.

Sheehy, Michael. *Divided We Stand: A Study of Partition.* London, 1955.

Singleton, Dale. "Housing and Planning Policy in Northern Ireland: Problems of Implementation in a Divided Community," *Policy and Politics* 13, no. 3 (1985): 305–26.

Smith, David J. *Equality and Inequality in Northern Ireland,* Part 1, "Employment and Unemployment," PSI Occasional Paper no. 39. London, 1987.

———. *Equality and Inequality in Northern Ireland,* Part 3, "Perceptions and Views," PSI Occasional Paper no. 39. London, 1987.

———. " 'No Substance' to Criticisms," *Fortnight* 258 (January 1988): 12.

———. Letter in *Fortnight* 260 (March 1988): 19.

———. "Policy and Research: Employment Discrimination in Northern Ireland," *Policy Studies* 9, no. 1 (July 1988): 41–59.

Smith, David J., and Gerry Chambers. "Positions, Perceptions, Practice," *Fortnight* 257 (December 1987): 18–19.

Smith, M. G. "Some Developments in the Analytic Framework of Pluralism." In Leo Kuper and M. G. Smith, eds., *Pluralism in Africa,* pp. 415–58. Berkeley, Calif., 1969.

Smyth, Clifford. "The DUP as a Politico-Religious Organization," *Irish Political Studies* 1 (1986): 33–43.

———. *Ian Paisley: Voice of Protestant Ulster.* Edinburgh, 1987.

Smyth, Martin. "A Protestant Looks at the Republic." In Fairleigh et al. (1975), pp. 25–35.

Stewart, A. T. Q. *The Narrow Ground: Aspects of Ulster, 1609–1969.* London, 1977.

Strauss, E. *Irish Nationalism and British Democracy.* London, 1951.

Sugden, John, and Alan Bairner. "Northern Ireland: Sport in a Divided Society." In Lincoln Allison, ed., *The Politics of Sport,* pp. 90–115. Manchester, 1986.

Sunday Times "Insight" Team. *Ulster.* Harmondsworth, England, 1972.

Tapsfield, Joan A. "In Search of Truth in Northern Ireland," *The Furrow* 34, no. 2 (February 1983): 95–8.

Taylor, David. "Ian Paisley and the Ideology of Ulster Protestantism." In Chris Curtin et al., eds., *Culture and Ideology in Ireland,* Studies in Irish Society, ii, pp. 59–78. Galway, Ireland, 1984.

Taylor, Rupert Langley. "The Queen's University of Belfast and its Relationship to the Troubles: The Limits of Liberalism." Ph.D. thesis, University of Kent at Canterbury, 1986.

——. "Social Scientific Research on the 'Troubles' in Northern Ireland: The Problem of Objectivity," *Economic and Social Review* 19, no. 2 (January 1988): 123–45.

——. "The Queen's University of Belfast: The Liberal University in a Divided Society," *Higher Education Review* 20, no. 2 (Spring 1988): 27–45.

Teague, Paul, ed. *Beyond the Rhetoric: Politics, the Economy and Social Policy in Northern Ireland.* London, 1987.

Todd, Jennifer. "Two Traditions in Unionist Political Culture," *Irish Political Studies* 2 (1987): 1–26.

Tóibin, Colm. *Walking Along the Border.* London, 1987.

Tovey, Hilary. "Religious Group Membership and National Identity Systems," *Social Studies* 4, no. 2 (1975): 124–43.

Townshend, Charles, ed. *Consensus in Ireland: Approaches and Recessions.* Oxford, England, 1988.

Trew, Karen. "Sectarianism in Northern Ireland: A Research Perspective." Paper presented at the British Psychological Society, Social Psychology Section Annual Conference, Canterbury, England, September 1980.

——. "Group Identification in a Divided Society." In Harbison, ed. (1983), pp. 109–19.

——. "Catholic-Protestant Contact in Northern Ireland." In Miles Hewstone and Rupert Brown, eds., *Contact and Conflict in Intergroup Encounters.* Oxford, England, 1986.

Trew, Karen, and L. McWhirter. "Conflict in Northern Ireland: A Research Perspective." In Peter Stringer, ed., *Confronting Social Issues,* pp. 195–214. London, 1982.

Ulster Unionist Party. *Devolution and the Northern Ireland Assembly: The Way Forward,* discussion paper presented by the Ulster Unionist Party's Report Committee. Belfast, 1984.

[UK Government]. *Northern Ireland: A Framework for Devolution.* London, 1982.

Van der Straeten, Serge, and Philippe Daufouy. "La Contre-révolution irlandaise," *Les Temps Modernes* 29, no. 311 (1972): 2069–104.

[Van Straubenzee]. *Report and Recommendations of the Working Party on Discrimination in the Private Sector of Employment* (the Van Straubenzee Report). Belfast, 1973.

Viney, Michael. *The Five Per Cent: A Survey of Protestants in the Republic* (repr. from the *Irish Times*). Dublin, 1965.

Violence in Ireland: A Report to the Churches. Belfast, 1976.

Waddell, Neil, and Ed Cairns. "Situational Perspectives on Social Identity in Northern Ireland," *British Journal of Social Psychology* 25 (1986): 25–31.

Walker, B. M. *Ulster Politics: The Formative Years, 1868–86.* Belfast, 1989.

Walker, Graham. *The Politics of Frustration: Harry Midgley and the Failure of Labour in Northern Ireland.* Manchester, 1985.

Wallace, Martin. *Drums and Guns: Revolution in Ulster.* London, 1970.

———. *Northern Ireland: 50 Years of Self-Government.* Newton Abbot, England, 1971.

———. *British Government in Northern Ireland: From Devolution to Direct Rule.* Newton Abbot, England, 1982.

Wallis, Roy, Steve Bruce, and David Taylor. *"No Surrender!" Paisleyism and the Politics of Ethnic Identity in Northern Ireland.* Belfast, 1986.

———. "Ethnicity and Evangelicalism: Ian Paisley and Protestant Politics in Ulster," *Comparative Studies in Society and History* 29 (1987): 293–313.

Walmsley, A. J. *Northern Ireland: Its Policies and Record.* Belfast, 1959.

Walsh, Brendan M. *Religion and Demographic Behaviour in Ireland,* Economic and Social Research Institute, Paper no. 55. Dublin, 1970.

———. "Trends in the Religious Composition of the Population in the Republic of Ireland, 1946–71," *Economic and Social Review* 6, no. 4 (July 1975): 543–55.

Watt, David, ed. *The Constitution of Northern Ireland: Problems and Prospects,* National Institute of Economic and Social Research, Policy Studies Institute, Royal Institute of International Affairs, Joint Studies in Public Policy no. 4. London, 1981.

White, Barry. *John Hume: Statesman of the Troubles.* Belfast, 1984.

White, Jack. *Minority Report: The Anatomy of the Southern Irish Protestant.* Dublin, 1975.

Whyte, John. "Interpretations of the Northern Ireland Problem: An Appraisal," *Economic and Social Review* 9, no. 4 (July 1978): 257–82.

———. *Church and State in Modern Ireland 1923–1979.* 2nd ed. (1st ed., covering 1923–70, pub. 1971.) Dublin, 1980.

———. *Catholics in Western Democracies: A Study in Political Behaviour.* Dublin, 1981.

———. "Why is the Northern Ireland Problem So Intractable?" *Parliamentary Affairs* 34, no. 4 (Autumn 1981): 442–35.

———. "Is Research on the Northern Ireland Problem Worth While?," an Inaugural Lecture delivered before the Queen's University of Belfast on 18 January. Belfast, 1983.

———. "How Much Discrimination Was There under the Unionist Regime, 1921–68?" In Tom Gallagher and James O'Connell, eds., *Contemporary Irish Studies,* pp. 1–35. Manchester, 1983.

———. "The Permeability of the United Kingdom-Irish Border: A Preliminary Reconnaissance," *Administration* 31, no. 3 (1983): 300–15.

———. "How Is the Boundary Maintained between the Two Communities in Northern Ireland?" *Ethnic and Racial Studies* 9, no. 2 (April 1986): 219–34.

———. "Interpretations of the Northern Ireland Problem." In Townshend, ed. (1988), pp. 24–46.

Wilkinson, Paul. "Maintaining the Democratic Process and Public Support." In

Richard Clutterbuck, *The Future of Political Violence: Destabilization, Disorder and Terrorism,* pp. 177–84. Basingstoke, England, 1986.

Wilson, Des. *An End to Silence.* Cork, Ireland, 1985.

Wilson, Thomas, ed. *Ulster under Home Rule.* London, 1955.

———. *Ulster: Conflict and Consent.* Oxford, England, 1989.

Wright, Frank. "Protestant Ideology and Politics in Ulster," *European Journal of Sociology* 14 (1973): 213–80.

———. "Case Study III: The Ulster Spectrum." In David Carlton and Carlo Schaerf, eds., *Contemporary Terror: Studies in Substate Violence.* London, 1981.

———. *Northern Ireland: A Comparative Analysis.* Dublin, 1987.

———. "Northern Ireland and the British-Irish Relationship," *Studies* 78, no. 310 (Summer 1989): 151–62.

Index

257